DALITS AND AFRICAN AMERICANS

DALITS AND AFRICAN AMERICANS
A Study in Comparison

S. D. Kapoor

KALPAZ PUBLICATIONS
Delhi-110052

Dalits and African Americans : A Study in Comparison
(Sociology)

Rs. 750

ISBN: 81-7835-260-5

Published in 2004 in India by
Kalpaz Publications,
C-30, Satyawati Nagar, Delhi-110052
E-mail : Kalpaz@hotmail.com

Laser Typesetting at : Shree Vaishnavi Creations, Delhi
Printed at : Chawla Offset Press, Delhi

Dedicated

to

Raj Nath Mahrotra

B.N. Khanna

and

Jyoti Swaroop Saxena

Contents

Preface

I have taken a circuitous route in coming to Indian reality, more particularly Dalit reality. Not that I was not conscious of it earlier but it was never brought into focus because of my preoccupation with English Studies. Surprisingly, it was my reading in African American literature that stirred my basic hostility against cruelty and injustice. Writers from Douglass to Toni Morrison sharpened my awareness and equipped me intellectually and emotionally to undertake a project of this nature. This awareness was reinforced by my reading in Dalit literature.

What particularly interests me is their journey towards a human terrain – both in life and literature – and the fight against those forces that prevent their journey. This journey involves two basic issues which are central to their existence: identity and freedom: to relate themselves to a complex of relationships and to move untiringly towards complete manhood.

My research in this field has had a sobering influence on me. It gave me new insights into human situation and revealed areas of experience that the mainstream literature has treated only perfunctorily. And with this insight the enclosures in the mind created by social and literary conditioning began to collapse. It took me sometime to disabuse my mind of the abstract universalities that were projected as truths unrelated to the specificities of their situation. In this process the oppressed both in India and America began to acquire a historical and human context.

In this journey they have had some support from non-Blacks and non-Dalits, although not all Blacks and Dalits admit this fact. Mark Twain and Prem Chand, for example, saw a human face behind the claptrap of race and caste stereotypes.

Two prominent thinkers who helped me acquire a framework for this project were: W.E.B. DuBois in America and Dr. Bhimrao Ambedkar in India. After reading them, the two oppressed groups could not be taken for granted. In fact the idea for comparing the two situations came to me at this stage.

The vision of a raceless, casteless and classless society that their literature projects took me to the commonality of experience. Which means that their experience cannot be taken in isolation, independent of the larger experience of which they are a part. Alice Walker, a prominent African American writer, once said that both black and white (by the same logic both Dalit and non-Dalit) are writing an immense story – the same story for the most part – with different parts coming from a multitude of different perspectives preparing a ground for a society free of cruelty and injustice. But in this the vision of the oppressed groups will be the guiding force.

S.D. Kapoor

Acknowledgements

This book is the outcome of a project financed by the University Grants Commission, New Delhi.

In the preparation of bibliography I was helped, among others, by Dr. Ranveer of Marathwada University, Aurangabad, The Editor of *Dalit Voice*, Bangalore and Professor Thorat of Jawahar Lal Nehru University, New Delhi. Sharan Kumar Limbale was gracious enough to send me a copy of his autobiography, *Akkarmashi.* Dr. G.L. Suthar, Director, Madhusudan Ojha Cell, JNV University, Jodhpur made me available *Manusmriti* and other books on Shudras and Untouchables from his library. I am grateful to Dr. Sharad Rajimwale, my colleague in the Department, for translating Sharad Patil's book *The Aesthetics of Non-Brahmin Literature* from Marathi into English. I am thankful to the Indian Institute of Advanced Study, Shimla for providing me an opportunity to interact with creative writers and scholars active in the field at a seminar on Recent Trends in Dalit and Black Writings held in 1997. I am also thankful to Professor Punalekar and his colleagues at the Centre for Social Studies, Surat for helping me crystallize my views on Dalits and also for placing me in a non-elitist ambience. I am thankful to the American Information Resource Centre, New Delhi and the American Centre for International Studies, Hyderabad for updating my bibliography on African Americans.

In the execution of my study I was helped by two of my scholars, Mr. Gaurav Mathur and Mrs. Shivani Kapoor. Mrs. Shivani Kapoor ably assisted me till the completion of this work.

I am also thankful to the Principal and Management of Onkarmal Somani College, Jodhpur for allowing me to have my project transferred to their College when the authorities of the JNV University, Jodhpur expressed their inability to provide infrastructural facilities to me.

I am thankful to my friends Mr. M.S. Maheshwari, Mr. Marudhar Mridul, Mr. M.D. Sharma, Dr. S.S. Tak, Mr. Deepak Banerjee, Professor O.P. Grewal and Professor H.L. Upadhyaya for their moral and intellectual support during the period of this project.

My wife gracefully put up with my erratic work schedule so that I could complete my work uninterruptedly. My son, Vikas Kapoor, saw to it that the manuscript is presented in a proper form.

S.D. Kapoor

Introduction

Comparisons between oppressed groups are not only natural but also sometimes necessary; natural because their struggle to reclaim the human space denied them for centuries is almost similar; necessary because the group that has taken a lead in reclaiming that space influences the other group in devising their strategies, far removed from the area of their operation. It is surprising how ideas travel from one country to another, without the assistance of any direct means of communication.

Indians have always evinced avid interest in the struggle of Black Americans and South Africans, including the people of Indian origin settled there, for equality and human dignity. Mahatma Gandhiji began his long struggle against the imperialist rule in South Africa where he resisted the dehumanizing system of apartheid

Jyoti Rao Phule was the first Shudra leader to recognize the great work done by the Americans in the liberation and elevation of 'Negroes'. So much so that he dedicated his book *Gulamgiri* (Slavery) to the good people of the U.S.A. "as a token of admiration for their sublime disinterestedness and self-sacrificing devotion in the cause of Negro Slavery". He also exhorted his countrymen to take their (white Americans) example as their guide to the emancipation of "their Shudra (and Ati-Shudra) Brethren from the trammels of Brahmin thraldom".

It was just proper for another great Dalit leader, Dr. B.R. Ambedkar, to have inscribed his book, *Who were the Shudras?* published a couple of decades later, to the memory of Mahatma Jyoti Rao Phule "who made the lower classes of Hindus conscious of their slavery to the higher classes and who preached the gospel that for India social democracy was more vital than independence from foreign rule".

On his part, Ambedkar was more forthright in his denunciation of the higher classes. In his essay, 'Hindus and Their Want of Social Conscience', he wrote that for Hindus the Untouchables have never been a problem. They do not weigh on their minds and do not become a subject of public debate. Occasionally, in the past ritual references were made by saints and preachers but their intervention did not alter their social status. As early as 1921 the Congress passed a resolution, as part of their programme of action, at the session held at Ahmedabad, to organize the Depressed Classes for a better life, to improve their social, mental and moral condition. But it was never implemented. The printed material on the Negro problem in America shows how much it is a problem of the whites. As compared to America, the amount of literature that exists on the Untouchable in India is negligible. According to Ambedkar, the reason for this is that the Americans have a social conscience while the Hindus have none. "Not having conscience, the Hindu has no such thing in him as righteous indignation against the inequities and injustices from which the Untouchable has been suffering. He sees no wrong in these inequities and injustices and refuses to budge. By this absence of conscience the Hindu is a great obstacle in the path of the removal of untouchability."

Ambedkar was directly exposed to the situation of Blacks in America during his stay at Columbia University, New York from 1913 to 1916. This was a period of ferment in Black community. It was characteristically called the Harlem Renaissance. Black writers were seriously examining their existence *vis-a-vis* the white society and devising ways to throw off the image of servility foisted on them by the white. DuBois' important book, *The Souls of Black Folk,* was published in 1903 and had the impact of a revelation on all those who read it. Booker T. Washington's book, *Up from Slavery,* which can be said to be the last of the slave narratives, was published in 1900 and contained the account of the pioneering work done by him at the Tuskegee

Institute. He was not a radical thinker like DuBois but emphasized gradualism and accommodation through industrial training. In other words, he was working within the system, preaching thrift and patience. DuBois, on the other hand, suggested ways of overcoming 'double consciousness' and 'double bind'. His words were a "counterpoise to Washington's feathery phrases of compromise". All this could not have been lost on Ambedkar.

I believe that Ambedkar's experience of Black America during the critical period of their struggle was a turning point in his life. The issue of caste segregation back home was beginning to acquire a framework. His critical abilities were at work when he read a paper, Castes in India : Their Mechanism, Genesis and Development, before the Anthropology seminar at Columbia on 9 May 1916. This paper was to become a basis for his longish essay, Annihilation of Caste, initially written for the Jat-Pat-Todak Mandal, Lahore as a presidential address, in which he systematically analysed the philosophy and the working of the caste system in India. In this he struck a blow at the Hindu Social Order. He plainly said that the Hindus observe caste system, not because they are inhuman or wrong-headed. They observe caste because they are deeply religious. Unless the sacredness of the notion of caste was rejected, untouchability could not be abolished. "You must destroy the sacredness and divinity with which caste has become invested. In the last analysis, this means you must destroy the authority of the Shastras and the Vedas". This sent shock waves among the executive members of the Mandal as also among devout Hindus who were not willing to go with Ambedkar that far, even though they wanted to abolish the caste system. Since Ambedkar was not prepared to remove the 'objectionable' portions from his address, the Mandal cancelled the annual conference and Ambedkar's address could not be read there. Ambedkar published it on his own.

In one of his essays Ambedkar quotes from Lala Lajpat Rai's book, *Unhappy India*, which in part was a refutation of the charges levelled against India by Miss Mayo in her book *Mother India.* In order to counter her argument, he gave a detailed "description of the lynching of the Negroes in the United States and the atrocities committed upon them by the members of the Ku Klux Klan". He made a comparison between the attitude of the Brahmins towards the Pariah and the attitude of the Klansmen towards the Negroes and found the latter more unjustifiable and more cruel. He wrote: "What are the caste cruelties of India put by the side of what the white man has done to the non-white people." On this Ambedkar comments that the atrocities practised by the Hindus upon the Untouchables were no less than those practised by the Americans upon the Negroes. "If those atrocities are not so well known to the world as are those practised upon the Negro, it is not because they do not exist. They are not known because there is no Hindu who will not do his best to conceal truth in order to hide his shame". (Vol. 5, Ambedkar; Writings and Speeches).

The identification with the Black American (African American) and South African runs so deep that the organizers of the Centenary Celebrations of Jyoti Rao Phule decided to invite Nelson Mandela, who happened to be visiting India during that period, to honour him as a crusader for freedom and to present him two important documents of Dalit struggle in India—*Slavery* by Jyoti Rao Phule and *Annihilation of Caste* by B.R. Ambedkar. Mandela could not find time to come for the celebrations and the two books were sent to him later.

The interest in African Americans has been kept alive by Dalit writers in Maharashtra. The African American writers were a source of inspiration to them particularly the treatment of suffering and identity in their works. Quite a number of African American writers have been translated into Marathi, Langston Hughes and James Baldwin in particular. Some of the translated plays have been staged. Like in America, autobiographies by Dalits have become a very powerful instrument in analyzing their situation and in explaining things to themselves.

The seminar on Recent Trends in Dalit and Black Writings organized by the Indian Institute of Advanced Study in 1997 gave a kind of legitimacy to this line of comparison. The participants made frequent references to African

American and South African writers and in some cases, direct comparisons were made. The issues debated were : the role of consciousness, its awareness and growth, and its manifestation in literature; 'relation of domination' and condition of powerlessness in relation to the other group. The most relevant question of protest and literature or 'anger and beyond' was also discussed along with the danger of sacrificing artistic integrity. Since their writings are drawn on a view of society seen from the bottom up, the 'periphery' questioning the 'core', they were shown to share a common frame of reference which included : 'symbolic violence' based on biological or social inequality, power and authority, visible or internalized: formation of a counter hegemonic discourse based on extra-literary concerns, leading to an alternative way of interpreting reality and the affirmation of a redefined identity.

Thus even the process of enslavement, which appears to have run a different course, could be seen in a larger framework of manipulating their lives enlisting racial and scriptural support. In America the Black race was painted as inherently inferior-pseudo scientific myths were invented to show the superiority of the white race. In India the Untouchables were painted as inferior on the basis of their birth in an *avarna* caste—an intricate web of Karmic laws was created to permanently condemn them to a lowly position in society. Despite the fact that both DuBois and Ambedkar proved through their attainments that they were in no way intellectually inferior to the so-called superior race or superior caste, their people remained at the same social level. The Dalits had been damaged to such an extent that they took a long time to develop resistance to this manipulation. According to Ambedkar, it is harder for the Untouchables to reach the level of consciousness because the manipulative strategies employed by the superior castes were backed by religion. The resistance to their situation was so weak that they never turned violent. It was different in the case of African Americans. The desire for freedom in them could not be beaten out of their system. Right from the beginning they revolted against direct slavery. They revolted on the ships when they were being taken to

America; they revolted when they landed on the shore of America. They revolted even after years of enslavement. In Alex Haley's *Roots* Kunta Kinte tried to run away a number of times from captivity. Finally, the master cut off his foot so that he could not try it again. The history of Black America is replete with hundreds of violent revolts in which they killed the white masters and got killed. The most violent of these were the ones led by Vasey, Prosser and Turner. In India there are no extant records of violent revolts by Dalits against their wretched condition. Apart from economic reasons, the most important reason was that the abstract conditioning had dulled their responses to such an extent that they became willing accomplices in their own degradation. The Karmic laws subjected them to a kind of duty that was its own reward. They could not think of any reward for their lowly work in this life. The graded social system had condemned them to social inequality. There was no hope for their liberation unless their existence was taken independent of Karmic laws. In other words, it meant that the social must be separated from the religious. The way secularism has been defined, and practised in that distorted form, shows how difficult it is, or has been made to be difficult, to separate the religious from the social. We have never pleaded for separation of temporal and spiritual power. Reacting to the practice of apartheid even in churches in South Africa, Mahatma Gandhiji made a distinction between the two kinds of untouchability—one that was practised in South Africa and the other, in India. In India, Gandhiji believed, the struggle to solve the problem of untouchability is likely to be much harder than in South Africa, although both are to be condemned, as untouchability in India is said to have religious sanction.

The struggle of both these groups exposes the contradictions in their respective society. America quite early in its experiment with a new society projected a kind of utopia, deriving its inspiration not from the past of Europe but from a projected future. Americans believed that in such a society there would be absolute equality of status and opportunity without the impediments of social hierarchy as in Europe. One of the early immigrants, St. Jean de

Crevecoeur in one of his letters to his people in France titled "what is an American?' wrote : "The rich and the poor are not so far removed from each other as they are in Europe... we have no princes for whom we toil and starve, and bleed : we are the most perfect society now existing in the world". In another letter he gave a graphic account of a slave who was subjected to torture by his supervisor for some indiscreet act. He was hung in a cage and exposed to the preying vultures who pecked him all over the body. Alex de Tocqueville in *Democracy in America* warned his countrymen of the uneasy relationship between the two races, which might be the cause of embarrassment and future danger facing the U.S. In India the inequality that the Dalits were condemned to live with coexisted with the high moral posture that the Hindus take. It is woven into the very fabric of Hindu society. The Dalit did not seem to exist for the caste Hindus. They are invisible for them with the result that they do not see them and have no qualm of conscience. This stark reality was made visible by Gandhiji and more particularly by Ambedkar. In 1950, in a speech Ambedkar said: "We are going to enter into a life of contradictions. In politics we will have equality and in social and economic life we will have inequality. How long shall we continue to deny equality in our social and economic life? How are Hindus going to deal with the Karmic law which is the central principle of Hinduism? Unless this contradiction is faced, inequality between the castes will persist." These contradictions could not be resolved through religion, despite the fact that Gandhiji combined asceticism and pragmatism. His personal conduct could not be imitated by others. If we continue to take religion with it, either we raise religion to the level of obsession or make it a mystique as in the case of Gandhiji. Poverty cannot be wished away by glorifying it; caste discrimination cannot be corrected by appealing to the conscience of the people alone. We have never taken it as a collective guilt and never taken collective measures to set it right. The evasion of it can never be a solution, and the incoherence in national life will persist.

In the Jubilee edition of his book, *The Souls of Black Folk,* published in 1953, W.E.B. DuBois made the bold statement, "The colour line is the great problem of the century". He was obviously referring to the Black race but by implication he was speaking for all those who were similarly placed. They were to set the agenda for the century. He did not stop at this but went on to talk of the larger ideological framework within which the colour problem existed. "But today I see more clearly than yesterday that back of the problem of race and colour lies a greater problem which both obscures and implements it and that is the fact that so many civilized persons are willing to live in comfort even if the price of this is poverty, ignorance and disease of the majority of their fellowmen; and to maintain that privilege men have waged war until today war tends to become universal and continuous and the excuse for the war continues to be colour and race." The excuse for the war changes. Now it is religion and it is being projected as 'The Clash of Civilizations.' In fact, it is a smoke-screen for brutal economic exploitation. And what about the contradictions that exist within the American society. According to Samuel P. Huntington, the core of American society, which is said to be a continuation of the Western society, is being threatened by other ethnic groups. It is another matter that DuBois could not provide a sound theoretical basis for the problem of colour and its functioning within the larger framework of capitalist society ; but he put his finger on the two issues involved, namely, colour and economic exploitation. B.R. Ambedkar, the undisputed leader of the Dalits in India, similarly talked of the twin challenges that faced his people: Brahminism and Capitalism. Time and again, he reminded his people that caste segregation could not be taken independent of economic problem, and he made some unsuccessful move in that direction. Teltumbde writes : "although there cannot be any doubt that he stood against Capitalism he could not articulate a sound theoretical basis for doing so." DuBois kept on struggling with the problem of race until he died. Similarly, Ambedkar kept on struggling with the problem of caste until he died.

The uniqueness of the experience of African American (Negro) or the unparalleled situation of the Dalit

(Untouchable) in India is true only in a limited sense. James Baldwin writes in *The Fire Next Time* "The American Negro is a unique creation; he has no counterpart anywhere and no predecessors. The Muslims react to this fact by referring to the Negro as 'the so-called American Negro' and substituting for the names inherited from slavery the letter X. It is a fact that every American Negro bears a name that originally belonged to the white man whose chattel he was". Dr. Ambedkar at one place wrote that the experience of the Dalit was unique because nowhere except in India there existed permanent segregation camps where hereditary slaves lived their wretched existence. Untouchability was, he believed, a unique phenomenon unknown to humanity except the Hindus.

Baldwin discovered in Paris that his colour did not matter to people there. He could move about without crutches. In Columbia University, America, Ambedkar was not treated as an Untouchable but an equal member of the academic community. Their uniqueness was confined to a particular social situation. Apart from that, if they continued to harp on the uniqueness of experience they would be playing into the hands of Muslims in America and orthodox caste Hindus in India. It is in the interest of vested powers to seal the choice of moving beyond categories. Frantz Fanon in *The Wretched of the Earth* wrote that the Blacks had two choices to deal with the stranglehold of colour : one was to make too much of the reality of colour; and the other was not to take any notice of it, thinking that it was like any other colour. The first choice might lead them into a blind alley. During the Black Power Movement, choosing the first option, they decided to have separate universities for Blacks, with black curricula, black history, black literature, black music, black folklore, black sociology and so on. The other experience was kept out of this curricula. In a couple of years they discovered that it was unrealistic to separate areas of experience which form part of mainstream experience. They then opened their university to non-Black courses and non-Black students. One fall out of this experience was that Black Studies became part of academic programmes in such reputed universities as Yale and

Harvard. In India, this line of thought has not been taken to the extremes, but it was the dominant thought among the Dalits in the last decade. We have opened universities in India after the name of Ambedkar—and renamed some—but here the faculty consists of both Dalits and non-Dalits. In important universities in Maharashtra, separate departments of Dalit Studies have been working for decades.

The two fallacies that their situation gave rise to—both in America and India, in America a couple of decades back-are : (1) exclusivism which means that the Black Dalit experience is the exclusive preserve of Black/Dalit and no non-Black and non-Dalit can represent it; (2) since their experience is unique, it cannot even be interpreted by others. Preoccupation with the two issues keeps the 'other' out of Black/Dalit mental and imaginative horizon. They may be right in a limited way. Transcendence has its limits and also the situation in which one is placed. There was a time when all avenues for representing themselves were blocked and they were represented by others. But such representation was selective and arbitrary and to a large extent ideologically determined. And it betrayed the point of view of the writer. Thus when Black/Dalit characters appeared in literature or even in performing art, they were stereotypes and always on the periphery, despite the fact that they were credited with some human qualities. Now that they have found their voice and can represent themselves they are naturally impatient to articulate their experiences which are inevitably strident and subversive. They wish to remove all impediments in the imaginative perception of reality and present it in the raw, unembellished. They have succeeded in carving out a space for themselves which forms the basis for a new discourse. But it cannot be denied that the ground for such a discourse was prepared by non-Black and non-Dalit writers. They sometimes had clairvoyance and reached a point where the human face of Black/Dalit was revealed. They also gave them a human reference. Mark Twain, that inimitable American writer, took recourse to irony to avoid being censored in his attack on racism.

Shelley Fisher Fishkin in her book, *Was Huck Black?* made the startling discovery that Huckleberry Finn's character (he is white) was modelled on Black characters. Even speech patterns he uses were taken from Black boys he knew in life. In her second book, *Lighting Out For the Territory,* Fishkin makes another discovery : it was a letter which was brought to her notice by an antique dealer, Nancy Stiner who Fishkin later discovered was Mark Twain's daughter. The letter was written by Mark Twain (Samuel L. Clemens) to Francis Wayland, dean of the Yale Law School financing the education of a Black student. Here is the text of the letter :

Dear Sir,

Do you know him? And is he worthy? I do not believe I would very cheerfully help a white student who would ask a benevolence of a stranger, but I do not feel so about the other colour. We have ground the manhood out of them and the shame is ours, not theirs, and we should pay for it.

If this young man lives as economically as it is and should be the pride of one to do who is straightened, I would like to know what the cost is, so that I may send 6, 12, or 24 month's board, as the size of the bill may determine.

You see he refers to you, or I would not venture to intrude.

Truly Yours,
S.L. Clemens

The person in question was a coloured man, Warner T. McGwinn, one of the Law School's first Black students. Later he rose to be a prominent lawyer. What is important in this case is that Twain felt that the whites should feel ashamed of the way they had treated Blacks in the country.

Comparable examples can be taken from Indian history. The Achut (Untouchable) number of Chand magazine was brought out in May 1927. Its editor, Nand Kishore Tiwari, was a Saryupari Brahmin. On the front page of the magazine he is shown sitting with a Hindi compositor, Banshi Lal Kori, an Untouchable taking food with him out of the same plate. One can only imagine how scandalized the *savarna* community must have been by this sacrilege on the part of Tiwari. One of the early stories by Prem Chand, Mandir, was published in the same number. The story was inspired by Ambedkar's campaign for entry into the Kala Ram Temple. It beautifully brings out the issues involved : the attitude of the upper castes, whose representative is the pujari (priest) and the anguish and helplessness of Sukhia, the untouchable mother for her ailing son; the inhumanity of the people who deny her access to the temple to pray for her son's life. Both the mother and the child die in their effort to enter the temple. Her fulminations against this segregation even in God's place did not move the conditioned *savarnas*. She finally rejects the *savarna* God.

Sooner or later, the categories of experience will have to go, but that will happen when the categories in the minds of people also disappear. Both Black and Dalits are fighting for the removal of these categories for a better social and political order. Antonio Gramsci at one place wrote that if an experience is historically created it can be historically explained and interpreted and also changed.

As in life so in literature the two groups start with a zero image of themselves. This zero image is inseparable from self concept because it was their self concept which was destroyed during the period of their persecution. It is an uphill task for them to restore this concept as it is inherent in the process of reshaping of reality. Besides, they have to contend with the contradictions within their groups, castes and sub-castes, lower class and middle class, and the process of moving upward; black skins and white masks. Carolyn F. Gerald writes : "We are black people living in a white world. When we consider that the black man sees white cultural and social images projected upon the whole extent of his universe, we cannot help but realize that a very great deal of the time the black man sees a zero image of himself. The black child growing into adulthood through a series of weekend movies, seeing white protagonists constantly before him projecting the whole gamut of human experience is, in extreme cases, persuaded that he too must be white, or (what is more likely) he experiences manhood by proxy, and in some one else's image".

Inevitably there is a conflict between the warring groups over the control of image. And this is the crucial phase for Black/Dalit writers, smashing of someone else's image, creation of a new image. But the associative power of imagination does not move into separate grooves. It is integrative. Ralph Ellison once said that in the world of imagination all colours meet. For that reason he said that he would like to be considered not just a black writer but a writer who happens to be Black, without compromising on the particularity of their experience. No white American could have written a book like *Invisible Man;* similarly no *savarna* could have written a book like *Akkarmashi.* Toni Morison in her book, *Playing in the Dark*, questions the set of assumptions on which the mainstream white literary tradition is based. She questions the content of the canonical American literature which emanates from a particular Americanness which is said to be free of, unformed and unshaped by the four hundred old year presence of first Black American and then African American in the U.S.A. Any concept of Americanness, she argues, cannot keep out the Africanist presence. Similarly, Dalit writers and critics are questioning the deliberate exclusion of first Untouchables then Dalits from the savarna imagination. Some of the writers are being subjected to new interpretation, like Dharmvir interprets Kabir differently. The concept of Indianness cannot keep out the presence of Dalits. Despite intellectual evasion by *savarnas*, the Dalits recorded their presence. Both Black/Dalit writers have reached a stage where they are obviously moving beyond 'anger', are just not confined to castigating the 'other' but exploring, as Maya Angelou said in an interview, other forms of evil. And here their role is vital for the future of the country in which they are placed. Ralph Ellison once said that the challenge before the Black writer is to run the full gamut of his humanity and this requires courage. Will they lose sight of the goal which they had placed before themselves or will they be guided by money values which are making other issues, if not redundant, at least less important? Will they keep alive the hope for a social, economic and political order in which discrimination on the basis of race, caste and gender will be a thing of the past? And in this they will have to guard themselves against market moralities and market cultures in which human relationship is pushed into the background.

1
From Bondage to Freedom

... the past is all that makes the present coherent and further that the past will remain horrible for exactly as long as we refuse to assess it honestly.

James Baldwin
Notes of a Native Son

One of the persistent delusions of mankind is that some sections of the human race are morally better or worse than others. This belief has many different forms, none of which has any rational basis.

B. Russell
Unpopular Essays

We live in a society that has still not freed itself of the mindset that condones brutal oppression and still believes that some races or castes are more equal than others. It was for this reason that the U.N.O. decided to have a world conference on "Racism, Racial Discrimination, Xenophobia and Related Intolerance" in Durban recently. Since the race war (and caste war) goes on as fiercely as ever, candour about blacks and whites (*savarnas* and *avarnas*) is necessary.[1] Candour is possible when one is able to reveal oneself, otherwise the incoherence about the past and about relationships will continue.

A study of the predicament of the African Americans and the Dalits necessarily takes us to the point in the past when the pernicious institutions of racism and casteism were established and later sanctified. Such a process will involve questioning the theories that were built around these institutions. It will be a journey into the past then back to the present so that the bits and pieces, the silences and gaps, of the painful journey of the two groups are put together very much like the journey undertaken by Alex Haley in *Roots* to Juffure where his ancestor Kunta Kinte was captured and brought to the U.S.A. It will put their predicament in proper perspective and enable us to deal with the vestiges of the past system that still stay with us, despite tangible gains achieved the world over in the name of human rights.

Our readings of the past, Frederic Jameson wrote in *The Political Unconscious*, are vitally dependent on our experience of the present. If we find the present oppressive, we will look for its causes in the past. If we believe that society is not likely to change, we will look for evidence in the past for this cynicism. If we delude ourselves with the thought that everything in the past was glorious, we will look for symbols in the past to glorify it, ignoring all social contradictions. The post modernist readings of the past lead us to the point where the fixity of any text – historical or literary – becomes problematic. Some go to the extent of discarding and obliterating the past or imposing neutral categories of thought on it. It is compounded by the belief that since the past cannot be captured in its totality it is no use going back to it. This is another way of evading crucial issues, which, if left unattended for long, come back to us with redoubled force. History could be the source of servitude or freedom. W.E.B. DuBois had this in mind when he stated that the twentieth century was the century of the colour line. And he was right, but the colour line has not been obliterated till today. Ambedkar once said that the ills of Hindu society cannot be set right as long as the caste hierarchy stays with us. Since we refuse to see the obvious and face the issues squarely, the twenty-first century might turn out to be the century of the Dalits.

Despite different approaches to the past, it is possible to have some kind of objectivity in its interpretation. Here one will have to make a distinction between history as record of facts and history as narration of those facts. What is happening now is that even facts are being falsified and shown as non-existent. For example, one cannot negate the fact that Africans were captured by toubobs and sold in the New World for hefty sums. Similarly, one cannot disregard the fact that in India, in a section of Hindu society, there was complete negation of human rights. For centuries, they were relegated to the status of non-human and kept outside the pale of relationship. In this sense the past will remain horrible as long as we refuse to assess it honestly.

Quite often, and without much thought, a specious argument is advanced that racism or casteism was invented to deal with a particular historical situation and in the changed political situation it is no longer necessary. But a system once invented and established, with racial or theological support, doesn't suddenly disappear with the change in historical situation. The attitudes that the old system created and the hidden laws that gave them legitimacy still persist and have acquired associations. And its consequences have further consequences. It requires a sustained political will and effort to change the entrenched attitudes. The U.S.A. took four hundred years to realize the simple fact that a human being (in this case, Blacks) is a human being. In India we took a millennium and a half to realize this simple fact (or have we?).

Thus our interpretation of the past, the struggles that the marginalized people in the U.S.A. and in India – Blacks and Dalits – made first for Civil Rights and then for Human Rights will largely be governed by what they have achieved in the present and what they have yet to achieve. It will involve questioning a certain set of assumptions both in life and literature, that denied them the right to acquire an identity in the racialized or casteist society. And those who should have represented them lacked, what Robert Penn Warren called, 'moral identity' and kept them out of their imaginative horizon or treated them condescendingly. It is surprising that in canonical American literature the white imagination is said to be unshaped by four hundred year old presence of first Africans and then African Americans in the U.S.A. The white writers failed to establish any meaningful relationship between the white and the overwhelming presence of Black ethnic group. Toni Morrison argues that any understanding of American literature must include the presence of Blacks in it, as it is not the exclusive preserve of the white.[2] In India the *savarnas* failed to establish any meaningful relationship between the dominant castes and the *avarnas* with the result that the *savarna* imagination seems to be unshaped by the overwhelming presence first of Untouchables, then *harijans* and now Dalits in canonical Indian literature. And even when they did appear, they had only marginal existence and were never credited with full human qualities. No account of Indian history and Indian literature is complete without the presence of Dalits in it.

Thus when we go back to the past we do so with certain perceptions about it. We try to frame questions to which we have found some answers in the present. "The most illuminating question might be, what were people not talking and thinking about which perhaps they should have been. The details of the past would be listened to with an ear attuned to silence."[3] The issues that the present has helped crystallize can give meaning to the struggles that the African Americans and Dalits made in the past. In the process some silences can be broken.

Fortunately, in the U.S.A. historical records of Blacks' painful experience in the New World are available right from the time the first shipload of slaves arrived in Virginia in 1619. In India there are no extant historical records that can help us reconstruct the past. The history of the Untouchables goes back to a millennium and a half. Whereas the origin of slavery in the U.S.A. can be conclusively established, with documents to support it, in India the origin of unntouchability lies buried in the unreclaimed past and is shrouded in mystery.

It is true that the history of the oppressed throughout the world, whether in the name of race and caste, has not run an identical course. Yet the broad framework of their struggle for liberation, both in life and literature, has been, more or less, the same. The differences are caused by the conditions of their existence, ideological formation of the ruling class and the ways devised by them to keep the oppressed in their place. The Untouchables or *antyajas* were separated from the dominant touchable groups and made to live in segregated quarters, making normal social interaction impossible. The Blacks who were the unwilling immigrants to the U.S.A. were segregated from the larger group on the basis of the pigment of their skin. They were made to live in ghettoes. The only way for them to exist was to submit ungrudgingly to the dictates of the dominant group. *"If you are black"*, wrote Le Roi Jones, "the only roads into the mainland of American life are through subservience, cowardice, loss of manhood. These are the white man's roads."[4]

Dr. Ambedkar calls the existence of the Untouchables an abomination. They were treated as an entity beyond human intercourse whose mere touch was enough to cause pollution. Untouchability among Hindus is a unique phenomenon. It is based on the concept of purity selectively. There were non-Hindu communities that were treated as impure, but they were, unlike Untouchables, never denied individuality. "The Hindus who touch them and become polluted thereby can become pure by undergoing purificatory ceremonies. But there is nothing that can make the Untouchables pure. They are born impure, they are impure while they live, they die the death of the impure, and they give birth to children who are born with the stigma of untouchability affixed to them. It is a case of permanent hereditary stain which nothing can cleanse."[5] In one of his essays Dr. Ambedkar makes a distinction between the conditions of slaves and

Untouchables. A slave, according to him, is conscious of his enslavement and to be conscious of slavery is the first and most important step in the battle for freedom. An Untouchable, on the other hand, is deprived of his liberty indirectly and has no consciousness of his enslavement. "It is slavery though it is untouchability. It is real though it is indirect. It is enduring because it is unconscious. Of the two orders, untouchability is beyond doubt the worse."[6]

In the U.S.A. slavery was practised only in the Southern States. In the North there was no apparent racial discrimination in the sense it existed in the South, although there too subtle ways werc devised to segregate them from the rest of the population by creating "the psychological distance."[7] For the whites, Blacks did not exist, were invisible. At best they were part of a landscape. In *American Hunger*, Richard Wright shows how he moves from the known terror (in the South) to the unknown terror (in the North).

In India the segregation between the upper castes and the Dalits was total despite geographical boundaries. Whereas in the U.S.A. the superiority of the Anglo-Saxon race gave the Blacks a character of inferiority, in India the upper castes, particularly the Brahmins, gave them an image of inferiority and hereditarily condemned them to stay at the lowest rung of the social order.

Albert Galloway Keller believed that slaves of African origin were fitted by temperament to servitude.[8] U.G. Weatherby held that the Negro belongs perhaps to the most docile and modifiable of all races.[9] This emphasis on racial superiority of the whites gave the Negro not only a character of inferiority but also denied their contribution to their economy and to the building of the nation. In fact, the white oppressor found in the character of the oppressed a full justification of his oppression. "Ignorance and depravity and the inability to rise from degradation to civilization and respectability are the most usual allegations against the oppressed. The evils most festered by slavery and oppression are precisely those which slave holders and oppressors would transfer from their system to the inherent character of their victims. Thus the very crimes of slavery become slavery's best defence. By making the enslaved fit only for slavery they excuse themselves for refusing to make the slave a free man."[10] Racism thus involved the assertion that one race was inherently superior or inferior independent of physical conditions and social factors. In other words, "it accepted the fact that the inequality is absolute and unconditional."[11]

The earlier defence of biological superiority came from religious preachers. In 1772 the Reverend Thomas Thompson published *The Trade in Negro Slaves on the African Coast in Accordance with Human Principles and the Laws of Revealed Religion.* In 1852 the Reverend Josiah Priest wrote *A Bible Defence of Slavery.* But a sounder theoretical framework for white racial superiority was provided by J.H. Hammond, a successful plantation owner from South Carolina. In a Senate speech on March 4, 1858 he propounded, what he characteristically called, 'The Mudsill Theory' based on a division of society into two clearly defined groups, one performing superior functions and the other performing inferiors ones, very much like the caste system in India. According to him "all social systems need a class to do the menial duties, perform the drudgery of life. There must be such a class so that the other class can make progress refinement and civilization. The white Americans found such a class in Negroes who, they thought, were eminently qualified in temper, rigor, and docility to perform such a function. The whites have given them a better existence by making them their slaves."[12] John H. Van Evrie provided an equally powerful defence of the superiority of the white race. He considered the Negro as belonging to a lower order of man and to a different species from the whites. He propounded 'The Plurality Theory' which meant that every man did not originate from a single centre of creation. "The Negro is a man but a different species of man who would no more originate from the same source as ourselves than the owl could from the eagle or the shad from the salmon, or the cat from the tiger, and who can no more be forced by human power to manifest the faculties or perform the purposes assigned by the almighty creator to the Caucasian man that can either of these forms of life be made to manifest the faculties other than inherently specified and internally impressed upon their organization."[13]

In India the priestly classes, if not the originators, (although Dr. Ambedkar argued so) were the perpetrators of the institution of Shudras and Ati-Shudras founded and maintained by unnatural means. Any inquiry into the caste hierarchy must start with a study of the Nineteenth Hymn of the Tenth *Mandala* of the *Rig-Veda*, a hymn which is known by the famous name of *Purusha Sukta*. It is argued by some scholars that this hymn was not part of the original but was an interpolation at a later date. In this the division of four classes is related to four parts of the body of the Virat Purusha. The Brahmana was his mouth; the Rajanya was made his arms; The Being called the Vaishya was his thighs; the Shudra sprang from his feet. Those who hold that it is a simple division of classes for the smooth functioning of society forget two simple facts. One is that in course of time certain functions performed by a particular class came to be fixed and that class came to be known by the function it performed. Dr. Ambedkar questions the rationale for dividing people on the basis of different parts of the body. He believes that it was a calculated design on the part of *savarnas* to keep certain classes at a certain level. The originators of this division could have shown this on the basis of the upper parts of the body or four Gods. "An explanation of the origin of the four *varnas* from four gods would have maintained equality of dignity by birth of the four classes."[14] But the *Purusha Sukta* did not adopt this line of explanation and suggested graded hierarchy "The part fixes the gradation of the class and the gradation in turn fixes the function of the class."[15]

The other fact is that it was given a divine sanction. No mortal could question it. Since it had divine sanction, it was given 'uncritical reverence'. The Vedas prevent people from rationally examining it as it is God's word, shruti. The same line is followed in *Manusmriti*. All that the successive generations have done is to preserve the theory of *chaturvarna* and not to question it. The Brahmins have been learned men, Ambedkar argues, and that is why they have not produced a Voltaire. Brahmins are not intellectuals. "There is a world of difference between one who is learned and one who is an intellectual. The former is class conscious and is alive to the interests of his class. The latter is an emancipated being who is free to act without being swayed by class considerations."[16]

It was left to a Dalit to systematically investigate the origin and functioning of the system of caste hierarchy – how the Shudras came to occupy the place they did and how the fifth class, the *avarna*, the Untouchables came into being. It was a matter of curiosity for Ambedkar how this rigid system was created and continued without any written law.

First the Shudras. Ambedkar's findings are that earlier the Shudras did not represent a *varna* but a class and a tribe. They were part of the Kshatriya *varna*. There are examples of kings who were Shudras. The Shanti Parva of *Mahabharat* mentions a Shudra king called Parjavan. In *Manusmriti* it is mentioned that the child of a Brahmin and a Shudra lady, if married a Brahmin could become a *savarna* in a couple of generations.[17] Ambedkar's theory is that the Shudra kings subjected the Brahmins to tyrannies and indignities as a consequences of which the Brahimns refused to perform the *upnayana* which gives *savarnas* the status of the twice-born. Thus they were pushed to the status of *avarnas*. The Brahmins when they gained ascendancy devised a system of pain and penalties to deal with the Shudras who became degraded and came to occupy a very low status in public life. In course of time, the word Shudra lost its original meaning of a tribe or class and became a general name for a low class of people.

One of the important findings of Ambedkar is the refutation of the accepted theory that the Shudras belonged to a different race, Anarya, and were forced to their present status by the Aryans who came from outside and subjugated them. Ambedkar finds no evidence in scriptures that the Aryan came from outside. This line of argument is being supported by a number of scholars. During the Vedic period, there was no colour discrimination . Besides, Aryans were both black and white. According to Ambedkar, it was a myth invented by the imperialists because it gave them a superior character. This myth was supported by philologists who propounded a common source for Sanskrit and other European languages. It suited the *savarnas*, particularly the Brahmins, as they claimed to be the representative of the Aryan race as against the rest of the Hindus who were said to be the descendants of the non-Aryans. Ambedkar does talk of the Nags in the South, but the differences between them and the Aryans were cultural rather than ethnic. The two race theory "helps them (Brahmins) to establish their kinship with the Europeans and share their arrogance and superiority."[18]

Ambedkar next turns to Untouchables. The origin of the obnoxious system of untouchability has not been conclusively established. "The origin of untouchability lies buried in a dead past which nobody knows. To make it alive, is like an attempt to reclaim to history a city which has been dead since ages past and present it as it was in its original condition. It cannot but be that imagination and hypothesis should play a large part in such a work."[19]

Quite often the origin of untouchability as a caste is attributed to the concept of purity and is seen in the framework of religious ideology. Ambedkar finds that this has also been the characteristic of non-Hindu primitive societies. Louis Dumont sees the caste system arising out of an ideology of purity being practised within an elaborate hierarchical system in which the Brahmins rule. But Ambedkar does not accept impurity as the basis of untouchability. Even in *Manusmriti* where *avarnas* are mentioned there is no reference to untouchability as an institution. There are, however, certain vile classes who live on the outskirts of the village, but they do not automatically become Untouchables. Ambedkar tries to trace the origin of untouchability to beef-eating on the part of the broken-men (the scattered men of defeated tribes) not part of the settled tribes. He establishes the thesis that untouchability began as a consequence of the struggle for supremacy between the Buddhists and the Brahmins in which the latter won. He places the date of origin of untouchability somewhere around 400 A.D. Fi-Hian who came to India in the Second Century mentions Chandalas and not Untouchables. According to Ambedkar, Chandalas were not yet Untouchables. In support of his argument he quotes from Bana Bhatt's *Kadambari* in which a Chandala king's daughter is described in glowing terms. But Huan-Suang who came to India in the 6th Century A.D. mentions scavangers and executioners who were Untouchables. Which means that the institution originated somewhere between the visits of the two travellers. Apparently, he does not attribute its origin to economic factors which the later historians do. D.D. Kosambi was the first to relate the emergence of caste to tribes and economic factors. His thesis has been supported by Irfan Habib in his book, *Essays in Indian History*. Irfan disputes the thesis of Louis Dumont that "caste ideology has been exclusively Brahminic in its development."[20] According to him the emergence of untouchability was a consequence of surplus men and leisure. He also questions the thesis of purity and pollution supported by religion in a structure of hierarchy on this basis. He finds no basis of the origin of caste in the four *varnas* as during the Vedic period there was neither any hereditary division of labour nor any form of endogamy. Kosambi had earlier established that the caste system arose out of some external process which relates to the process of freeing of the tribal elements into a general society. This, according to him, lies at the very foundation of the most striking Indian social feature namely caste.[21] The food gatherers and the mixed jatis that arose out of the unsanctioned relationship between the *varnas* were outside the pale of four *varnas*.[22]

Since they were excluded from taking to agriculture and their own original or altered occupations were of minor or seasonal importance, they became a large reservoir of unfree, servile, landless labour available for work at the lowest cost to peasants as well as superior land holders. Thus the entire caste hierarchy was built around an elaborate system of exploitation in which the beneficiaries were the upper castes. Concepts of purity and pollution were a rationalization of this basic fact.[23] But even Irfan Habib does not dispute the fact that the Brahmins have played a key role in universalizing the caste system and integrating it into the dharma. Since they were at the top of the hierarchy, they made the caste system and Brahminism inseparable. Another important element which strengthened the hereditarily ordained caste system was the doctrine of Karma. Evidence of this doctrine is found both in *Manusmriti* (Ch.11: 24,26) and in Buddhism. "The Karma doctrine or the belief in the transmigration of soul which formed the bedrock of Buddhist philosophy was an ideal rationalization of the caste system, bearing a belief in its equity even among those who were its greatest victims."[24]

Ambedkar attacks the "pernicious notions" of caste hierarchy in India which were founded on the Shastras. In America and other countries the class composition was based on economic and social considerations. The white Americans needed cheap labour on plantations as they seemed physically not strong enough to do the work there. The Blacks fitted the requirement admirably. The rationalization of the institution of slavery came much later. Slavery had no foundation in religion. Untouchability, although it did give economic advantages to the Hindus, was primarily based on religion. The economic and social interests change with time but that is why slavery has disappeared from the face of the earth and untouchability has not. Untouchability has religious sanction. "If the Hindu observes untouchability it is because his religion enjoins him to do so. If he is ruthless and lawless in putting down the Untouchables rising against the Established Order, it is because his religion not only tells him that the Established Order is divine and therefore sacrosanct but also imposes upon him a duty to see that this Established Order is maintained by all means possible. If he doesn't listen to the call of humanity, it is because his religion does not enjoin him to regard the Untouchables as human beings. If he does not feel any qualms of conscience in assaulting, looting, burning and other acts of atrocities against the Untouchables, it is because his religion tells him that nothing is sin which is done in defence of the social order."[25] Mahatma Gandhi also accepted the fact that in India untouchability was based on religious sanction. On the occasion of the hundredth anniversary of the death of William Wilberforce, considered the father of the Abolition of Slavery Act passed by the British Parliament, Gandhi sent the following message:

"India has much to learn from the heroes of the abolition of slavery for we have slavery based upon supposed religious sanction and more poisonous than its Western fellow,"[26] He reiterated the same point in a rejoinder to a brief newsletter sent by C. F. Andrews visiting South Africa, exposing the practice of racial discrimination even in the churches in operation there. "It is, however, worth noting the distinction between the two untouchabilities. In South Africa it is based upon colour prejudice and has no sanction either in religion, or in law. In India unfortunately, it is claimed by a large number of Hindus to have religious sanction and we know that it has also the sanction of law. The Indian untouchability is, therefore, much worse than the South African. Both are, no doubt, equally mischievous, so far as the victims are concerned. Both deserve equal condemnation. Only, in India, it seems that the fight is likely to be much harder than in South Africa."[27] Gandhiji was guarded in his view as to religions sanction of untouchability. There were differences between Gandhi and Ambedkar over the removal of this sanction. Gandhiji did not go along with Ambedkar in removing these sanctions. He made it complicated by making a distinction between *varna* and caste, accepting *varna* as the basis of Hinduism. The differences surfaced when Ambedkar wrote an extended essay, 'Annihilation of Caste' for the Jat Pat Todak Mandal, Lahore. In it he examines *chaturvarna* dharma and finds that there cannot be a more degrading system of social organization than the *chaturvarna*. "It is the system which deadens, paralyzes and cripples the people from helpful activity."[28] During the Maurya period, it was completely annihilated, but when the Brahmins came into power, it was resurrected. Besides, such a system cannot be enforced without the sanction of law. "How are you", he argues, "going to compel people who have acquired higher status based on birth without reference to their worth to vacate that status? How are you going to compel people to recognize the status due to a man in accordance with his worth, who is occupying a lower status based on his birth."[29] It was also questioned by Sant Ramji of Jat Pat Todak Mandal whom Gandhiji quotes in his article in Harijan. "For all practical purposes in Hindu society caste and *varna* are one and the same thing, for the function of both of them is one and the same, i.e. to restrict intercaste marriage and interdining."[30]

Ambedkar finds Gandhiji's definition of *varna* restricted to 'ancestral calling' without relating it to work unsatisfying. The acceptance of one's ancestral calling irrespective of natural aptitude is not only impractical but also indefensible. "If the Mahatma believes as he does in everyone following his or her ancestral calling, then most certainly he is advocating the caste system and that in calling it the *varna* system he is not only guilty of terminological inexactitude, but he is causing confusion worse confounded."[31]

The most surprising aspect of this system of *chaturvarna* and caste is that the custodians of this social organization never thought it fit to examine it. The victims became so passive that they never thought of questioning the Established Order. Their status remained the same over the centuries and, what is more, the victims themselves became accomplice in the inhuman system. They tolerated it, and never mought of rebelling against it. In other countries, people rose against social evils, but not in India. With the result that they were completely disabled for direct action and accepted their servitude as 'inescapable fate.' They lost the capacity for natural response. Even when they were subjected to violence, they did not resort to counter violence. Here is an instance quoted by Ambedkar from The Times of India of August 29, 1946. "The Harijan quarters of a village in Kaira district are reported to have been raided by caste Hindus on suspicion that the Harijans were causing the death of cattle by witchcraft. It is alleged that about 200 villagers armed with sticks rounded the Harijan quarters and tying an old woman to a tree, burnt her feet. Another woman is reported to have been belaboured. The Harijans evacuated the village in panic, but Mr. Chhotabhai Patel, Secretary of the District Harijan Sevak Sangh who was apprised of the incidents has brought back the Harijans to the village and applied to the authorities for their protection."[32]

The conditioning went on at various levels: at the level of physical violence, mental violence as well as religious violence. The last one makes them different from African American. In the U.S.A. religion was enlisted to lend support to racism, but it did not damage them to the extent it damaged the Untouchables in India. In a very subtle manner the concept of purity and pollution was combined with the concept of non-violence which, surprisingly enough, got India its independence.

In the 1920s Ambedkar rejected communism as a solution to the ills of caste segregation. He, however, accepted the broad objectives of socialism but did not accept the means of violence to achieve those ends. It is not surprising that towards the end of his life he defended Buddhism on that very ground. "During the radical years of the 1930s however there was no such rejection of Marxism on the grounds of violence. The thrust of Ambedkar's attack was against the religiously inspired non-violence of Gandhism. In fact the main point of his criticism of violence was always that communist led strikes and actions were often 'adventurous' that they needlessly harmed the weakest section of the working class and Dalits and sacrificed people's lives in campaigns that tried to be militant for the sake of militancy. In fact, it upheld non-violence more as a strategy than as a principle, and it rejected Gandhian non-violence-as-religious principle."[33]

Ambedkar himself admitted in his essay 'The Revolt of Untouchables' that the movement of the Untouchables against the injustice of the Hindu social order falls into two stages. The first stage was marked by petitions and protests. The second stage was marked by open revolt in the form of direct action against the Hindu Established Order. The movement from the first attitude to the second was necessitated by the realization that the petition and protest had failed to change the Hindu attitude towards them. Despite the Government notification giving them equal rights to the use of public utilities and institutions they continued to be discriminated against. So they chose the second alternative of direct action but that too fell short of violence.

Dr. Ambedkar lists two examples of direct action to strike a blow at the Hindu social order. One was the right to water from public watering places, in this case the Chawdar Tank. Some 2000 Untouchables marched in a procession through the main streets and for the first time drank water from the Tank. Predictably, there was violent reaction from the caste Hindus who heaped all sorts of atrocities upon them for daring to pollute the water. The Untouchables were not deterred, in fact, their resolve for exercising this right to civil liberties was strengthened. The battle was fought in the court and the judgement was given in favour of the Untouchables. Similarly, they resorted to direct action in seeking entry to the famous Hindu temple at Nasik, the Kala Ram Temple. But the most important example of direct action that took place at Mahad on December 20, 1927 was the burning of the *Manusmriti* which embodies the spirit of inequality which is at the base of Hindu society. Ambedkar compares it with the fall of Bastille which was the embodiment of the spirit of the ancient regime in France. "The burning of the *Manusmriti* by the Untouchables at Mahad on December 20, 1927 is an event which has the same significance and importance in the history of the emancipation of the Untouchables which the fall of Bastille had in the liberation of the masses in France and Europe."[34]

The revolt of the Dalits in such cases was more in the nature of passive resistance and peaceful defiance. M.S. Gore calls it 'an ideology of protest.'[35] Even such direct action was not tolerated by caste Hindus who organized themselves and attacked the Dalits on the basis of a rumour that the Dalits were planning to enter another temple called Vireshwar. A serious riot was averted by the leaders of Depressed classes, who held them back. Other methods of repression were devised by the caste Hindus to halt the forward march of the Dalits for equality, sometimes ways that could hardly be called unlawful. When the Bombay Government passed orders (1935) requiring the admission of the children of the Untouchables in public schools, the caste Hindus "withdrew their children from public schools, as they did not like their children sitting with those of the Untouchables and getting themselves polluted."[36] Even the Dalit Panther Movement in Maharastra, formed on the pattern of Black Panther Movement in the U.S.A. did not have the radicalism the latter had. They were not militant enough to counter violence done to them by the upper castes. Besides, they remained isolated from the other radical groups. "They used to gather with rustic arms at the places where atrocities were reported, thus creating a temporary atmosphere of fear in those places. While the Black Panthers carried sophisticated arms because of legal sanction and their easy availability in the U.S., the Dalit Panthers carried rustic weapons."[37] It did give them a kind of self-confidence which was reflected in the use of violent language conveying simmering discontent. They, however, realized that they might not achieve the desired results through militancy. Slowly the movement petered out.

John Hope Franklin has recorded in *A Brief History of the Negro in the U.S.A.* that the first Negroes that came to the New World were not from Africa but from Europe. It was in the 14th Century that Europeans began bringing Africans into Europe, believing that they were liberating Africans from heathenism. The Spanish and Portuguese explorers brought Negroes with them to the U.S.A., so did the French. But it was in 1517 that steps were taken by the great Spanish Bishop Bartholome to establish slavery in The New World. During the 17th and 18th Centuries, the slave trade was controlled by Dutch, French and English companies leading to competition among them. By that time the Spanish slave trade had become an important economic institution, the companies setting up trading posts for capturing Africans in collusion with African leaders. The story of Kunta Kinte's kidnapping by the slatees and the toubobs could be replicated a million times. The Africans thus caught were transported to the New World in ships, sometimes 'tightly packed', depending upon the captains of slaves. "Usually they were packed so close that they had no room even to sit upright during the entire voyage. In some instances they were packed close together like books on a shelf."[38] An imaginatively reconstructed account of the journey of slaves has been graphically given by Alex Haley in *Roots*. The most striking feature of this process of enslavement was that the African never meekly submitted to the force of slave catchers. "Perhaps the most poignant aspect of the transaction was the resistance that the slaves put up to their forced sale and incarceration on the 'floating prison.' Fierce wars broke out between tribes when the members of one sought to capture members of another for the purpose of selling them to traders. Even after the slaves were sold and chained, it was necessary to guard them heavily lest they make a futile attempt to escape and injure or kill themselves in the process. One trader remarked that the Negroes were "so wilful and loth to leave their own country that they have often leap'd out of the canoes, boat and ship into the sea, and kept under water till they were 'drowned.' They preferred a watery grave or to be devoured by sharks to enslavement in some faraway land."[39]

The journey of slaves in slave ships under abominable conditions did not succeed in breaking the spirit of the slaves. They burned with humiliation and murderous rage even though they were unable to set themselves free. Kunta Kinte in *Roots*, and others who were being taken to the U.S.A., vowed to themselves that they would kill at least one toubob before they got killed. Some of them, after attacking the toubobs, jumped into the sea. "Kunta knew that he would never see Africa again. He could feel clearly now through his body against the planks, a slow, rocking motion, sometimes enough that his shoulders and arms or hips would press against the brief warmth of one of the men he was chained between. He had shouted so hard that he had no voice left, so his mind screamed it inside : kill toubobs – and their traitor black helpers."[40] Even occasional lashes could not subdue his spirit. Later, when he was sold at auction, he resented the way his body was examined by the prospective buyers. He tried to run away from slavery four times. Each time he was caught and brought back to his master. Last time the toubob chopped off his right foot so that he could not run away from the farm again. Besides, it would be an example to other slaves who might be nursing similar ideas. In one of his letters to his people back home in France, Crevecoeur has given a chilling account of a slave hung in a cage in midair. He was bleeding all over, his eyes were empty sockets, eyes being taken out by preying vultures who pecked him all over the body. The supervisor told the visitor, "The laws of self preservation rendered such executions necessary."[41] Not all blacks meekly surrendered to such violence inflicted on them. Some of them continued to indulge in violent crimes. James W. Clarke writes that violence begets violence. He systematically analyses how the culture of violence originated and how it has become an integral part of Black culture as it was of white culture. The Black culture of violence was fed by the memories of the injustices done to their ancestors in the last four hundred years. "......it was the belief of whites in their biological superiority that was the central tenet in a cluster of values and beliefs that framed and supported a regional culture of violence that targeted Blacks."[42] This supremacy was part of the agricultural economy of the South and this engendered a mindset that found expression in counter violence. In Herbert Aptheker's *American Negro Slave Revolts,* which was originally published in 1943 and later in 1987, one finds records of such revolts as expression of their rage, anger and desire for freedom. E.D. Genovese in his book *From Rebellion to Revolution : Afro-American Slave Revolts in the Making of the Modern World* gives detailed accounts of slave rebellions to show how innumerable Afro-Americans, preferred death to painful existence of slavery. Clarke lists other writers who have re-examined American history from this point of view. He suggests that in order to break the cycle of violence some kind of a moral transformation is required. "Without a rededication of spousal and parental responsibilities, all have agreed, government programs alone – no matter how essential, how benevolent or how punitive – will fail and the future of the black community and even American democracy will remain in jeopardy."[43]

"The most unremitting despotism" on the part of the whites and "degrading submission" on the part of the Blacks formed attitudes that created lasting ills.[44] And these lasting ills have vitiated the normal relationship between the two races. Alexis de Tocqueville was the first to point out that the uneasy relationship between the races was the cause of embarrassment and future dangers facing the U.S. "Hitherto whenever the whites have been the more powerful, they have kept the Negroes down in degradation or in slavery. Everywhere the Negroes have been stronger, they have destroyed the whites; and that is the only reckoning there has ever been between the two races."[45]

The first recorded instance of organized slave resistance occurred on September 13, 1663 in Virginia. And the first actual insurrection took place in 1712, when the slaves set fire to a building in New York City. However, the rebels were captured and some of them were hanged. There were other instances of conspiracy and in some cases the masters died at the hand of their slaves. "In 1742 seven Negroes were executed for the murder of their master. Others were convicted for committing the act of sabotage, such as arson, stealing of property and the brutal treatment of livestock."[46] In 1800 a planned attempt was made by Gabriel Prosser, supported by a thousand slaves, to destroy the town and their masters. They were armed with clubs, scythes, homemade bayonets and few guns. The inclement weather and the betrayal by his own followers, subverted the plan, and a large number of Blacks, along with Prosser, were captured and hanged. In 1822 a free Negro Denmark Vesey of Charteston, South Carolina, supported by thousands of slaves planned to attack the armouries to capture arms, but, like in the earlier case, the plan was leaked out, and a large number of them were arrested and, including Vesey, executed. The most dreadful of insurrections was spearheaded by Nat Turner in Virginia on August 21, 1831. Turner became a symbol of black rage and black freedom. The first day itself some 60 whitemen were killed, including Turner's master and his family. In a counter attack a large number of Turner's followers were captured and hanged. Turner was later caught and executed after a couple of days. His confession is a significant document giving rise to differing opinions on it. The insurrection sent shock waves throughout the white world. After the incident some States required slaves to go to churches of their masters. They also banned slave preachers so that such incidents were not repeated. Nat Turner was a preacher. Slave laws were made more stringent. These insurrections established at least one thing: that they were not willing to put up with their miserable existence any longer. Such revolts on the part of slaves and repression by whites continued down to the Civil War. After the Civil War the level of relationship between the two races changed. The Southerners found it difficult to accept the fact that they were now without traditional cheap labour in the form of slaves.

In the South, the existence of a large number of free Negroes proved to be a source of embarrassment to the slave holders, since their existence undermined the very foundation on which slavery was built. The speech that Huckleberry Finn's father Pap makes in *The Adventures of Huckleberry Finn* shows the conflict in the minds of the Southerners during that period. The free Negroes and the Anti-Slavery Societies were putting pressure on the Government to abolish slavery. William Llyod Garrison brought out a journal, *Liberation*, in 1831 and enlisted the active services of ex-slaves who would narrate their experiences at meetings. Negroes also published journals like *Freedom's Journal, The North Star* and the *Anglo-African*, apart from many autobiographies written by ex-slaves. The most important among them was Frederick Douglass who wrote three versions of his autobiography. Despite concerted efforts on the part of Anti-Slavery Societies, it was difficult to combat the environment of violence created by the whites.[47] Many Negro leaders moreover counselled violence, if no other approach against slavery was successful. "In 1834 the Negro convention adopted a resolution that represented the views of an increasing number of Negroes. In part it declared that those who, without crime, are outlawed by any government can owe no allegiance to its enactments.... We advise all oppressed to adopt the motto, Liberty to Death?"[48]

The Civil War raised hope in Blacks as they began to believe that their freedom was inseparable from the war. They enthusiastically enlisted themselves as volunteers for the war. During the Civil War itself the slaves began to leave the plantations. The whites feared uprisings. Increasingly, the war came to be identified with anti-slavery movement. In 1865 chattel slavery was abolished and in 1866 Civil Rights Act was passed.

But attitudes did not change with the passing of the Act, although the victory of the North over the South was a watershed in American race relations. The Southerners devised other ways to retain free Negroes so that the plantation system did not suffer. Ku Klux Klan became a terror for the Negroes. The climate of violence that was created put the free Negroes on the defensive. Their reaction alternated between demands for Civil Rights and outright violence.

The issues concerning race relations were crystallized by leaders like DuBois and Marcus Garvey, the latter launched a back-to-Africa movement. Some leaders favoured integration and assimilation on equal terms; some others demanded separatism.[49] The emergence of Martin Luther King Jr. in the mid 20th Century raised hopes for those who favoured assimilationism. His slogan, 'we shall overcome' was drowned in his blood when he was assassinated. The emergence of Malcolm X at this point of time in American race history marked a change in the strategies adopted by Blacks for achieving full freedom. Instead of non-violent means the emphasis was on violent means. The demand now was not for Civil Rights but for Human Rights.[50] "The rage pretended to sleep, but it never slept. The merest touch of a feather was enough to bring it howling, roaring out."[51]

A philosophical basis for violence was provided by Frantz Fanon in *The Wretched of the Earth.* He wrote: "At the level of individuals, violence is a cleansing force. It frees the native from his inferiority complex and from his despair and inaction. It makes him fearless and restores his self-respect."[52] The streak of violence can be attributed to their fearful enslavement and its perpetuation by other means. Arbitrary acts of white brutality have left emotional scars which also contributed to the culture of violence. The most recent manifestation of it was the beating up of a black man by white cops in full view of the public in Los Angeles, and the subsequent riots that broke out as a consequence of that act of brutality. The simmering violence in American culture is a fact that can be ignored by both races at their peril.

The resistance to the manipulation of the lives of Blacks and Dalits differs because of historical and economic conditions of their existence. It is apparent that such manipulation damaged their psyche and caused a split in their personality. They were made to accept the worldview of their masters, although reluctantly. The process of liberation of both these oppressed groups began with the struggle over the nature of reality. It involved the questioning of reality imposed on them and then redefining it so that they not only moved out of the fixed place given to them but also acquired new frames of reference. The whites and the *savarnas* could help them in this process if they could devise ways to help them deal with their nature of reality. James Baldwin wrote: "I did not intend to allow the white people of this country to tell me who I was and limit me that way and polish me off that way."[53]

Dr. Ambedkar questioned the 'inherent' right of the *savarnas* to define Dalit reality, to create a social structure of graded inequality which deprived them of the opportunities to break out of that structure educationally, economically and culturally. Their growth was forever stunted, their dreams, blurred and their ambitions circumscribed. Their struggle to break that stranglehold shows that they are no longer at the receiving end and are demanding what is theirs by right. This is reflected in the changing appellations which define and redefine their existence.

In America, African Americans were first called Negroes, which initially denoted a race different from the white. Soon the ethnic label was supplemented by a contemptible expression 'Nigger'. The appellation Negro, however, continued to exist alongside 'Nigger' and retained its meaning of racial difference. Malcolm X writes in his Autobiography that the white boys called them 'Nigger', 'Darkee', 'Rustus' and 'Coons' and they were convinced that these were their natural names.[54] Gradually even the word Negro acquired a negative connotation. White American, including creative writers like Faulkner and Mark Twain, used Negro and Nigger interchangeably and no one objected to it. DuBois, however, felt that their suffering would not be reduced by change in the appellation. He felt that there was nothing wrong in a name, and the word Negro would mean the same by any other name as the meaning of the word changes with its usage. The word 'quaker', for example, was once used in a pejorative sense, which is no longer the case now. DuBois in *The Souls of Black Folk* signifies the moment when the American Negro began to reject the idea that the world belonged to white people only. It was during the Harlem Renaissance that Black writers began to separate those aspects of their existence that made them different from the whites. They underscored the fact that they were different from their masters. In fact, these aspects gave them a distinct character and a distinct identity within the mainstream white culture and identity. For the first time the Black writers emphasized that the Negro was a historical entity as well as a human being and this fact was kept away from him. "The power of the white world is threatened whenever a black man refused to accept the white world's definition."[55]

The questioning of the definition of their existence threw up a number of appellations. 'Coloured' was one and 'Black' was another. It suggested that these appellations were as respectable as 'white' and there was no history behind them. In other words, they were different but not inferior. This was a radically changed perception of reality. The National Conference on Power passed a resolution to the change from Negro to African American or Afro-American. The Negro Teachers' Association of New York changed its name to the African American Teachers' Association. The New York Amsterdem News announced that it would no longer use the word Negro. The Philadelphia Leaders used the term 'OPPRESSED AMERICAN' which was scorned by Samuel Cornish. He said that since Indians are called Red Indians and whites are called white Americans, and since they are no different from them, they should be called Coloured Americans. In Ghana in a press conference Malcolm X used the appellation Negro and he was quickly and firmly corrected. The Ghanians said that Afro-American has greater meaning and dignity. Malcolm X sincerely apologized and as long as he was in Africa, he never used the word Negro again. Le Roi Jones and Larry Neal write : "The word 'Black' was used by the English to describe a free man of color, while Negro was used to designate a black slave."[56] This questioning of their existence in America and changing appellations used indicate the political awakening in this ethnic group. This took the entire issue of relations between ethnic groups in America to a political level, although the racial aspect could not be completely ignored. They were in contact with two levels of existence simultaneously. They kept contact with the continent of their origin, in whatever form it was possible, and the country of their forced adoption. In the last decades of the Twentieth Century the common appellation to describe the Negro in the U.S.A. was either Black or African American. And in their process of acquiring full human status, they do not want to shun either. In this sense colour becomes not only a political reality but also a cultural reality. Although the fight over the nature of reality still continues, they have reached a stage where they are redefining the larger reality of which they are a part. "The power to define comes when we can take that turn and give it back to those who gave it to us. Now if they choose to call us that (nigger), that's fine. We don't have to acknowledge it or turn our head when they say it, and it will die out. I think it is important that we reconnect with the African term, which we have. This is a little radical in some people's opinion, but a lot of people claim to be African American. I don't even claim that. I say African born in America, because that describes my condition. And a lot of people have problem with that."[57]

Likewise in India, the appellations used for the one time Untouchables chart out their history until they reach a stage of political consciousness. They took two millenniums to realize that their problem was not just a caste problem but also a political one. The effort of those who want to exploit their situation is to push it to the caste fold. The appellations 'Untouchable', 'Antyaja', 'Panchama' defined their existence when the upper castes had complete control over their lives. Like the Negro, they had no say in defining the nature of their reality. The *savarnas* prescribed the limits of a*varna* existence, the mode of their living, the level of communication with them and the impossibility of change. For centuries they accepted this image of themselves, this definition of their existence, although dissenting voices were raised by saints who were both religious and social reformers. Lord Buddha was the first to question the hierarchy of social existence on the basis of birth. Swami Dharmateerth writes in *History of Hindu Imperialism* that the Brahmins consolidated their power and even rewrote certain scriptures, added certain portions to the existing ones according to their design. The imposition of the Mugal rule which seemed to represent an egalitarian order did not help the Untouchables much in improving their lot. In the name of preservation of culture and religion the Brahmins forced other castes to withdraw themselves into a rigid hierarchical order. The Untouchables were uncomfortable with the reaffirmation of this unhappy categorization, but all they could do was to appeal to the conscience of the *savarnas*. Even those who got converted to Islam remained at the lowest rung of the ladder.

It was with the advent of the British and the consequent resistance against the imperial rule that attempts were made to redefine their existence in social terms. It was during this period that ideas released by the Enlightenment helped social reformers and thinkers to reassess and reexamine the rigid caste structure in India. In the 19th Century these ideas took the form of a movement. Almost simultaneously, in all parts of the country, social movements sprang up posing a challenge to the hegemony of the upper castes. But most reformers who took up their cause never rejected the religious framework. Jyoti Ba Phule in Maharashtra was the first Shudra to raise a banner of revolt and shook the very foundation of caste structure. He questioned the code of conduct prescribed not only for lower classes but also for women. In fact, he did pioneering work in this field and others who came after him built up on that. In a way, he anticipated both Ambedkar and Gandhi, the latter called him Mahatma Phule, and the former dedicated his book *Shudras* to him. He unceasingly worked for the uplift of *avarnas* and the widows. Although he questioned the rituals and established Satya Shodhak Samaj, he operated within the larger framework of religion. Apart from humanizing religion, he called his religion Sarvajanik Satya Dharma which, to a large extent, was governed by rational thought and which sought to create a world family based on human rights. In such a religion, there would be no domination of one group by another. He also examined the past, although his interpretation was not entirely acceptable. He looked for religious and political equality in past history. Phule found that the root of the social decline of Hindu society could be traced back to social slavery of thousand years.[58] But Phule continued to use the appellation 'Untouchable' or 'Ati-Shudras'. He wrote a booklet *Asprashyanchi Kaifiyat* (The case of the Untouchables) presenting an imaginary account of a Mahar and Mang urging Queen Victoria on a tour to India to visit their locality. One could say that in him the reality of the Untouchables is struggling to free itself from the stranglehold of sacred religion.

The same struggle can be seen in the life and movement of Narayan Guru in Kerala. He belonged to the Ezvah caste, somewhat equivalent to the caste of Jyotiba Phule. Quite early in life, he reacted to social discrimination between the lower and the upper castes. He spent most of his life in the company of the Untouchables and the backward classes. He made no distinction between one caste and another. He attacked the rigidity of social and religious practices by having a separate Shiva temple and by establishing a centre for weavers in order to support his movement of equality. To strengthen his movement, he set up a school and a library. Like Phule he continued to use the term Untouchable. On his birthday in 1921 he gave two messages to the people : one was that there is one caste, one religion and one God; the other that alcohol is poison and one should abstain from it and stop manufacturing it. But religion was never pushed into the background.

Another great revolutionary who effectively worked for the removal of social evils like untouchability was E.V. Ramaswami Periyar. He was an atheist. He called upon all those who were keen on doing justice to the backward and depressed classes to burn the *Ramayana* and the *Manu Dharmshastra* which gave legitimacy to social evils. He was the one who changed the appellation from Untouchables to depressed classes. The British Government also favoured this appellation.[59] Periyar changed the scope of his struggle by including all non-Brahmins, Christians and Muslims to challenge the rigid caste system. He went to the extent of saying that Brahmins and non-Brahmins form two opposing groups, a line which was later developed by Ambedkar. He observed that caste practices were being followed in all institutions including schools and Khadi Boards. To counter this domination, he formed, what is called, Self Respect Movement. It was a powerful social movement and contributed a great deal to the destruction of caste structure in Tamil Nadu. Later he dissociated himself from the Congress leadership on its apparent Brahminic bias on the issue of caste discrimination in schools. Thus he saw the problem of the depressed classes in purely social and political terms. "Ramaswami debunked Brahminsim from the standpoints of rationalistic atheism and social criticism. His cultural and ideological onslaught on the traditional social structure did go a long way to legitimise it and to expose it as nothing but greed for exclusive power."[60]

Gandhiji's use of the appellation Harijan for the Untouchables was part of his concept of Hindu society. He believed that the upper classes would realize the irrationality of segregating one caste from the other castes and barring all intercourse. He believed in the goodness of men and appealed to their conscience. In spite of his firm commitment to the amelioration of the lot of the Harijans, he was still operating within the religious framework. Ambedkar was unhappy with the appellation Harijan. When it was brought to the Assembly in Bombay for discussion and approval, Ambedkar opposed it. But despite his opposition and that of some members of the Labour Party, it was passed by the Assembly. Nehru was quick to point out that Gandhiji was trying to apply value system of the medieval society to present day reality. Gandhiji was defining their existence from the point of view of an enlightened Hindu who wanted to provide them status within the Hindu fold without disturbing the tenets of Hindu religion. This was questioned by Ambedkar who provided a new framework which was social and political and not religious. For quite sometime he continued to use the appellation depressed classes which was the official appellation used by the British. At places he used the phrase oppressed groups which suggested the hegemony of the upper castes sanctioned by the *varna*shrama dharma. It also enabled him to relate them to other oppressed groups, making them part of a world-wide movement that began after the World War. He was aware of Dalit Muslims and Dalit Christians but did not make efforts to organize them under a common banner. The Colonial Government set up a schedule in which reservations were to be provided for the untouchable castes. Ambedkar later used the term scheduled castes, which did not include other backward castes. It is surprising that the word 'Dalit' was first used by Jyotiba Phule and later by Swami Vivekanand, but it acquired its new connotation only in the 1970s, when it was used by Dalit writers. Dalit has a secular and even economic connotation. Gangadhar Pantawane defines it succinctly in the following words: "To me dalit is not a caste. He is a man exploited by the social and economic traditions of this country. He doesn't believe in God, Rebirth, Soul, Holy Books teaching separatism, Fate and Heaven because they have made him a slave. He does believe in humanism. Dalit is a symbol of change and revolution."[61] Dalit here clearly means the suppressed and the exploited people and is in consonance with the larger connotation given to the depressed people by Ambedkar. It gained currency during the Dalit Panther movement in the 70s. Gradually it came to include the scheduled tribes and other backward castes. The Bahujan Samaj Party has changed it to Bahujan in order to include a large majority of those who belong to lower castes. Kancha Ilaiah has combined Dalit and Bahujan to include all those people and castes who form the exploited and suppressed majority.[62] On the basis of appellations used by the Dalits and African Americans one could construct the history of their struggle as also the direction it should take. For defining and redefining themselves is part of their process to rehabilitate themselves. If they relent in their struggle, they would be defined by others. Now the invisible forces that are redefining and reshaping our lives in economic terms are making the task of the Dalits and African Americans more difficult. DuBois, Richard Wright and James Baldwin were the names given by their former masters. DuBois traces his ancestry and discovers that DuBois was a successful plantation and slave owner and his surname was given to him. The names were given to them under circumstances not of their choosing. "It is particularly problematic because it is not just your name but your family, your tribe. When you die, how can you connect with your ancestors if you have lost your name? That's a huge psychological scar. The last thing you can do is to take another name which is yours because it reflects something about you or your own choice."[63] Le Roi Jones changed his name to Amiri Baraka; Malcolm severed all connections with his past by adding X to his name; Cassius Clay became Mohammad Ali. Toni Morrison feels that a part of that had to do with 'cultural orphanage.' The renaming and redefining is not an individual choice. It has something to do with the process of deconstructing and reconstructing reality in order to be able to operate within it.

The question of power has always been in the background while defining their predicament: the power to define the future of their caste/race; the power to have a say in the running of the country; the power to change the very structure of society; the power to choose an ideology that will help not only a particular caste or race but all those havenots who have been at the receiving end. Dalit and Bahujan have political connotations but have not acquired the force that comes with political power. Their prominent leaders fear that the reality of caste or race will be ignored if they subordinate it entirely to class formation. At the same time they know that their situation is related to power which is concentrated in the hands of the whites or superior castes. When Ambedkar talked of widening the area of their struggle, he had this aspect in mind.[64] Similarly, for Malcolm X, the struggle for black freedom was neither social nor moral; it was between the white haves and the black havenots. And if the oppressed wanted to breach the power of the oppressor, he must either acquire power or align himself with power.[65] At the same time Malcolm X was conscious of "institutionalized racism" and felt that the liberals treated the Negro as a symbol and a victim and not as a man. The fact is that unless the peculiar nature of casteism or racism is taken into account, the larger formation of class will be delayed and will fail to achieve its desired end. In India it was not until the second congress of the CPI in 1948 that the reality of caste was taken into account by the communists, but even then Ambedkar was considered a reformist and separatist leader. Ambedkar considered Untouchables, Shudras and tribals as natural allies to combine for the destruction of the Hindu social order. But this did not happen and the Untouchables were completely isolated. What was more. They were opposed by the very classes who ought to be their natural allies.[66] Ambedkar tried to forge a common front with workers in factories in Bombay, in a limited way, of course, but he soon realized that they were segregated on the basis of their work. They were for example never placed in the weaving section. In America, racial discrimination was apparent even in the Communist Party. Richard Wright once went to New York to attend a meeting of John Reed Club, the party's literary wing. He was shocked to find that there was no accommodation reserved for him in the hotel where other delegates were lodged. His problems did not end there. Since he wanted to be a different kind of communist who shaped people's feelings and awakened their hearts, he was called a Trotskyite and branded an independent intellectual not toeing the party line.[67]

But that does not mean that the uniqueness of their experience whether in India or in America and the interests of the larger groups cannot be combined. As in America, Indian intellectuals are beginning to see the reality of caste and its place in the common interests of people similarly placed. Nursing their unique experience might lead them to believe that there are no parallel situations and no oppressed people in other parts of the world. This might also lead them to have contempt for those liberals and progressive non-Dalits and non-Blacks who largely agree with them and want to work with them to dismantle the oppressive system. Stephen Spender in a piece on James Baldwin writes: "If the Negro problem is resolvable, the only useful way of discussing it is to consider American Negroes in a situation comparable to that of workers and Negroes elsewhere (like Dalits in India). To write as though Negroes do not exist anywhere except in America, is to induce despair, to suggest that in America white and black cannot become integrated to the (rather limited) extent to which they have been, for example, in Brazil. It is in fact playing in the hands of black Muslims whose position is that America – world even – has to choose between having nothing but black or nothing but white people by which it is meant that it would be undemocratic to have nothing but the black majority."[68] Both Baldwin and Ambedkar were greatly agitated by the disparity between the situation of their people and the people for whom they worked. Even the terminology used by them for describing their situation and how they were deprived of their liberty and human existence is not only identical but goes beyond the predicament of their people.

Spender does not mean to say that one should be blind to their human aspect and should define their existence only in economic and class terms. Once class formations take place, property relations will be defined in human terms. The reason why the slogans of the

French Revolution never became a reality was that the means of production were concentrated in a few hands. Ambedkar was in no doubt that this would have to change. He warned the people in parliament that if economic inequalities were allowed to continue, the exploited might destroy the very structure on which parliamentary democracy was based.[69] During the past fifty years these inequalities have increased and can be remedied only if economic equality is ensured. According to Ambedkar this could be done by an organized body of workers which would include Dalits and other deprived sections of society. He could not say as much but it meant that the caste issue would have to be part of a larger class issue. James Baldwin sounded a similar warning when he wrote in *The Fire Next Time* that if racial and related disparities continued, the Blacks might ring down the curtain on the American scene.

In African American history there are two distinct strains : one leaning towards nationalism leading to separatism, and the other towards assimilationism. The strain of nationalism was represented by DuBois through Marcus Garvey, Elija Mohammad, Malcolm X, Eldridge Cleaver, Stokely Carmichael to Louis Farrakhan. They take this strain back to African American slaves who managed to forge an alternative world view capable of supporting either a spiritual or 'national' liberation movement. The process was strengthened with the collection of accurate information about their group history and culture.[70] Negro intellectuals have supported either one strain or another.[71] Some of them went to the extent of saying that they were a separate nation within a nation and identified themselves with the third world countries that were struggling to become free from colonial rule. Disagreeing with the major changes made by Elija Muhammad's son after Elija's death, in Nation of Islam, Louis Farrakhan emphasized "his belief in the continuing need for a race-specific theology and a self-defining, separatist approach to economic and social relations."[72] He found the establishment of a separate nation-state as impractical. He discussed the Nation of

Islam's People Organized for Economic Rebirth (P.O.W.E.R.) and urged his people to come out of that state of mind and work for the real thing that is economic empowerment. In India, the history of the Dalits has always moved towards assimilationsim, although the other strain was not altogether absent. Although Ambedkar identified Dalit exploitation and caste discrimination with Hinduism which sanctioned the *varna* system, he was at best a social reformer. When his efforts to find the rightful place for the Dalits within the Hindu fold failed, he decided to reject Hinduism and embraced Buddhism along with a large number of his followers. But it is not considered a break with Hinduism by many thinkers as Buddhism is taken as an offshoot of Hinduism. Ambedkar once told Gandhiji that though he differed from him on the issue of untouchability, he would take an appropriate decision at the opportune time. "I will choose only the least harmful way for the country. And that is the greatest benefit I am conferring on the country by embracing Buddhism; for Buddhism is a part and parcel of Bhartiya culture. I have taken care that my conversion will not harm the tradition of the culture and history of the land."[73] According to Rajgopalachari Ambedkar's so-called conversion to Buddhism was more anti-Hinduism than the acceptance of the gospel of Buddhism. It was Ambedkar's last demonstration of anger. Nonetheless a large majority of them remained within the Hindu fold and their struggle for the annihilation of caste distinction still continues. Their fate seems to be inextricably linked with the Hindus. The problem of the Dalits is more complicated because they are part of the same ethnic stock, contrary to what the British scholars say. They are Hindus and yet not Hindus. They believe in Hindu religion, yet are not free to practise it like other Hindus. One reason could be that unlike Blacks, they do not belong to a separate racial stock. Besides, all along they have found solace in the cultural strength of Hindu religion minus caste. Some half-hearted efforts have, however, been made as is revealed in the book, *History of Hindu Imperialism* by Swami

Dharma Teertha as also in Kanchan Ilaiah's *Why I am Not a Hindu* and Dr. Dharmvira's books on Kabir, but these efforts never developed into a movement. The literature written by Kabir, Chokhamela, Nandnar, Ravidas and others is claimed equally by Dalits and non-Dalits. Their goal was never separatism but integration on more human terms. A spurt of it could be seen in Dr. Ambedkar's demand for a separate electorate and he succeeded in getting it from the Britishers. But Gandhiji opposed it on the ground that Dalits were an integral part of Hindu religion and thus there was no need for a separate electorate for them. Dr. Ambedkar relented when Gandhiji went on a fast unto death. There is an element of reconciliation in his assertion that "only when the Hindu Society becomes a casteless society that it can hope to have the strength enough to defend itself. Without such internal strength Swaraj for Hindus may turn out to be only a step towards slavery."[74]

The mood of African American has also swung towards reconciliation. Representative African American writers like Toni Morrison, Cornel West, Henry Louis Gates Jr., Alice Walker and Maya Angelou are working for a society in which they will be both African and American. They want to clear the pallid stream of American life, its lust for wealth, its market morality and humanize America so that they have their place in America like any other ethnic group. And in this race differences and class differences will have to be grouped together so that one does not know where one ends and the other begins.

References

1. Gore Vidal, *At Home,* New York, Random House, 1988, p. 286.
2. Toni Morrison, Playing in the Dark: Whiteness and Literary Imagination, William Morrow, New York, 1992, pp.4-5.
3. M. Andrew Scott, Henry George, Henry Adams and The Dominant American Ideology, SAC – 76, 1977, p. 237.
4. Le Roi Jones, Home: Social Essays, New York, William Morrow and Co., 1960, p. 85.
5. Dr. Babasaheb Ambedkar, Writings and Speeches, Education

Department, Government of Maharashtra, 1989, Vol.7, p. 266.

6. Babasaheb Ambedkar, Writings and Speeches, Vol. 5, p. 15.
7. Richard Wright, American Hunger, Harper and Row, 1977, p. 13.
8. Albert Galloway Keller, Colonization, Boston, 1907, p. 145.
9. U.G. Weatherby, "The West Indies as a Sociological Laboratory" in American Journal of Sociology XXIX, 1923-24, p. 242.
10. Frederick Douglass, quoted in The Future of the Race by Henry Louis Gates Jr. and Cornel West, Alfred Knoff, New York, 1996, p. 2.
11. Juan Comas, Racial Myths, Ionesco, Paris, 1953, p. 49.
12. Leslie Fishel Jr. and Benjamin Quarles, The Black American: A Documentary History, Glen View, Illinois, Scott Foresman, 1970, p. 59.
13. *Ibid.*, p. 60.
14. Ambedkar, Writings and Speeches, Vol.7, p. 33.
15. *Ibid.*, p. 32.
16. *Ibid.*, p. 240.
17. Manusmriti, Introduction by R.N. Sharma, Chaukhamba Sanskrit Sansthan, Delhi, 1998, 10:65.
18. Ambedkar, Writings and Speeches, Vol.7, p. 86.
19. *Ibid.*, p. 44.
20. Irfan Habib, Essays in Indian History, Tulika, 1979, p. 169.
21. D.D. Kosambi, An Introduction to the Study of Indian History, Bombay, 1956, p. 25.
22. See Manusmriti, ed. Dr. R.N. Sharma Chapter 10:12, 20, 24, 31, 32, 34, 36, 37.
23. Irfan Habib, p. 166.
24. *Ibid.*, p.168.
25. Ambedkar, Writing and Speeches, Vol. 5, p. 90.
26. Baren Ray, Gandhi's Campaign Against Untouchability, 1933-1934, Gandhi Peace Foundation, New Delhi, 1996, p. 42.
27. *Ibid.*, p. 43.
28. Ambedkar, Writings and Speeches, Vol. I, p. 63.
29. *Ibid.*, p. 59.
30. *Ibid.*, p. 84.
31. *Ibid.*, p. 93.
32. Ambedkar, Writings and Speeches, Vol. 5, p. 33.
33. Gail Omvedt, Dalits and the Democratic Revolution, Sage Publications, New Delhi, 1994, p. 227.
34. Ambedkar, Writings and Speeches, Vol. 5, p. 255.

35. M.S. Gore, The Social Context of an Ideology, Sage Publication, 1993.
36. Ambedkar, Writings and Speeches, Vol. 5, p. 263.
37. Lata Murugukar, Dalit Panther Movement in Maharashtra, Popular Prakashan, Bombay, 1991, p. 203.
38. John Hope Franklin, "A Brief History of the Negro in the United States" in The American Negro Reference Book, ed. John P. Davis, Prentice Hall, New Jersey, 1967, p. 6.
39. *Ibid.*, p. 5.
40. Alex Haley, *Roots*, Picador, 1997, p. 156.
41. J. Hector St. John Crevecoeur, Letters from an American Farmer, Gloucester, Mass. Peter Smith, 1968, p. 178.
42. James W. Clarke, The Lineaments of Wrath: Race, Violent Crime in American Culture, Transaction Publishers, New Jersey, 1998, p. 6.
43. *Ibid.*, p. 293.
44. Thomas Jefferson, Notes on the State of Virginia, Boston, 1801, pp. 240-241.
45. Alexis de Tocqueville, Democracy in America, Double Day Anchor, New York, 1969, Original 1838, p. 342.
46. Franklin, p. 11.
47. S.D. Kapoor, "Aspects of Violence", in Jodhpur Studies in English, Vols. III and IV, 1990, pp. 33-41.
48. Franklin, pp. 35-36.
49. See Harold Cruse, The Crisis of the Negro Intellectual: From Its Origin to the Present, William Morrow and Co., 1967.
50. The Autobiography of Malcolm X (with the assistance of Alex Haley), Rept. Penguin Books 1976, p. 258.
51. James Baldwin, Tell Me How Long the Train's Been Gone, Dell Publishing, New York, 1973, p. 89.
52. Frantz Fanon, The Wretched of the Earth, Penguin 1973, p. 74.
53. James Baldwin, The Fire Next Time, Dell Publishing, new York, 1969, p. 95.
54. Malcolm X, Autobiography, p. 83.
55. James Baldwin, The Fire Next Time, p. 95.
56. Larry Neal and Le Roi Jones, Black Fire: An Anthology of African American Writing, William Morrow and Co., 1968 p. 180.
57. Randall Kenan, Walking on Water: Black American Lives at the Turn of the 21st Century, Alfred Knoff, New York, 1999, p. 484.
58. Tark Tirth Lakshman Shastri, Jyotiba Phule, National Book Trust, India, 1996, p. 77.

59. M.A. Gopalkrishnanand, Periyar: The Father of the Tamil Race Emerald Publishers, Madras, 1996.
60. G.Aloysius, Nationalism Without a Nation in India, O.U.P., 1994, p. 60.
61. Quoted by Zelliot in From Untouchable to Dalit, Manohar Publishers, New Delhi, 1998 (Rep), p. 268.
62. Kancha Ilaiaih, Why I am Not a Hindu, Somya, 1996, Preface pp. VI-IX.
63. Danielle Taylor Gutherie (ed) Conversations with Toni Morrison, University of Massachusetts Press, 1994, p. 126.
64. See Ch.7 'Ambedkarism': The Theory of Dalit Liberation in Gail-Omvedt, Dalit and The Democratic Revolution, Sage Publication, New Delhi, 1994, pp. 223-259.
65. Malcolm X, the Man and His Times, quoted in the Introduction to the Autobiography of Malcolm X, p. XXIII.
66. The Untouchables: 'Children of India's Ghetto' in Ambedkar, Writings and Speeches, Vol. V. pp. 115-116.
67. Richard Wright, American Hunger, Harper and Row, 1997, p. 107.
68. Fred L. Standley and Nancy V. Burt, (ed) Critical Essays on James Baldwin, C.K. Hall and Co., Boston, 1988, p. 256.
69. Ambedkar, Writings and Speeches, Vol. 13, p. 1216.
70. William L. Van De Burg, (ed.) modern Black Nationalism, New York University Press, 1997, p. 5.
71. Harold Cruse, The Crisis of Negro Intellectual, 1967 op.cit.
72. Modern Black Nationalism, p. 315.
73. Quoted by Dhananjaya Keer in Dr. Ambedkar: Life and Mission, Popular Prakashan, Bombay 1999, p. 498.
74. Ambedkar, Writings and Speeches, Vol. I, p. 80.

2
The Process of Liberation

The major thing that binds us - there may be others because I don't dwell on it quite that much - is the clear identification of what the enemy forces are, not this person or that person and so on, but the acknowledgement of a way of life dreamed up for us by some other people who are at the moment in power, and knowing the ways in which it can be subverted. That is a connection. We know who he is. What separates us are the things that separate all people, one of which is the way you identify what the problems are and the disguises in which they appear.

An Interview with Toni Morrison by Christina Davis in Conversations with Toni Morrison

But while I am prepared to bear with the imperfections and shortcomings of the society in which I may be destined to labour, I feel I should not consent to live in a society which cherishes wrong ideals or a society which having right ideals will not consent to bring its social life in conformity with those ideals. If I am disgusted with Hindus and Hinduism it is because I am convinced that they may cherish wrong ideals and live a wrong social life. My quarrel with Hindus and Hinduism is not over the imperfections of their social conduct. It is much more fundamental. It is over their ideals.

B.R. Ambedkar
in Annihilation of Caste
Vol. I,
Ambedkar Writings and Speeches

The process of liberation of Dalits and African Americans from invisibility to visibility from a non-human to a human status and the attainment of complete manhood has not been simple. It has been painful and prolonged. It has been painful because at each stage of their struggle they are reminded of their lurid past and the indignities they were subjected to; it has been prolonged, more in the case of Dalits than in that of African Americans, because they had to fight against an invisible wall of segregation supported by entrenched attitudes despite changes in historical situation. The attitudes that racism and casteism have put in them cannot be jettisoned out of their system at one stroke. The ruling ideology in its innumerable manifestations does not concede the human space that ought to be theirs by right. The history of African Americans since 1866 and of Dalits since 1948 has been the history of struggle to reclaim that space. The psychological distance is not allowed to be bridged and that is why it is taking so long.

Broadly speaking, their struggle for liberation has moved through three stages, prolonged or shortened depending upon the force of ruling ideology and the situation in which they were placed. The first stage is that of attaining consciousness of their predicament, that is how they acquire the knowledge that they are being treated differently, not because God willed it so or because of some inherent imperfection in them, but because of the manipulation of those who have complete control over their lives. The second stage comes when they question this categorization and struggle to come out of it. The third stage comes when they reject the false image imposed on them and try to redefine themselves.

To the African Americans the level of consciousness came early. Since they were forcibly brought to America, they carried the consciousness of a free land, although the whites tried to beat this out of their system. But the fact is that they never accepted their fate in an alien land and were unhappy with the structures imposed on their lives. Besides, their more fortunate brethren who lived in the Northern part of America and were exposed to liberal thought provided a contrast to their existence. The awareness of their predicament was kept alive not only by the possibility of a free life but also by memories of the past which were passed on from generation to generation. It is interesting to know how the vestiges of their parent culture in the form of words stay with them. In *Roots* by Alex Haley, the descendants of Kunta Kinte have been using certain words – 'Ko' and 'Bolongo', for example – for generations and these provided tenuous connection with the land of their origin. Alex Haley was able to locate the exact place in Africa where these words were spoken and from which his ancestor was kidnapped. When Frederick Douglass wanted to know from his elders why they were slaves and the whites were not, he was told that they were trapped into it by the wily whites and their native supporters. This awareness was sharpened by the contradictions between the professed ideals of the land and the denial of those ideals to one segment of their society. Later, when Douglass managed to become free, he gave lectures in America and in England in which he effectively brought out the double standards that the whites followed.

In the case of Dalits the process of acquiring consciousness of their predicament was protracted. It was only in the mid-Twentieth Century that they became conscious of the fact that it was the system that was responsible for their miserable state and not the Dalits themselves as they had been made to believe. Despite this consciousness, in some of them, the lurking fear remained that by demanding equality they were violating some divine law. Even in the past voices were raised against it but they were not strong enough to dismantle the system and the philosophy behind it. From Buddha through Chokhamela, Kabir, Ravidas, Mahatma Phule to Ambedkar all ripped open the façade that they themselves were responsible for their lowly state, but the façade remained a reality. Nonetheless, the ground was prepared on which a secular democratic equalitarian structure could be raised, although it was not easy to dislodge the abstract image that had become part of their psyche.

Frederick Douglass seems to be speaking for all his people who were slaves when he poured out his heart's complaint at the sight of moving multitude of ships standing on the banks of Chesapeake Bay:

"Those beautiful vessels, robed in white and so delightful to the eyes of freemen, were to me so many shrouded ghosts, to terrify and torment me with thoughts of my wretched condition. I have often, in the deep stillness of a summer's Sabbath, stood all alone upon the banks of that noble bay, and traced with saddened heart and tearful eye, the countless number of sails moving off to the mighty ocean. The sight of these always affected me powerfully. My thoughts would compel utterance, and those, with no audience but the Almighty, I would pour out my soul's complaint in my rude way with an apostrophe to the moving multitude of ships."

"You are loosed from your moorings, and free. I am fast in my chains, and am a slave.... You are freedom's swift winged angels that fly around the world. I am confined in bonds of iron."[1]

The countless ships moving off to the ocean are freedom's swift-winged angels whereas he was chained in bonds of iron to the moorings of his master. Unlike those ships, he has no hope to sail freely through the ocean of life. He was so desperate that he even questioned the existence of a just God. But he was convinced that slavery was man-made and not God made and it was left to them to alter it.

Similarly, Chokhamela, a 14th Century Mahar poet-saint, questions the concept of impurity, which is said to be the basis of untouchability, relating it to a universal concept.

The only impurity is in the five elements.
There is only one substance in the world.
Then who is pure and who is impure?
The cause of pollution is in the creation of the body.

He goes on to give 'impurity' a wider meaning in which the distinction between the so-called pure and the 'impure' is obliterated, or at least is made meaningless.

In the beginning
At the end
There is nothing but pollution.
No one knows any one who is born pure.
Chokha asks in wonder,
Who is pure?[2]

It is apparent that the division of people on the basis of purity and impurity is a contrived one and is not God-given. But the individual lamentation of a Douglass or a Chokhamela did not automatically get converted into group consciousness which becomes the basis for liberation. The consciousness is firmly established when their people believe that they "have had a common history: have suffered a common disaster and have one long memory."[3] It then leads them to the questioning of existing relationships in terms of new reference and new connection. The irrational and the abstract are replaced by the rational and the concrete. It is a drastic change in perception. Douglass represents this change in his autobiography. When no longer in bondage, he wrote a letter to his former master, Mr. Auld from a position of equality. "I am myself; you are yourself; we are two distinct persons, equal persons. What you are I am. You are a man, so am I. God created both, and made us separate beings. I am not by nature bond to you, or you to me."[4] But even as he wrote this letter, a large majority of Blacks, including his brothers and sisters, were still in captivity. In the other part of the letter, Douglass posed the question of suffering in human terms, imagining the reversal of roles of the master and the slave. "How, let me ask would you look upon me were I, some dark night in company with a band of hardened villains, to enter the precincts of your legal dwelling, and seize the person of your own lovely daughter, Amanda, and carry her off from your family, friends and all the loved ones of her youth, make her my slave – compel her to work, and I take her wages – place her name on my ledger as property – disregard her personal rights – fetter the powers of her immortal soul by denying her the principle of learning to read and write – feed her coarsely – clothe her scantily, and whip her on the naked back occasionally, more and still more horrible, leave her unprotected – a degraded victim of the brutal lust of fiendish overseers who would pollute, blight and blast her fair soul."[5]

The formation of group consciousness takes a long time. In America, as in India, to some extent at least, it was left not entirely to the victims, leaders and thinkers to forge such a consciousness; the enlightened whites through their anti-slavery campaign, underground railroad – whether overt or covert – contributed their might to the creation of a common platform, although some of them risked their lives. The culmination came during the Harlem Renaissance when a group of writers sought to interpret their predicament, independent of their masters. They separated those aspects of their existence that gave them a distinct ethnic character. With this there was a spurt of creative activity in all forms, literature, music, folk lore and art and painting. It raised other issues of culture and identity to which we shall turn later.

In India group consciousness, leading to an understanding of their situation, was formed in the 19th Century but its full force could be seen in the early 20th Century when Gandhiji emerged on the Indian political scene as a leader. He identified himself with the poorest and the dispossessed and became their undisputed leader. But his leadership did not work for empowering them which could only be done by attacking the entrenched social structure. And those who wanted structural change and empowerment were pushed to the periphery in the name of nationalist movement as though the two were antithetical. If Gandhiji had waged a two-pronged war – against the imperialists and against the feudal lords in villages - the history of the Dalits would have been different. It would then have acquired a solid base for political consciousness along with moral consciousness. The ambivalence of the Hindu leaders to the Dalit problem began right there. This could be more clearly seen in the working of the Congress Party which had an elitist character. Jawahar Lal Nehru admitted as much after attending the Bankipore Session of the Congress in 1912. It was very much an English-knowing upper-class affair as he wrote in his autobiography later. The Working Committee of the Congress Party drew up a programme, including the programme of organizing the Depressed classes for a better life, providing them schooling and other facilities as early as 1921. It was endorsed by the Congress Party. In 1922 practical measures were suggested by the Committee and it was desired that a sum of 2 lac be raised for the purpose. But funds were never made available. In 1923 at Poona a resolution was passed leaving the entire issue of the Depressed classes in the hands of the All India Hindu Mahasabha. Swami Shradhanand, who was a dedicated Arya Samajist and was devoted to the removal of untouchability, resigned from the chairmanship of the Committee. The letters exchanged between him and Moti Lal Nehru make interesting reading.[6] The upper and middle classes that formed the leadership wanted to maintain the status quo which meant that the lowly classes, urban and rural, participated in nationalist agitation only under the hegemony of the propertied classes. Surprisingly enough, Gandhiji provided a space which was exploited by these classes to further their interests. Jyoti Rao Phule had anticipated this in the 19th Century itself when he questioned the leadership of the Aryan Brahmins.[7] Pavan K. Varma writes that the leaders of the Congress Party while apparently made public announcements in favour of the Depressed classes, in fact indulged in double speak. "Gandhiji personally involved the masses without empowering them. The peculiar paradox of a powerful political movement against the external force and the absence of radical transforming change in the internal domain is explained by the organization and strategy of mass mobilization adopted by the Congress and capitalized on Gandhiji's hidden appeal."[8] Despite the fact that Ambedkar had emerged as a leader by the thirties, he could not match Gandhiji's appeal. But he did what no other leader – Dalit or non-Dalit – could do.

The Dalits had finally thrown up a leader who would provide not only group consciousness but would also analyze the entire gamut of their experience, and raise the right issues for their liberation. It involved the issue why they have reached the stage they have and what should be done to change it.

I strongly feel that in his approach to the Dalit issue and the strategies evolved for achieving their liberation, Ambedkar was influenced by W.E.B. DuBois. He was at Columbia University in the second decade of the last century and it is unlikely that he might not have heard of DuBois who had by then established himself as a thinker. His *The Souls of Black Folk* which appeared in 1903 became an instant success. Ambedkar does not mention DuBois anywhere in his writing and the only reference I found in books on Ambedkar, was a letter written by him to DuBois (full name not given) on July 2, 1946 in which he requested him to send some papers which would be helpful in taking the question of the Untouchables to the U.N.O.[9] What DuBois did for his people was to systematically examine the entire race question, the damage that racism had caused to their psyche and what should be done to come out of it. With the publication of *The Souls of Black Folk* "Negroes of training and intelligence, who had hitherto pretended to regard the race problem as of strictly personal concern and who sought individual salvation in a creed of detachment and silence found a bond in their common grievances and a language through which to express them."[10]

DuBois identified the problem, particularly the problem that arose in the aftermath of Emancipation. Time and again, the Blacks were made to realize that they were different in their life and longing because they were shut off from the white world by a vast veil. "The shades of the prison-house closed round us all; walls strait and stubborn to the whitest, but relentlessly narrow, tall and unscalable to the sons of night who must plod darkly on in resignation, or beat unavailing palms against the stone, or steadily, half hopelessly, watch the streak of blue above"[11] Such a world does not yield self-consciousness to them but allows it to be shaped by the other. DuBois caught this conflict admirably. "It is a peculiar sensation, the double-consciousness, this sense of always looking at one's self through the eyes of others, of measuring one's soul by the tape of a world that looks on in amused contempt and pity. One ever feels his two-ness, - an American, a Negro; two souls, two thoughts, two unreconciled strivings; two warring ideals in one dark body, whose dogged strength alone keeps it from being torn asunder".

"The history of the American Negro is the history of this strife, - this longing to attain self-conscious manhood, to merge his double self into a better and truer self. In this merging he wishes neither of the older selves to be lost. He would not Africanize America, for America has too much to teach the world and Africa. He would not bleach his Negro soul in a flood of white Americanism, for he knows that Negro World has a message to the world. He simply wishes to make it possible for a man to be both a Negro and an American without being cursed and spit upon by his fellows, without having the doors of opportunity closed roughly in his face."[12]

I have given this longish quotation because it forms the essence of the Negro problem. With DuBois group consciousness gets firmly established. The 'double consciousness' caused the split in their psyche which led to 'moral degeneracy'. Identifying the problem is one part; the other part is dealing with it so that they can finally reach the stage of self-conscious manhood. This is the most difficult part of their struggle as the forces that created that split keep pulling them down. Once their inner self is whole and their society is rid of racism, they can move towards graces of civilization. DuBois wanted to raise his people to the level of civilization as quickly as possible. In this process education played a very important role. And the kind of education he had in mind was different from the kind that was being given to them at Tuskegee Institute run by Booker T. Washington. "Technical skill will produce artisans but not men. Men we shall have if we make manhood the object of the work of the schools – intelligence, broad sympathy knowledge of the world that was and is, and of the relation of men to it – this is the curriculum of that Higher Education which must underlie true life."[13] Besides, education was not simply a matter of school; it was also a concern of the family, and the group life and the social class. In his essay 'The Talented Tenth' he outlined what he wanted his people to do in this field. He wanted at least ten per cent of bright young men to be trained in the best manner possible so that they in their turn bring others up, a kind of 'ethical role' for the talented people. "Men of America, the problem is plain before you. Here is a race transplanted through the criminal foolishness of your fathers. Whether you like it or not the millions are here, and here they will remain. If you do not lift them up, they will pull you down. Education and work are the levers to uplift a people. Work will not do it unless inspired by the right ideals and guided by intelligence. Education must not simply teach work – it must teach life. The talented tenth of the Negro race must be made leaders of thought and missionaries of culture among their people. No others can do this work and the Negro colleges must train men in it. The Negro race, like all other races, is going to be saved by its exceptional men."[14]

The Talented Tenth would give overall leadership to their community, directing their thought and social movements. DuBois gave an ethical role to them assuming that they would subordinate their individual interests to larger interests of their community. As was feared, this group turned elitist, abdicated their responsibility and imitated the standards and aspirations of the white middle class. DuBois was forced to reexamine his thesis of the talented tenth in a memorial address which he gave at the Grand Boule Conclave in 1948. "I assumed that with knowledge, sacrifice would automatically follow. In my youth and idealism, I did not realize that selfishness is even more natural than sacrifice. I made the assumption of its wide availability because of the spirit of sacrifice learned in my mission school training."[15]

He modified his thesis so as to move from individuals motivated by personal freedom to group leadership. Such a leadership would include not only economic but also cultural aspects. Lest people misunderstand him, he explained that he was not advocating pride in biological race but pride in a cultural group, integrated and expanded by developed ideals. In order that such a group functioned for the preservation of their culture, it was imperative that there should be an end to the socio-economic conditions in which most blacks existed. The group would enlarge the scope of their culture and include other culture groups so that grounds could be prepared for a world culture. "The concept of a group-leadership, not simply educated and self-sacrificing, but with clear vision of present world conditions and dangers, and conducting American Negroes to alliance with culture groups in Europe, America, Asia and Africa and looking toward a new world culture. We can do it. We have the ability. The only question is, have we the will?" [16]

The process of liberation charted out for his people by Ambedkar followed almost the same pattern. Ambedkar appeared on the national scene when their existence was being defined for them and all they were expected to do was to fit into that pattern, and trust the goodness of their *savarna* leaders. Like his predecessor, Jyoti Rao Phule, he could see the danger of following that line. Just as DuBois had identified the problem for his people, Ambedkar did the same. "The power of the privileged class" he wrote, "rests upon lies which are sedulously propagated among the masses. No resistance to power is possible while the sanctioning lies, which justify that power are accepted as valid. While the lie which is the first and the chief line of defence remains unbroken, there can be no revolt. Before any injustice, any abuse or oppression can be resisted, the lie upon which it is founded must be unmasked, must be clearly recognized for what it is. This can happen with education."[17]

The privileged classes would not sacrifice their class interests for general interests and would emphasise only moral transformation of the Hindus with quickening of their conscience. Ambedkar exposed the lie on which it was based. Ambedkar wanted his people to see that it was a fraud that was passed off as truth. Once the Dalits reach a stage where they recognize the falsity of artificial class barriers, they can move on to a position of equality. Whereas the concept of race could easily be explained, it was not so easy in the case of castes in India as it had divine basis. The restructuring of the social order was possible only after the sacred basis of caste was destroyed. Thus exposing the lie involved questioning the entire social system that the Hindus had built up over the centuries. And annihilating it required a radical change in the attitudes of Hindus. "The destruction of caste does not, therefore, mean the destruction of physical barrier. It means a notional change. Caste may be bad. Caste may lead to conduct so gross as to be called man's inhumanity to man. All the same it must be recognized that the Hindus observe caste not because they are inhuman or wrong-headed. They observe caste because they are deeply religious."[18]

Lest he should be misunderstood, Ambedkar said that it is not a question of discarding the Shastras; it is a question of undermining the authority with which caste is invested as Buddha and Nanak did. The Jat Pat Todak Mandal for which his essay 'Annihilation of Caste' was written did not understand the distinction he had made. Exhorting the members of the Mandal he wrote: "You must have courage to tell the Hindus that what is wrong is their religion – the religion which has produced in them the notion of the sacredness of the caste. Will you show that courage.?"[19] The organizers of the Mandal couldn't muster up the courage to accept Ambedkar's logic and the meeting was cancelled. In the beginning of his seminal essay, Ambedkar talks of the two classes of social reformers. One class consisted of political reformers and the other of the socialists. The two should have been complementary to each other but they became two hostile camps. The hostility went to such an extent that those who were for political advancement turned indifferent to social reform. Socialists in their emphasis on economic reforms made it more complicated. Ambedkar firmly believed that social emancipation was a precursor to political and economic emancipation. In fact, in the past social and religious revolution provided a basis for political revolution. "I can't see," Ambedkar wrote, "how a Socialist State in India can function for a second without having to grapple with the problems created by the prejudices which make people observe the distinction of high and low, clean and unclean.... Turn in any direction you like, caste is the monster that crosses your path. You cannot have political reform, you cannot have economic reform, unless you kill this monster."[20] And this would be possible only when the Depressed classes were treated not as a religious minority but as a political minority. Here the approaches of DuBois and Ambedkar become different. Whereas DuBois emphasized cultural and racial aspects to bring about homogeneity and solidarity, Ambedkar believed that their future lay in acquiring power through political means. His demand for a separate electorate for his people and his disagreement with Gandhiji over this shows the direction in which he wanted his people to move. This he did even at the cost of earning the displeasure of Indians that he was working against the interests of the country. Ambedkar has been more sinned against than sinning. He could never give up the cause of the Dalits. Even when he sided with the British for getting political power for his people, he knew that they were doing it to their advantage. In his Presidential address to the All-India Depressed Classes Congress in August 1930, he said : "I am afraid that the British chose our unfortunate conditions, not with the object of removing them, but only because such a course serves well as an excuse for retarding the political progress of India.... No body can remove your grievances as well as you can, and you cannot remove them unless you get political power in your hands. No share of this political power can come to you as long as the British Government remains as it is. It is only in a Swaraj Constitution that you stand any chance of getting the political power into your hands without which you cannot bring salvation to your people."[21]

Ambedkar knew that without social reform, political reform was incomplete. He, therefore, waged a two-pronged battle. One was against those aspects of Hindu religion that gave sanctity to the doctrine of *chaturvarna*; and the other to empower his people so that they participated in the political process for amelioration of their condition. But during the battle, the crusade against caste segregation gained an upper hand, and the process of bringing about institutional change through political power was delayed. So determined was he to get status for his people that he sided with the British to earn separate electorate for his people, only to surrender it under the pressure of Gandhiji's fast. He later settled for joint electorate. The wily British used him to counter the force of Gandhiji. He had demanded 50% of the representation granted to Muslims for the Scheduled Castes in the Interim Government. His fervent appeals failed and they were denied representation in favour of the Congress. The British did precious little for the improvement of their condition. "So far as social reform was concerned, the untouchables found themselves under a Government distinguished in no vital respect from those native Governments under which they had toiled and suffered, lived and died through all their weary and forgotten history. From a political standpoint, the change was nominal. The despotism of the Hindus continued as ever before. Far from being curbed by the British High Command, it was pampered. From a social point of view, the British accepted the arrangements as they found them and presented them faithfully in the manner of the Chinese tailor, who when given an old coat as a pattern produced with pride an exact replica, rents, patches and all."[22]

Since Ambedkar was impatient to get for his people human rights, he fell into the trap of the British who had their own interests to serve. It is debatable if his getting separate electorate for his people would have solved their problems. The independent India was being promised a secular political structure by Nehru but Ambedkar was skeptical of the role of caste Hindus in their liberation. He saw some hope when he was called upon to be the Chairman of the Constitution Drafting Committee. He believed that through the Statutes and Law the status of Dalits as equal citizens would be upheld and they would finally be assimilated into the Hindu society on the basis of liberty, equality and fraternity which would not be mere slogans but would become facts of life. His speech in the Constituent Assembly spelt that out.

"These principles of liberty, equality and fraternity are not to be treated as separate items in a trinity. They form a union of trinity in the sense that to divorce one from other is to defeat the very purpose of democracy. Liberty cannot be divorced from equality, equality cannot be divorced from liberty. Nor can equality and liberty be divorced from fraternity...."

"I remember the days when politically minded Indians resented the expression 'the people of India'. I am of opinion that in believing that we are a nation we are cherishing a great delusion. How can people divided into several thousands of castes be a nation? The sooner we realize that we are not as yet a nation in the social and psychological sense of the word, the better for us. For then only we shall realize the necessity of becoming a nation and seriously think of ways and means of realizing the goal. The realization of the goal is going to be difficult – far more difficult than it has been in the United States. The United States has no caste problem. In India there are castes. These castes are anti-national in the first place because they bring about separation in social life. They are anti-national also because they generate jealousy and antipathy between caste and caste. But we must overcome all these difficulties if we wish to become a nation in reality. For fraternity can be a fact only when there is a nation. Without fraternity, equality and liberty will be no deeper than coats of paint."[23]

Ambedkar was never tired of repeating the slogans of the French Revolution. But in France itself they had lost their force as the bourgeoisie that took over soon gave up their revolutionary character. In India the struggle was to begin. He was sharp enough to realize before long that the conversion of slogans into reality was not that easy. It became clear to him when he piloted the Hindu Code Bill through which he sincerely wanted to correct some of the ills of Hindu Society. Initially he had the support of Nehru, but when it was vehemently opposed in the Parliamentary Committee, he first modified it and finally withdrew it at the behest of Nehru himself. His disillusionment began at this point. The hidden forces that he had been talking about were too powerful for him to contain. On this issue he resigned from the Cabinet.

Like DuBois he believed that part of the problem of his people emanated from ignorance, and they must be made aware of the importance of education which would form the basis of their long-drawn struggle through organization to agitation. He formed the People's Education Society and its colleges. He also brought out a weekly in 1920, *Mooknayak* (DuBois edited *The Crisis* for a number of years) which underwent a number of mutations – it became *Bahishkrit Bharat, Samata, Janata* and finally *Prabuddha Bharat.* He also prepared ground for the formation of a political party, the Republican Party of India which later split on ideological grounds. Ambedkar was so enmeshed in the problem of caste that he had not much time left to attend to the related problem of institutional change, which alone would take care of economic and psychological aspects of their problem. He did try to enlarge the scope of their struggle but a common front could not be created. The communists initially were reluctant to concede that caste existed as a reality. They did so only in 1948. They never agreed to work with Ambedkar who was called a separatist leader by them. They were convinced that the interests of Dalits lay in joining hands with the other exploited sections as the victory of the democratic revolution would emancipate them from social degradation and slavery. The communists attributed caste discrimination to bourgeois divisiveness and were not adequately equipped to deal with caste contradictions. Things were crystallizing but before the two issues of caste and class could be reconciled at a political level, Ambedkar died.

DuBois, like Ambedkar, was a crusader for the cause of his people. As Cornel West argues in his piece on DuBois: 'Legacy of The Talented Tenth' that despite his tireless effort to raise the educational, political and economic level of his people, he was working within the Enlightenment worldview. "DuBois was never alienated by black people – he lived in black communities where he received great respect and admiration. But there seemed to be something in him that alienated ordinary black people. In short he was reluctant to learn fundamental lessons about life – and about himself – from them. Such lessons would have required that he at least momentarily believe that they were or might be as wise, insightful and 'advanced' as he; and this he could not do."[24]

He had unwittingly become part of the elitist culture which aimed at correcting things through excellence for which criteria came from the ruling class. West goes on to point out the intellectual defects of DuBois' endeavour: First, "he believed that the highbrow culture was inherently humanizing and that exposure to and immersion in great works produce good people – the other was that the educated elite he had put his faith in could transcend their individual and class interests and more easily act on behalf of the common good than the uneducated masses."[25] The myth of highbrow culture leading to goodness was exploded during the Second World War when millions of Jews were killed by those who were steeped in highbrow culture; similarly, the faith in the missionary zeal of the educated elite was belied when they moved to accept the middle class values of the white. His enlargement of the scope of the fight of the blacks by including diaspora communities in other parts of the world in a common cause could not solve the problem. He did want his Talented Tenth to have expert knowledge of modern economies and socialist means to provide leadership. But their knowledge was not part of an ideology that worked for institutional change. Like Ambedkar, DuBois' efforts fell short of the desired ideal that could end twin oppression of race and economic forces. The selfishness of people and the desire to take advantage of their community in order to further their own interests could be controlled through a philosophical framework and institutional change. Ambedkar did provide a philosophical framework for fighting against Brahminism – that is the forces that opposed liberty, equality and fraternity – but not against economic oppression, though he did talk of fighting against it. He was not very different from DuBois in enlarging the scope of struggle, but was constricted by entrenched economic forces. His acceptance of Buddhism in a secular garb was not enough. Despite the fact that both of them were towering personalities, they were governed by the alternatives available to them during their times: American optimism in the case of DuBois and political and intellectual culture released by the French Revolution in the case of Ambedkar. The strategies they devised were not sufficient to deal with the fast-paced world capitalism which undermined their efforts to create a human, social and political order devoid of social and economic exploitation. At the ripe age of 95 DuBois left America for Africa, thoroughly disillusioned. "I cannot take any more of this country's treatment. We leave for Ghana October 5th and I set no date for return.... Chin up and fight on but realize that American Negroes can't win."[26] Ambedkar was similarly disillusioned. While withdrawing the Hindu Code Bill, he wanted to make a statement to the Parliament but the Chair insisted on precensoring the statement. Even in Swaraj his mouth was gagged. At the end of his career he found himself and his people suffering from "the same old tyranny, the same old oppression and the same old discrimination which existed before."[27]

But they had laid solid foundation for the ongoing struggle against race and caste oppression. In America,

DuBois' contribution is being critically examined and reevaluated like H.L. Gates Jr. and Cornel West did; in India the followers and admirers of Ambedkar are apotheosizing him so that the relevance of his thought in the changed socio-historical context cannot be properly examined.

One exception is Anand Teltumbde who in his book, *Ambedkar in and for the Post-Ambedkar Dalit Movement,* subjects Ambedkar and his legacy to a critical reevaluation. According to him Dalit Movement has lost its revolutionary character. The obsession with casteism has overshadowed the class issues. The revolutionary component in Ambedkar's thought found expression for a while in the mass movement led by Dada Saheb Gaikwad, Ambedkar's long-time associate and trusted companion. But within the larger movement he was dubbed a communist. The Dalit Movement represented by different icons of Ambedkar has moved in a number of directions. Teltumbde does not apotheosize Ambedkar; instead he finds lacunae in his zone of thought. For example, Ambedkar lacked methodological tools to deal with the problems facing his people. He relates it to his inability to articulate a suitable ideology for the Dalit Movement. One reason for this was that he was skeptical of Marxian methodology, and concentrated more on the oppressive nature of their caste situation. He was aware of the economic problems but he hardly had the time to attend to them. He had once said that the caste problem could be tackled if the religious basis of caste was undermined. He was looking for a religion that would ensure social equality. The choice was between Sikhism and Buddhism, and finally he chose the latter. Ambedkar could not think of a system without religion. He even equated Buddha's approach to private property with that of Karl Marx ignoring historical factors responsible for such a situation. He called upon his followers to choose between the gospel of Buddha and the gospel of Marx. In such a choice caste and class issues could not be combined.

The most difficult stage of their struggle comes when both Dalits and African Americans have to deal with the 'contrived self' or what Pierre Bordeau calls "internalized oppressive beliefs," or "doxa". In an interview with Terry Eagleton he explains it in concrete terms : "There are many things people accept without knowing. I will give you an example from our society. When you ask a sample of students what are the main factors of achievement at school, the further you go down the social scale, the more they believe that those who are successful are naturally endowed with intellectual capacities. And the more they accept their exclusion, the more they say 'yes', I was no good at English.... French.... and mathematics. Now it is a fact, and in my view an appalling fact. One that individuals do not like to accept. It doesn't mean that the dominated individuals tolerate everything; but they assent to much more than they know. It is a formidable mechanism, like the imperial system, a wonderful instrument of ideology much bigger and more powerful than television or propaganda. This is internalization of oppressive beliefs."[28] And the struggle to come out of it takes innumerable forms. Once James Baldwin went to a restaurant and was curtly told by the waitress 'Negroes are not served here.' Baldwin could not contain his anger as this denial of facility to him at a public restaurant. It challenged his very existence as a human being. He got so enraged that he threw a water jug at the lady and ran away for life with white crowd chasing him. He somehow managed to escape to his room. They wanted to murder him and he wanted to kill them. It is not an isolated incident as it revealed the hidden attitudes of the two races that had been in operation through the centuries.

Anger is one response to the situation; the other could be concealment of one's feelings and withdrawal. In Baburao Bagul's story, 'When I Concealed my Caste', both these responses are present. The first choice is the assertion of oneself even at the cost of risking one's life; the other is the suppressed desire to become part of the middle-class respectability by concealing one's caste. The first choice is born out of anger and resentment against the system that has given them the sense of inferiority, a desire for change is in the background. The second choice is guided by a desire to find a place within the system by artificially containing the contradictions within. The second choice is difficult to resist as it offers a dream of comfortable, secure existence once one moves up the social ladder. There has been a significant section in India – as in America – that has striven to become what is called 'Dalit Brahmins'. Once they are there, they try to acquire the attitudes of the new class. They begin to maintain distance from their close relatives. This distance satisfies a psychological need and they feel happy that they are part of the dominant class. There are two Dalit characters in Bagul's story surrounded by upper caste people, Kshatriyas and Brahmins. One character displays the caste label and dares the caste people to treat him differently so much so that he becomes a terror to them. The other character conceals his caste, poses to be a Brahmin in speech, dress and demeanour. His behaviour convinces the two upper caste characters that he is a Brahmin and is treated like one. He is given a room in a Kshatriya household and is treated with respect. Another character who is taken in by his projection of a different self adores him and, what is more, wants to understand poetry with his help and learn other graces from him. But all along he feels uncomfortable with this mask and wishes he could act and behave like Kashinath, the other Dalit character. He even secretly admires Kashinath's courage. He knows he cannot conceal his caste for long as he has to produce his High School certificate in the office. He thinks of resigning and going back to Bombay but the fear of poverty prevents him from resigning. One day the Brahmin character invites him to his place for food. At his house, his wife touches his feet. Ramcharan, the Brahmin, gives him a bath and both feed him with respect. He is given a bed and after meals he sleeps comfortably. But people get wind of the concealment of his real caste. They barge into Ramcharan's house and beat him mercilessly, Ramcharan's wife meekly complaining that it was not his fault. At that very moment, out of nowhere, Kashinath, his caste fellow, appears on the scene and rescues him from the caste fanatics. The story ends there but raises deeper psychological contradictions which are to be resolved because they have been internalized.

In the U.S.A. the assertion of black self took Blacks to the extreme of rejecting everything that belonged to the white race or that could be claimed by both races. This culminated in the Black Power Movement. Separating themselves from the larger culture, they took pride in whatever belonged to them, their music, folk culture, history and their literature, as also part of their physical appearance. They even decided to have a separate university with their own curricula, keeping out the culture and history of the dominant race. Frantz Fanon wrote in *The Wretched of the Earth* that there are two ways one could deal with the problem of colour: either one takes too much notice of it or not at all. That is either one takes pride in one's colour or takes it like any other colour. But the difficulty is both these choices cannot be put in neatly divided categories. It is another matter that, before long, they rejected this experiment and opened up their institutions to other ideas. But the pressure this move exerted on the dominant race could not be disregarded. Now Black Studies is part of the academic programme in such prestigious universities as Harvard and Yale. The important aspect of it all is that the collective experience and collective knowledge of Blacks are getting acceptability on their terms. The components of their identity had started taking shape. The Talented Tenth seemed eager to accept the American mainstream identity and culture and in the process were discredited. The educated classes in the Dalit samaj had more or less behaved in the same manner. In a speech in 1956 Ambedkar observed : "The educated – highly educated class (from Dalit – Shoshit Samaj) have betrayed me. I had expected that after acquiring education – higher education, they will serve the society. But I see a crowd of clerks who are engaged in feeding their own stomach."[29] One fall out of it was that the stereotyped image into which the Blacks/Dalits seemed trapped was being transformed into a more humane image by relating themselves to the complex of relationship.

Frederick Douglass and Alexander Crummel, who were called his mentors by DuBois, had provided the larger framework within which Blacks sought to operate. From Douglass DuBois took the concept of the fundamental equality of all members of the human species; from Alexander Crummel he got the concept that Blacks must be absorbed in civilization without ignoring the distinctiveness of their racial qualities, that is graces of civilization as well as racial pride. Blacks in America, according to Crummel, were a nation set apart in their country. Later this thought became the basis of a united front of all oppressed nations of the world. In India Dalits were also called a nation within a nation. When DuBois shifted his focus in his revised address on The Talented Tenth, he had both these aspects in mind. And it was not difficult to achieve it as over the centuries Blacks had preserved their internal histories and external treatment which are the sources of their identity. These also separate them from the white race. DuBois posed the question of their identity thus:

"What, after all am I? Am I an American or am I a Negro? Can I be both? Or is it my duty to cease to be a Negro as soon as possible and be an American? If I strive as a Negro, am I not perpetuating the very cleft that threatens and separates black and white America? Is not my only possible practical aim the subduction of all that is Negro in me to the American? Does my black blood place upon me any more obligation to assert my nationality than German, or Irish or Italian blood would?"

"Here, it seems to me, is the reading of the riddle that puzzles so many of us. We are Americans, not only by birth and by citizenship, but by our political ideals, our language, our religion. Further then that, our Americanism does not go. At that point we are Negroes, members of a vast historic race that from the very dawn of creation has slept, but half awakening in the dark forests of its African fatherland. We are the first fruits of this new nation the harbinger of that black tomorrow which is yet destined to soften the whiteness of the Teutonic today."[30]

The questions who am I? What am I? Where do I belong? are gnawing questions as they at once take them to the inner space that was fractured during the period of their enslavement. Besides, it is also related to the question of self which has a moral connotation. That is why they keep looking back to Africa for support, which may not be there in tangible form but is there in some form. And these supports are to be created even if they are elusive. James Baldwin dealt with this dilemma by saying that whatever else a black man is he is part white and part black. That is the riddle that DuBois talks about. It was easy for other ethnic groups to preserve their cultural identity in the process of becoming Americans. It was not so in the case of Blacks as they were not a homogeneous group when they were brought to America. Whatever cultural memory they were able to preserve did not form a coherent whole. Julius Lester writes that Blacks were made to forget all aspects of their collective memory and were kept on the periphery of white culture. They were made to forget their history and were given a history of pain and suffering. They were made to give up their religion and were made to accept the religion of their masters, although not always on the basis of equality. They were made to forget their language and were given a garbled version of English. Their language grew along different lines as it was not based on its rudiments. In course of time their language acquired a character of its own. One could get some idea of it from the slave narratives that the ex-slaves wrote as also from the novels written by white writers portraying black characters. The language Jim uses in *The Adventures of Huckleberry Finn* has a distinct flavour, defying all standard rules of grammar. But people cannot live in a vacuum. The necessity of their existence forces them to create a framework of relationships. This could be seen in the cultural forms that developed – blues, spirituals and jazz. And these are distinctly American products and have no parallel in their ancestral homeland. They are part African and part American and cannot be separated at that level. Alex Haley who goes to Africa to look for his roots in his book of the same title *Roots* brings this out forcefully. With the help of some experts in African languages, he was able to identify the area from which his ancestor was kidnapped. He managed to reach the village, Juffure, in Gambia and was excited to meet his clansmen. But when he tried to communicate with them he found that he did not understand anything that was being communicated except through an interpreter. At the same time he was surprised to know that the village *griot* (oral historian) could narrate the details of the day Kunta Kinte was kidnapped from the village. The seventy odd people of the village formed a wide human ring around him suggesting that he was one of them. The women who had their infant children within cloth strings across their backs came one by one and put their babies in his arms. Later, he understood the meaning of this ceremony from a Harvard University Professor, Dr. Jerome Bruner. He told Haley: "You didn't know you were participating in one of the oldest ceremonies of human kind, 'the laying of hands.' In their way they were telling you 'through this flesh which is us, we are you, and you are us'."[31]

In the midst of people who were jet black he felt a 'terribly shaming feeling' and felt impure. The people of Juffure were seeing a Black American for the first time. "They hadn't been looking at me as an individual, but I represented in their eyes a symbol of the twenty-five million of us black people whom they had never seen, who lived beyond the ocean."[32] Yet he could not obliterate the distance of three centuries between him and the people of Juffure as his experience in America had alienated him from the parent culture. But the connection had been established at some level and the vestiges in the form of words and memories provided that connection. In the mosque to which he was taken, he said to himself : "After I have found out where I came from, I can't understand a word they are saying. Later, the crux of their prayer was translated for me: Praise be to Allah for one long lost from us whom Allah has returned."[33]

In India Dalits faced a different problem of identity and culture. Unlike the Blacks, they could not go back to a separate ethnic stock as they intersect with the dominant group at various points even though it has not been established that they belong to the same ethnic stock. There was no hiatus in their existence in the form of language, history and religion. Like the Blacks they were denied full access to the cultural and mythological resources of the mainstream culture. There religion was the same although they could not go close to the deity in the temple. Prem Chand in a story, 'Temple', published in the 1927 special issue of *Chand* magazine devoted to Untouchables dramatizes this relationship. An untouchable widow has the belief that her ailing son can be cured if she offers prayers at the feet of God. She pawns her bangles to buy things for the prayer, and then pays another rupee to the *pujari* to get a talisman to put round her son's neck. Her efforts to go to the deity fail and she is beaten up and left to die with her son outside the temple. Mulk Raj Anand in his novel *Untouchable* presents this conflict through the character of Bakha. When he learns that the temple priest has lustful designs on his sister, he is filled with anger but is prevented by the elders from taking the extreme step which might violate the caste code. Similarly, the history of the *savarnas* was supposed to be their history yet they had no role in it. Narayan Guru in his own humble way decided to have their own Shiva temple, when his people were not allowed entry into the *savarna* temples. Even the *savarna* literature did not give them a human face. They spoke the same language but were denied sophisticated use of it. They were not allowed to learn the alphabet to read the scripture, or even listen to the sacred word. In this they were no different from the Blacks in America. Thus Dalits were kept on the fringe of the dominant Hindu culture and were fed on the crumbs thrown to them by the caste Hindus. If these resources of identity are not available to them, they have either to reclaim them or create new resources to rehabilitate themselves and define themselves or interpret their experience in a new context.

Dr. Ambedkar tried to provide a framework for understanding Dalit identity in the context of the entire Indian history. His approach was secular, in a wide sense of the term, rather than sacerdotal. Towards the end of his life, he was working on a theory which he tentatively called 'Revolution and Counter Revolution in Indian History.' In it he argues that Buddhism was as great a Revolution as the French Revolution. It was not merely a religious revolution but became a social and political revolution. "In this work the particular interpretation of the social origins of the Shudras and the untouchables were put in a much broader, more fundamentally conceived historical context in which the conflict between Buddhism and Brahminism is represented as a civilizational clash in the process of social evolution in India."[34]

Ambedkar's unfinished book, *Revolution and Counter-Revolution,* was on the one hand a critique of the social history of India, on the other a questioning of the rationale of broad Indian identity and culture. Even now it is believed that the core of Indian identity is still intact and it has been preserved over the centuries. Ambedkar explodes this belief in his thesis developed in the book. First, he questions the almost sacred belief that there has been a common Indian culture and a common Indian identity. Then he goes on to posit that instead of one monolithic India, there have been three Indias: Brahminic India, Buddhist India and Hindu India, each with its own culture. Before the Muslims invaded India Brahmins and Buddhists were engaged in a mortal conflict over the nature of reality and social organization. This conflict was a conflict between two perceptions about life and two ways of organizing social and political reality. The counter-revolution began with the ascension of Pushyamitra to the throne, which resulted in the political triumph of Brahminism over Buddhism. But this revolution of Pushyamitra was not merely a political revolution, as it launched a campaign of persecution against Buddhism which could be likened to the persecution launched by Mohammad Gazni against Hinduism. It helped Brahmins consolidate their position. It is not surprising in this context that a new code of law in the form of *Manusmriti* was promulgated during that period. After the support of the Buddhism weakened, the laws became more rigid. Ambedkar then catalogues the deeds and misdeeds of triumphant Brahmanism.

"(1) It established the right of the Brahmins to rule and commit regicide. (2) It made the Brahmins a class of privileged persons. (3) It converted the *Varna* into caste. (4) It brought about a conflict and anti-social feeling between the different castes. (5) It degraded the Shudras and the women. (6) It forged the system of graded inequality and (7) it made legal and rigid the social system which was conventional and flexible."[35]

.By questioning the existence of a dominant nationalist tradition, Ambedkar is separating those aspects of Dalit experience that mark them out from the non-Dalit. At the same time, the history of nationalist tradition cannot be separated from the history of those who were not part of it. Those who did not contribute to the Brahminic view of social organization were systematically excluded, as for all practical purposes they did not exist for them. Ambedkar provided a basis for a new interpretation of nationalist tradition which became the basis of a non-elitist interpretation during the freedom movement and later in the form of subaltern studies. They not only rejected the imposed nationalist concept but also asserted that they were never part of the dominant Hindu identity. But this is taking an extreme position which cannot be sustained as Dalit identity intersects with non-Dalit identity at important points. Ambedkar developed this thesis further when he examined the composition of the smallest unit of the country, the village. Instead of strengthening the dominant nationalist concept, it undermined it. Speaking on the Village Panchayat Bill in Bombay Legislative Council in 1932, he said: "If India has not succeeded in building up a national spirit, the chief reason for that in my opinion is the existence of the village system. It made all people saturated with local particularism, with local patriotism. It left no room for larger civic spirit. None whatever. Under the ancient village panchayat, India, instead of being a country of a limited people, became a loose conglomeration of village communities with no common tie except common allegiance to a common king."[36] In the absence of a larger civic spirit, a kind of imagined ideal state was imposed on village life. Such an imposition concealed the division and contradictions that existed in village life. Along with it, Ambedkar questions the unquestioning acceptance of a never-changing village life and the idyllic picture of their existence. The village remained the same under successive attacks from the Pathans, the Mughals and the British as though their coming did not matter to them. Ambedkar believed that no one could take pride in the villages for the role they played in the history of the country. The only thing that could be said about them is that they saved themselves from the turmoil. And no one bothered to know at what level they remained intact and undisturbed, may be at a parochial level. Ambedkar felt that the village republics were the cause of destruction of India. The values that are associated with village life-passivity and lack of protest – have contributed to that destruction. Analysis and examination of the social system were impossible and change under such conditions was unthinkable. And passivity and lack of protest were raised to the level of a philosophy. Ambedkar thus provided a framework for Dalit identity and a separate line of development of Indian society. In fact, while defining Dalit identity, he was defining the larger Indian identity. Ambedkar's movement for social equality was another revolution against the counter revolution of the Brahmins. The various movements that he led were part of that revolution for radicalizing Indian society. The conversion of Ambedkar and his followers to Buddhism was the culmination of that process of radicalism. The non-Hindu identity came to be established. The immediate outcome of it was that the Dalits refused to perform the duties traditionally assigned to them which they had always resented and which included carrying away dead animals from the village. The defiance of the traditionally-defined duties invited persecution but the Dalits were determined and stuck their ground and some of them left the village. The assertion of a different identity brought about changes in social formation.

The problem of the Dalits, like those of Blacks, was that their identity could not be completely separated from the mainstream identity but it was a separation of some aspects of their existence. Through this effort they were humanizing Hindu India just as Blacks were humanizing the United States of America.

The question of Black identity has been bothering Black thinkers and writers ever since the Harlem Renaissance which provided the framework in the context of which Black existence could be evaluated. They were also conscious of the points at which their experience could not be separated from the white America. In fact, the presence of Blacks in America had modified the image of America as a white nation. In an essay published in *Time magazine* in the 60s, Ralph Ellison wrote that the concept of a lily white America not only unacceptable to Blacks but was also unrealistic. He pointed out that many aspects of Black culture have become part of white American culture. Music and paintings that are being projected as American to the outside world are the major contribution of Black Americans. Jazz is not just Black music but American music. Similarly, Black literature in its own way provides aspects of American experience that are found missing in mainstream literature. Which means that at some level of imagination the experience cannot be separated. Ralph Ellison said at one point that at the level of imagination all colours meet. This, however, does not mean that the Blacks have merged their identity with white America. They are in a way providing a corrective to the American ideal which is composed of extreme individualism. In its place they have a sense of community which is basic to Black experience.

Henry Louis Gates Jr. says in an interview that black and white cultures do not exist in separate blocks. One cannot say when one culture ends and the other begins. Apart from that, there are numerous subcultures in America and to put one above the other is to miss the composite nature of American society. Irving Howe argues in *The Limits of Ethnicity* that it would not be proper to call one culture as the dominant one and the others as marginal. The entire struggle of Black Americans is to partake of the generality of American culture and retain their particularity. In recent years, as Todd Gitlin argues in The *Twilight of American Dream*, the pressures against a single coherent American identity always strong have intensified. Black Americans, in their desire to find a place for themselves have questioned the entire enterprise of the American nation supported by the American Dream which is said to be part of the American collective unconscious. They have also questioned the enforcement and realization of American ideals which they thought were supported by the basic tenet of equality of men. James Baldwin writes in *The Price of the Ticket*: "We are the strongest nation in the world but that is not for the reason that we think. It is because we have the opportunity that no other nation has of moving beyond the old world concepts of race and class and caste, to create finally, what we must have had in mind when we first began speaking of the New World. But the price of this is a long look backward whenever we came and an unflinching assessment of the record."[37]

Because of the contradictions between the professed ideals and actual social formations, there was a deflation of the American Dream. In fact, the categories of race and caste pushed the dream into the background. Richard Wright questioned the very direction the American Society had taken. He wanted fellow Americans to consider whether any ideals existed beyond the accumulation of wealth. Thus Black Americans could see America and its ideals the way white Americans did not particularly because of the peculiar situation in which they were placed. This gave them a double perspective.

They were both inside it and outside it. "They are capable of identifying themselves with the fantastic ingredients of this society but lie also forever outside the culture, an invisible strength, an observer."[38]

The peculiar situation enables them to expose not only the inadequacy of the American Dream but also provide some kind of correction. In an article published in the *Utopian Imagination,* I discussed the three postulates of the American Dream : (1) sense of history, (2) sense of community and (3) the idea of success. In all these three the perceptions of Black Americans were different.[39]

When Europeans came to the new land they believed that they were leaving the past history behind and creating new history. As Robert Frost said it was a fresh start for the human race. In fact, negation of history became its first principle. It, however, gave them an advantage over Europe in as much as they sought to create a society without hierarchy. Unlike Europe there were no lords separated from the vast majority of people. They belonged to the same class. "And this has been the great problem of the U.S., the wish to escape history.... They wanted to be outside history. That is why they have the ingenuity, the kind of generosity, and at the same time a kind of incomprehension."[40] It also led to a sense of disinheritance and lack of cultural memory which meant that the majority of young Americans were cut off from the possible roots because of different background, immigration, not a purely native background.[41] Black Americans, on the other hand, have preserved not only their history but also the history of America. In fact, white Americans could see their images in the black history.

Similarly, the emphasis on individualism, and restless acquisitive nature of white Americans, forces them to withdraw from a stable communal world into a world of isolation. Tocqueville points out that American individualist, "severs himself from the mass of his fellows and draws apart with his family and friends so that after he has formed a little circle of it he leaves society at large to itself."[42] Thus the relation between the individual and the community as also the connection between the past and the present is tenuous, leading to a kind of alienation from the entire mass of people surrounding them.

Black Americans have been able to preserve in their own way their sense of history and community which the dominant culture has been negating in the name of the 'melting pot'. Richard Wright put it very succinctly asking his countrymen to pose the right issues. "Our America is frightened of facts, of history, of process, of necessity. It hugs the easy way of damning those whom it cannot understand, of excluding those who look different and it salves its conscience with a self-draped cloak of righteousness.... I do share these traits of character and I really do not think that America, adolescent and cocksure, a stranger to suffering and travail, an enemy of passion and sacrifice, is ready to probe into its most fundamental beliefs."[43]

Despite the fact that thinkers like Emerson and Thoreau gave individualism a spiritual dimension, the sense of togetherness and community is not part of the 'portable cosmos' which white Americans carry within themselves. As against this, the Blacks never severed connection with their community. DuBois in his autobiography writes : "My discussion of the concept of Race and of the white and the colored world, are not to be regarded as digressions from the history of my life; rather my autobiography is a digressive illustration and exemplification of what race has meant in the world in the nineteenth and twentieth centuries. It is for this reason that I have named and tried to make this book an autobiography of race rather than merely personal reminiscence with the idea that peculiar racial situation and problems could best be explained in the life history of one who has lived them. My living gains its importance from the problems and not the problems from me."[44] The third tenet of the American Dream – success – which has been the moving force behind American society has also been examined by Black Americans and found wanting in human content. They point out that the myth of success and the land of opportunities cannot be taken as independent of the complex forces that operate in their society. It conveniently ignores the fact that the larger corporations not only crush the individuals but also destroy the self-made success which is the basis of the American concept of happiness. A perceptive writer like Mark Twain could catch this contradiction in American society when he wrote in his autobiography how the ignorant and the inexperienced so often and so undeservedly succeed when the informed and the experienced fail.[45]

Langston Hughes, in a poem calls it a stupid plan in which 'dog eat dog, and mighty crush the weak'. But the white Americans are so passionately committed to it that they are not willing to examine it. The ordinary American has so completely identified himself with the symbols and goals associated with the myth of success that if he fails, he blames some inadequacy in himself rather than the system.

Thus Black American writers provide a different perspective on the American Dream. For one thing, they point out that no one is clear about the nature of the Dream, although it is obvious that it is for the privileged and those already made. For another, they point out the contradictions which have become more glaring now. They point out that something has gone wrong but no one quite knows where. "None knows where we are going; we seem to be headed in several directions at once. The strain is made a good deal more unbearable by the fact that Americans passionately believe in their avowed ideals amorphous as they are and are terrified of waking from a radiant dream."[46]

By its very nature Dream is an ideal beyond awareness, beyond complete comprehension, coupled with a hunger for its realization. Irving Howe in *The American Newness* calls it a mist, a climate and a thin presence. Dream is shaped by intangibles which become part of the national psyche. These intangibles are sustained by myths, sometimes by sanctified books. Even when it is not consciously pursued for historical reasons, it exists in a subterranean form. It is modified in the light of new historical experiences but the contours remain almost the same. This happened during the Mughal rule in India and later during the British rule. Whereas the Muslims got Indianized somewhat, the Britishers were never integrated into the Indian ethos, although the force of liberal ideas that they brought with them could not be disregarded. It was during the British rule and the resistance provided to it that a secular dream began to take shape which existed side by side with the dream that had become part of the Hindu psyche. The two components of the Great Indian Dream – justice symbolized in the character of Ram and catholicity in the form of world as an extended family – and which included Muslims and Christians in it were given a new focus. The place of the Dalits was never specified but they were taken to be part of the dream. Mahatma Gandhi secularized the dream, although he kept calling it Ram Rajya and emphasized 'Satyagraha' to achieve truth and discipline. His effort to make it all inclusive was surreptitiously exploded by the British and questioned by Dalit leaders like Ambedkar. Despite that, Gandhi became a symbol of a composite India that does not encourage sectarian approach to the formation of the new nation. The contestations began over the formation of the nation and the ideal the nation should put before itself.

American Dream foundered on the fault line of race; Indian Dream, similarly foundered on the fault line of caste. The Dalit mind was never without fear and they could not hold their head high. Ambedkar was sharp enough to understand that unless the explicit and implicit goals of society were subordinated to the liberation of the Dalits they had no hope for a better future. He questioned the belief that some Great Man would bring about improvement in their social condition. "The conflict, hereafter, will not be between the British and Indians, but between the advanced castes of India and backward classes. No borrowed or hired person who does not belong to your class can further your welfare by the least degree.

You must get rid yourselves of internal divisions and organize yourselves strongly."[47]

In the thirties and the forties Ambedkar saw the liberation of Dalits in political terms. He did not give it up entirely, but after 1951 he gradually got disillusioned and saw no hope for his people in politics divorced from religion. In 1950 itself at the inauguration of the Buddhist Temple he stated that he would henceforth devote the rest of his life to the study and dissemination of the ideals contained in Buddhism. Hinduism was rooted in an abstract philosophy which proclaimed the unity of all people but indulged in social practice of inequality. Buddhism, on the other hand, Ambedkar believed, shunned abstract philosophy and proposed a philosophy based on social equality between human beings with compassion as its core value. Thus Buddhism satisfied Ambedkar's social as well as religious needs. Somehow Ambedkar had come to believe that religion was essential for establishing equality. Defending his choice of accepting Buddhism as his religion, he said: "This religion tells me to work for the well-being of all, for their happiness and the fostering of love for all. This religion should be accepted not only by men but by the Gods as well.... If we leave aside a few communists, there is no one in the world who does not want some religion. That which promises equal opportunity to all is the true religion. The rest are all false religions."[48]

Ambedkar here is treading a thin ground. The danger in reconciling religious and the social or economic is that one might surrender the latter to the former as we have seen it happening in some countries. In this, Ambedkar was part of the Indian tradition which did not separate the two against which Ambedkar himself had waged a battle. Despite this it goes to Ambedkar's credit that he never gave up the struggle for economic reorganization of society. Quite early in his career he wanted to bring about changes in the existing land relations so that the exploitative system could be corrected at that level. But his bracketing of religious, moral and material aspects cannot be accepted unreservedly, without support of an economic philosophy. Ashoka's renunciation of violence and acceptance of non-violence as a creed as propounded by Buddhism did not automatically bring about change in property and land relations. For want of a theoretical formulation, independent of religion, it could not be achieved. It is in this background that he makes a comparison of Buddha and another theoretician Karl Marx in his essay Buddha or Karl Marx. He knows the difficulty "of a comparison or a contrast between two such personalities divided by such a lengthy span of time and occupied with different fields of thought."[49] Both accept the equality of all men and both want to reconstruct society. Both accept that everything is subject to change. Whereas in Buddhism it is moral force that brings about change, in Marx it is dialectical materialism that is the moving force behind change. This is the major point of contrast between the two which cannot be ignored. Both are against private property: whereas in Buddha its accumulation causes sorrow to people and must be done away with according to moral force, in Marx it is the basis of exploitation and domination. The ideal state, according to Marx, can be achieved by nationalizing means of production, which will put an end to exploitation. Buddha and Ambedkar do not go along with this line of thinking. There is a gap in Ambedkar's thinking which shows in the concluding part of his essay. "It has been claimed that the Communist Dictatorship in Russia has wonderful achievements to its credit. There can be no denial of it. That is why I say that a Russian Dictatorship would be good for all backward countries. But this is no argument for permanent Dictatorship. Humanity does not only want economic values, it also wants spiritual values to be retained. Permanent Dictatorship has paid no attention to spiritual values and does not intend to.... Man must grow materially as well as spiritually. Society has been aiming to lay a new foundation (it) was summarized by the French Revolution in their words, Fraternity, Liberty and Equality. The French Revolution was welcomed because of this slogan. It failed to produce equality. We welcome the Russian Revolution because it aims to produce equality. But it cannot be too much emphasized that in producing equality society cannot afford to sacrifice fraternity and liberty. Equality will be of no value without fraternity or liberty. It seems that the three can coexist only if one follows the way of the Buddha. Communism can give one but not all."[50] Ambedkar does make a distinction between moral values and spiritual values. But such distinction between moral values and spiritual values cannot hold as the former derives its sustenance from the latter. Moral values do not exist in a vacuum and a contextless world and they cannot be enforced without changing the capitalist system. If religion tries to change the capitalist system, it will have to change its entire philosophical basis. Religion by its very nature cannot have a scientific basis. But an important fall out of his study of the two thinkers was that it sought to question the Great Indian Dream at crucial points. The problem that the post independent India is facing is that moral and religious aspects are invariably mixed up and they come in conflict with similar values held by people belonging to different faiths. Like the concept of Indian nationalism, the concept of Indian Dream is being modified. It cannot completely disregard the religious concept that has always been in the background. While questioning the Indian Dream rooted in a religious framework – apparently presented as non-religious – Ambedkar accepted the religious basis in a secularized form. With the result that the sacred and the secular jostle for supremacy and it seems unlikely that it will be resolved soon. The religious basis, however secularized, could lead to division in the society and then some sections of the society will always be left out. The intellectuals who should be exposing the lies take an ambivalent stance. The ambivalence is nothing new but a carry over of the past attitudes with the result that social justice and coexistence do not have a sound scaffolding. The basic human rights of about 13% of the people are compromised in the name of mainstream religion. In his book, *Riddles in Hinduism*, Ambedkar undermines the character of an ideal ruler symbolized in the character of Ram. He did not succeed though, but it did reveal his anger and disgust with the components of the Indian Dream. In this context, he talks of the deception of the mainstream religion, its evasion of issues and also its obsolescence. The glorification of the past added to this evasion. In the present context religion in this sense can become a smokescreen for realizing some political goals. Ambedkar questioned the Dream because it did not assure Dalits a place in it and made his people see the falsity of the claim that the great Indian culture makes of large-heartedness and catholicity. *In India: A Million Mutinies Now*, Naipaul holds that innumerable little mutinies are taking place across the country. This is happening because India is awakening to history, at least in some sections of it, resulting into new knowledge of things. He links it to the growth of a 'critical intelligence'. In an interview with Dileep Padgaonkar he said: "What is happening in India is a mighty creative process. Indian intellectuals who want to be secure in their liberal beliefs may not understand what is going on. But every other Indian knows precisely what is happening. Deep down he knows that a large response is emerging, even if at times this response appears in his eyes to be threatening."[51] It is too early to say whether this new response is heading towards a new organization of society. But one cannot deny the fact that there is an upsurge in the country, particularly in the depressed classes, but this upsurge might also be used to condone the violent acts of the mad fringe in the Hindu society. And later incidents proved it and Naipaul had to give a clarification. But the upward movement of the lower classes is forcing some reshuffling of caste/class structure.

The Dream that was projected during the freedom movement was of an inclusive kind. It gave rise to a unified idea of the country which was later codified in the constitution and to which Naipaul refers. But during the five decades of independent India the 'unified idea' has weakened. This unified idea or national idea should not be confused with Ram Rajya. It was a secular national idea which received a set-back from, what Romila Thapar calls 'exclusionist nationalism'. In fact, Indian society came to be seen in terms of its constituents "as majority and minority communities defined by religion."[52] Ambedkar could foresee this when he told the Britishers that even after India became independent, Dalits would be at the mercy of the *savarna* if no structural changes were made.

In this process, the concept of secularism was the first to be undermined. And there appeared extremists in each dominant religious group sticking up their group against the other with fatal consequences. The concept of secularism has been maligned and beaten out of shape. Yet in a country composed of diverse religious groups, there is no alternative to it. The surprising thing is that even those who swore by secularism became ambivalent as also those who called it 'pseudo secularism.' In fact, distorting meanings of concepts to the extent of making them irrational became one of the prime concerns of political parties. As a consequence, nationalism, which had given flesh and sinew to the freedom movement, degenerated into narrow sub-nationalisms. During the struggle for freedom, religion was a component of nationalism but it was subordinated to, what might be called, composite nationalism or secular nationalism. As Octavio Paz said that the new brand of emerging nationalism is political corruption of nationalism. Frantz Fanon had warned the Third World countries to be wary of this trend, as revolutionary nationalism might degenerate into spurious nationalism.

Both Dalits and African Americans have to contend with forces that either defer the Dream or cause its blurring. Thus they are forced to partake of a Dream that is not theirs. The situation is compounded by the forces released by globalization and liberalization which appear to be great equalizers, but leave their problems untouched. Once they are sucked into its vortex, the oppressed cease to be less agitated about the issues that have been so dear to them. The life of contradictions continues to exist although its force is minimized somewhat. In India the political parties that claimed to espouse the Dalit cause, are themselves in disarray. The caste issue and the issue of status get so entangled that one fails to deal with them. The rage exists but its force is blunted. The target against which the Dalits have been fighting is being shifted.

Something similar is happening in America. Toni Morrison in her latest novel *Paradise* shows that the problem for African Americans is how to reconcile the racial past with the void of the present. While the memories of the past continue to haunt them, the present does not help them deal with it. The larger society also does not help them find ways of reconciling to it.

Will colour, like caste, become irrelevant in America?. Will miscegenation, like interdining or intermarriage that Dr. Ambedkar talked of, become a means to that end? Podhoretz once argued : "The wholesale merging of the two races is the most desirable alternative for everyone concerned. I am not claiming that this alternative can be pursued programmatically or that it is immediately desirable as a solution.... What I am saying, however, is that in my opinion Negro problem can be solved in the country in no other way."[53] There is a kind of desperation in his optimism but how do they help in dealing with the vestiges of the past which still exist in their minds.

The desire for change of goals sounds feeble. What DuBois said half a century ago, is still valid. "What do we want? What is the thing we are after? Do we want to be Americans, full fledged Americans, with all the rights of other American citizens? But is that all. Do we simply want to be Americans? Once in a while through all of us there flashed a clairvoyance, some clear idea of what American reality is. We who are dark can see America in a way that white Americans cannot. And seeing our country thus, are we satisfied with its present goals and ideals." [54]

Jennifer Hochschild subjects the ideology of the American Dream to intense scrutiny, and apart from examining different tenets of the American Dream *vis-à-*

vis the African Americans, also examines the role of O.J. Simpson, Colin Powell and Louis Farakhan and discovers disturbing images being thrown up by their roles. Colin Powell, for example, who ran for President, was not supported by as many Blacks as whites and for quite sometime could not decide if he was a Democrat or a Republican. The Million Man March that supported O.J. Simpson's act of murder revealed that a majority of Blacks could rally round a black person. The unfortunate thing is that America even now is marked by "the permanence of racism", in which despite recurrent waves of immigration, the Africans will always be the faces at the bottom of the well. Hochschild finds differences at the level of policy proposal rather than at the level of commitment and this makes the Blacks ambivalent towards the Dream. "The ideology of the American Dream still holds sway over the minds of the people of America despite the flaws like the hollowness of materialism, the degeneration of community, the hypocrisy of claims to equal opportunity and the selfishness of the lucky."[55] The ideology also operates differently in different classes. A large number of African Americans who move up the social ladder support the ideology in their own way. On the other hand, the poor African Americans who are strategically placed provide a serious challenge to the ideology. The difficulty of bringing together Black and poor white on a common struggle against this ideology arises because of their holding different opinion. Their conditions invalidate the comparison between the two groups. It is in the case of the poor African American that the gap between promise and practices between the national idea and its realization is so wide.

Despite this, the U.S.A. is passing through a phase when the idea of isolationism and separatism seems to have been pushed into the background and a move towards multiculturalism is being supported by both Black and white thinkers. For a change, the battle is being fought at the level of culture as though culture alone would set things right. Cornel West and Henry Louis Gates Jr., two prominent African American intellectual leaders, support this move towards cultural integration. In an interview with Larry Ward Gates Jr. said that like most people who take the study of culture seriously, he distrusts boundaries. He emphasizes the impure and relational nature of African American culture, the acceptance of which would lead to what he called a 'critical trust' to appreciate what was of significance in white culture, and African American culture. Toni Morrison in her own way underlined the contribution made by African Americans to American culture and literary imagination. According to her the presence of Black in white imagination cannot be disregarded, as it is the central fact of American history. Shelley Fisher Fishkin in her books *Lighting Out for the Territory and Was Huck Black?* underscores the fact that the experiences of the two races cannot be put in two separate compartments. African American presence is so integral to American culture that without this component they would lose part of their identity or sensibility. Todd Gitlin goes to the extent of saying that if the white American does not know the larger history, which means the people of colour, the western and the non-western they would remain ignorant. "The student of any color who doesn't read Douglass or Ellison misses the core of American history and literature as much as the one who omits Hawthorne, Melville, Emerson, Whitman or Twain. Serious multiculturalism is not a children's party where party favours are passed out to every one to celebrate his or her contribution; it is reintegration into superior integration."[56]

But the uneasiness about reintegration remains and this causes a kind of shuttling between despair and hope. This uneasiness has been caught by Cornel West in conversation with some of the most outstanding figures in politics, religion and arts in the U.S.A. in a book titled *Restoring Hope.* The editor of the book Alvin Shawn Sealey in his introduction seems hopeful of a genuine American sentiment and tries to relate the restoration of hope in African American to philanthropy and altruism.[57] He, however, admits that, unlike other immigrants, African

Americans have been subject to the debasing and largely unrelieved burdens of racism and racial discrimination. Yet together with those who are concerned with the American condition, they have managed to move towards a position of greater equity and possibility even as their enemies of fairness and justice would have them remain in a state of impoverishment and despair. Cornel West is not as optimistic as Sealey and finds that there are bleak prospects in Black Americans. In fact there haunts a spectre of despair in the late 20th Century America. To live is to wrestle with despair, yet never to allow despair to have the last word. Bill Bradley, one of the persons interviewed, makes a distinction between optimism and hope and finds "optimism somewhat synthetic and hope a much deeper concept. Optimism rests in the belief that tomorrow will be a little bit better than today. Hope sustains in the darkest of hours. Hope goes to the core of human personality and our common humanity and the belief that things can be better than they are. Hope is something that empowers a people, a nation, all humanity."[58]

But the basis of sustaining this hope is constantly eroded, for it hides a stark reality that of poverty and unemployment. In the U.S.A. 94 per cent of the wealth is cornered by 20 per cent of Americans. The remaining 80 per cent of the population is struggling for 6 per cent of the wealth. This can be removed only by restructuring the economic and political system. If the African Americans are satisfied with a slightly bigger slice of the cake, the entire struggle for a better and more human world will lose its meaning and with it the effort to humanize the social and political structure. In other words, if they fail to bring about democratic socialism, they will, including Dalits, be defeated by their former masters. The failure will mean the failure of their quest for equality which means that they are as good as the others, the whites and the *savarnas*. They will fail to reach the level of man making (Ambedkar) or complete manhood (DuBois). They will continue to be trapped in the cave which separates them from the larger humanity.[59] The

Dalits need another Ambedkar who will break the Ambedkar icon and form issues that will serve not only immediate but also long term gains. This will prepare the ground for structural change or democratic socialism.The political parties that seek to end social injustice or economic exploitation seem to have subordinated the two to some kind of apparent Dalit unity. The attitude of gradualism and a kind of renunciation and passivity have become part of their psyche. The struggle requires a constant updating, an examination of what they have achieved, where they have gone wrong and what they should do to achieve their goal. The Dalits hope that the simmering discontent will throw up a new leadership that will complete the unfinished task of Ambedkar.

References

1. Frederick Douglass, Life and Times of Fredrick Douglass: The Complete Autobiography, Rept., 1962, Collier Books, pp. 125-126.
2. Chokhamela, in An Anthology of Dalit Literature ed. Mulk Raj Anand and Eleanor Zelliot, Gyan Publishing House, New Delhi, 1992, p. 5.
3. W.E.B. DuBois, Dusk of Dawn: An Essay Toward an Autobiography of Race concept, Shocken Books, New York, 1968, p. 117.
4. Frederick Douglass, My Bondage and My Freedom, Arno Press, N.Y. 1968, p. 423.
5. *Ibid.*, pp. 427-428.
6. Ambedkar Writings and Speeches, Vol. 5, pp. 287-328.
7. Collected works of Mahatma Jotirao Phule, Vol. II, Education Department, Govt. of Maharashtra, Bombay 1991, p. 29.
8. Pavan K. Varma, The Great Indian Middle Class, Penguin 1988, pp. 9-10.
9. A.M. Rajasekhariah: B.R. Ambedkar, The Politics of Emancipation, Sindhu Publication, Bombay, 1971, p. 216.
10. Saunders Redding in Introduction to the Study of The Souls of Black Folk by W.E. B. DuBois, Chicago, 1931, p. IX.
11. W.E. B. DuBois, The Souls of Black Folk, A.G. Mc Clug 1931, p. 3.
12. *Ibid*, pp. 3-4.

13. Cornel West and Henry Louis Gates Jr. eds. The Future of the Race, Alfred A Knopf N.Y. 1996, p. 132.
14. W.E.B. DuBois, The Talented Tenth Published in The Future of the Race, pp.156-157.
15. *Ibid.*, p.161.
16. *Ibid.*, p.168.
17. Ambedkar Writings and Speeches, Vol. 5, p. 399.
18. Ambedkar Writings and Speeches Vol. 1, p. 68.
19. *Ibid.*, p. 69.
20. *Ibid.*, p. 47.
21. Quoted by A.M. Rajsekhariah in B.R. Ambedkar, The Politics of Liberation, Sindhu Publications, Bombay 1971, p. 65.
22. Ambedkar's letter to Mr. A.V. Alexander in Ambedkar Writings and Speeches, vol.10, pp. 497-498.
23. Quoted by Justice V.R. Krishna Aiyer in Dr. Ambedkar and The Dalit Future, pp. 32-33.
24. The Future of the Race, p. 58.
25. *Ibid.*, p. 68.
26. *Ibid.*, p. 111.
27. Quoted by Rajsekhariah, p. 323.
28. New Left Review, No. 191.
29. Ambedkar at Ramlila Ground, Agra March 18, 1956.
30. The Future of the Race, pp.124-125.
31. Alex Haley, Roots, Picador, London, 1977, p. 680.
32. *Ibid.*, p. 677.
33. *Ibid.*, p. 680.
34. Gail Omvedt, Dalit and The Democratic Revolution, Sage Publication, 1994, p. 246.

    Contrast this with Nehru's integrationist thesis in his autobiography discussed by M.S. Gore, in An Ideology of Protest.
35. Ambedkar Writings and Speeches, Vol. 3, p. 275.
36. Ambedkar, Vol. 2, p. 106.
37. Todd Gitlin, The Twilight of American Dream, Metropolitan Books, 1995, p. 35.
38. James Baldwin, The Price of the Ticket, St. Matin Marrek, 1985, p. 318.
39. S.D. Kapoor, "American Dream and Black Experience" in The Utopian Imagination eds. Jasbir Jain and Santosh Gupta, Printwell Jaipur, 1991, pp. 41-54.
40. Octavio Paz, Partisan Review (1), 1986, pp. 64-85.
41. Czeslaw Milosz, The Southern Review, 1985, p. 101.

42. A.D. Tocqueville, Democracy in America, Vol. 2, Alfred Knopf, 1968, p. 98.
43. Richard Wright, American Hunger, Harper and Row, 1977, p. 40.
44. W.E.B. DuBois, Dusk of Dawn: An Essay Toward an Autobiography of a Race Concept, Schocken Books, 1968, p. 221.
45. Mark Twain, The Autobiography ed. Charles Neider, A Perennial Classic, 1959, p. 254.
46. James Baldwin, The Price of The Ticket, p. 16.
47. Quoted by M.S. Gore in The Social Context of an Ideology, p. 213.
48. *Ibid.*, p. 220.
49. Ambedkar Writings and Speeches Vol. 3, p. 441.
50. *Ibid.*, pp. 461-462.
51. *The Times of India*, July 18, 1993.
52. India: Another Millennium, ed. Romila Thapar, Viking 2000.
53. Commentary, Feb. 1967.
54. Quoted by Harold Cruse in the Crisis of Negro Intellectual, p. 39.
55. Jennifer L. Hochschild, Class and the Soul of the Nation Facing upto the American Dream, Princeton University Press, N. Jersey, 1995, p. XVIII.
56. Todd Gitlin, The Twilight of the American Dream, Metropolitan Books, Henry Halt and Co. N.Y., 1999, p. 145.
57. Restoring Hope, Cornel West in conversation on the Future of Black America. Ed. Kelvin Shawn Sealey, Beacon Press, Boston, 1997, p. XVII.
58. *Ibid.*, p. 45.
59. *Ibid.*, p. 75.

3
Consciousness and Literature

In the course of their development, Negro Americans have come to share a heightened group consciousness.... The once diverse peoples and their progeny through centuries of common experience in America, have been welded into a distinct political entity, increasingly organized, characterized by greater unity than any other capable minority, with a strong sense of 'belongingness'. In short there has been developed in America a new people - the Negro people—with organizational forms and a group consciousness peculiarly its own.

It was inevitable that this people with its special memories and sentiments and aspirations should develop its own body of esthetic experience.

Wilkerson
Quoted by Hazel Arnett Ervin in
African American Literary Criticism
Twayne Publishers, 1999

We younger artists who create now intend to express our own individual dark-skinned selves without fear or shame. If white people are pleased, we are glad. If they are not, it doesn't matter. We know we are beautiful. And ugly too. The tom-tom cries and the tom-tom laughs. If colored people are pleased we are glad. If they are not, their displeasure does not matter either. We build our temples for tomorrow, strong as we know how, and we stand on top of the mountain, free within ourselves.

Langston Hughes
The Negro Artist and
the Racial Mountain (1926)

Dalit and African American literature is the outcome of a heightened group consciousness which provides a frame of reference in the form of "special memories, sentiments and aspirations." It relates its experience to all those cultural forms – music, folk literature, *abhangs*, blues and spirituals – that gave sustenance to their lives but were never part of the mainstream life. It was during the Harlem Renaissance that African Americans separated those aspects of their experience that needed articulation. In the case of Dalits this awareness came with Ambedkar during the thirties but it acquired force in the fifties and the sixties. This was the beginning of a vibrant literature that has acquired its own depth and dimension that could be the envy of any national literature.

Both Wilkerson and Hughes in the two quotes given above establish a definite connection between consciousness and its manifestation in literature. Consciousness, like experience and feeling, is a flexible term and its meaning ought to be delimited in the context of Dalit and African American experience. Unlike the consciousness of the whites, African American consciousness is not the product of historical forgetfulness. It is the full baggage of historical experience that they carry with them, like the Black American in *Invisible Man* who was evicted from his hovel. He collected things that took him to his past – part of a chain, a certificate of free Negro and pictures of the leaders. Unlike *savarna* consciousness which suffered from selective amnesia about the past, Dalit consciousness collected bits and pieces that were thrown as crumbs by the *savarnas*. What rankles in them are the unpleasant memories of their ancestors. Ralph Ellison wrote in *Shadow and Act* that African American consciousness was a product of their memory, sustained and constantly reinforced by events and by their hopeful suspension of final judgement as to the meaning of their governance. In other words, it meant recognizing themselves as themselves; for this reason their consciousness developed along different lines. Similarly, Dalits kept their part of history and by implication *savarna* part of history also alive. Consciousness in their case is total perception of reality which forms their world view. The process of opinion forming and evaluation of experience cannot be separated from consciousness, although it may not be visible initially. In this sense consciousness as reflected in literature gives Dalits and African Americans an understanding of their predicament, of the social order of which they are a part and their place in it.

One of the cardinal facts of the past century and it continues in the present is the dominance of history and politics over all aspects of human reality, including the world of imagination which encompasses the human landscape. In fact, as Thomas Mann once said, in our times the destiny of man presents its meaning in political terms. And here politics is taken in its widest sense of organizing structures that create human situation or otherwise. In a way literature performs an ideological function. And mostly ideology is pressed into service at a level that can be perceived only if one carefully studies the ideological forces working during that particular period. In *Culture and Imperialism* Edward Said posits that literature participated in Europe's overseas expansion. It helped project an image, in imaginative terms, of the imperialists as superior to the natives in whose interests the imperialists stayed in their country. Its continuation and its rejection can be seen in India as well as in the U.S.A. The new literary discourse, both in the U.S.A. and in India, is questioning the role of the 'core' as against the 'periphery'. In fact, it is pushing the 'core' out of its privileged position. It is also looking for an alternative way of organizing reality and the world. The reversal of roles points to a new direction but new obstacles are being created to prevent the formation of revolutionary consciousness. The oppressed writers across the globe represent this shift in the consciousness of once colonized people – and those colonized within the colonized – particularly in the sense of pushing the world in a certain direction and in the sense of altering people's ideas about the society they should strive for.

Literature in this context cannot remain neutral and thus cannot be defined in absolute terms as it exhibits the same traits that characterize Dalit and African American in real life, including their changing status in society. Apart from dealing with the inequities of social structure, their literature also deals with the complex structure of race and caste. Thus literature for them is not an irrational and mysterious phenomenon, the result of an extraordinary inspiration and genius separated from other men and from ordinary life. It is "a particularly precise and coherent expression of the problems which pose themselves to ordinary men in their daily lives and of the ways in which they are led to resolve them."[1] What is important is isolating problems and then giving them precise and coherent expression. This is possible when the experience becomes a structured whole subordinated to an appropriate form.

There are three levels at which consciousness operates in literature. First, it is historical consciousness in the form of collective experience; second, it is actual consciousness which includes emerging and residual consciousness; and third, possible consciousness. In the process of structuring of experience historical consciousness is harmonized with actual consciousness. The possible consciousness grows out of the synthesis of historical and actual consciousness and suggests the direction such experience should take: the possible consciousness should not appear superimposed or contrived. In fact, a sense of human community should grow out of it. It must not destroy all possibilities and potentialities of human reality. In Alain Robbe-Grillet's novel *The Erasers* the characters are subordinated to 'massive homogeneity' in which the possibility of human growth is almost absent. Grillet seems to apply the same laws of self-regulation to the fictive world as one finds in real life, which means that the way the fictive world is organized is no different from the way we organize our real world. It is pure mechanical organization. What is missing in the novel is possible consciousness.

The fusion of three levels of consciousness is not easy for most Dalit and African American writers as they are pitted against, what might be called, official consciousness which sanctions a particular kind of perception and ordering of reality. The official consciousness ought not to have any place in their special memories. Their distinctiveness lies in the fact that free decision is possible and they can create the situation they want and need. For achieving this, they will have to be in contact with their real self, an image of themselves not a false image. "The image we have of ourselves", Carolyne F. Gerald writes, "controls what we are capable of doing.... We cannot block out the Black-White struggle for control of image and create a utopianized world of all Black reflections. Our work at this stage is clearly to destroy the zero and the negative image, myths of ourselves by turning them inside out. To do this we reverse the symbolism and we use that reverse symbolism as the tool of projecting our own image on the universe."[2]

There is a deliberate attempt to break that image in the context of pressing and gnawing realities and to replace it by an image that suggests a positive view of themselves and of their destiny. Ralph Ellison's *Invisible Man* questions all forms of authority and the falsehood supported by it through symbols. He is kept on the run by the white who had promised to get him a job. He succeeds in breaking that falsehood when he learns that the white wanted him not to see through the design. Le Roi Jones put it succinctly and in ideological terms in *Home: Social Essays*. "If there is ever a Negro literature, it must disengage itself from the weak, heinous elements of the culture that spawned it, and use its very existence of a very profound America. But as long as the Negro writer contents himself with the limitation of the useless ugly elegance of the stunted middle class mind, academic or popular, and refuses to look around him and 'tell it like it is' preferring the false prestige of the Black bourgeoisie or the deceitful acceptance of buy and sell America, something never included in the legitimate cultural tradition of his people, he will be a failure and, what is more, not even a significant failure, just another dead American."[3]

The true African American literature will free itself not only of the 'ugly elegance of the stunted middle class' mind but also of the false prestige of the Black bourgeoisie supporting the image of 'buy and sell America'. It will then assume a self-conscious role representing the cultural status of its people.

A comparable movement in Dalit literature in India, in Maharashtra in particular, began in the early seventies when Dalit literature was supported by a militant ideology of Dalit Panthers. The Times Weekly supplement of November 25, 1973 took notice of this shift in their imaginative creation and published some literary creations. It was a voice of protest "against the middle-class Hindus who have monopolized cultural expression." (Dileep Padgaonkar)

In the white/*savarna* imagination, the criteria for judging their experience were always different as though their pain and suffering were of no consequence. In fact, as Richard Gilman wrote in *The Confusion of Realms,* their birth, death, pain and suffering were not considered proper natural elements but as unsanctioned realities to be experienced on sufferance and without communal acknowledgement. By pointing out that their experience is not the same as that of their masters, they are questioning what Stokely Carmichael called, "the dictatorship of definition, interpretation and consciousness."[4]

The interplay of these three forms of dictatorship could be seen in Dalit and African American literature more forcefully in the latter. *Mulatto* by Langston Hughes which was written during the thirties of the last century deals with the life of Colonel Norwood, a white plantation owner in Georgia, a Southern State in the U.S.A. A brown woman, Cora Lewis, has been Colonel Norwood's mistress for thirty years and mother of many children fathered by Norwood. The Colonel is very pleased with Cora's management of the household and he in turn treats her children well, sending them to school and having them trained for jobs. But Robert, one of Cora's sons, who, in appearance and complexion, looks exactly like Norwood, is not willing to accept the manipulation of his life, particularly after his exposure to education. He considers himself a natural successor to Norwood and even calls him his 'Papa'. As such, he shows the consciousness of a liberated person and defies all discriminatory practices and behaves as though he is no different from the whites. He drives Colonel's car and comes to the house through the front door which no Black man is allowed to use. When his brother Williams warns him of the consequences of his rebellious act, he tells him: "I might stay here and teach some of you darkies to think like me, may be till it gets too much for the old Colonel --but no more bowing down to – not Robert Norwood.... Nobody's gonna fix a place for me. I'm old man Norwood's son." Nobody fixed a place for him. Even his mother Cora's persuasion is not enough to dissuade him from accepting the reality of his situation. Norwood gets complaints from his people about his intransigent behaviour in public. Norwood tries to curb his insouciance but Robert would have none of the superior attitude of Norwood. The conversation between Robert and Norwood brings out the interplay of consciousness and interpretation into sharper focus.

Norwood : .... Now, I'm going to let you talk to me, but I want you to talk right.

Robert : What do you mean 'talk right'?

Norwood : I mean like a nigger should to a white man.

Robert : Oh! But I'm not a nigger, Colonel Tom. I'm your son.

Norwood : You're Cora's boy.

Robert : Women don't have children by themselves.

Norwood : Nigger women don't know the fathers. You're a bastard.

[Robert clenches his fist. Norwood turns towards the drawer where pistol is, takes it out, and lays it on the table. The wind blows the lace curtain at the windows and sweeps the shadows of falling leaves across the paths of sunlight on the floor.]

Robert : I've heard that before. I've heard it from Negroes, and I've heard it from white folks.

Now I hear it from you.[slowly] You're talking about my mother.

Norwood : I'm talking about Cora, Yes. Her children are
bastards.

Robert : [quickly] : And you are their father. [Angrily] How come I look like you, if you are not my father?

Norwood : Don't shout at me, boy. I can hear you. [Half-smiling]
How come your skin is yellow and your elbows rusty? How come they threw you out of the post office today for talking to a white woman? How come you are the crazy young buck you are?

Robert : They had no right to throw me out. I asked for my money back when I saw the broken tubes. Just as you had no right to raise that cane today when I was standing at the door of the house where you live, while I sleep in a shack down the road with the field hands.[slowly] But my mother sleeps with you.

Norwood : You don't like it?

Robert : No, I don't like it.

Norwood : What can you do about it?

Robert : [After a pause] : I'd like to kill all the white men in the world.

Norwood : [Starting] : Niggers like you are hung to trees.

Robert : I'm not a nigger.

Norwood : You don't like your own race? [Robert is silent] Yet you don't like white folks either?

Norwood asks him to leave the room through the kitchen but Robert defies him. Norwood is so enraged at this challenge to his authority that he picks up the pistol.

Norwood : You Black bastard! [Robert goes towards him calmly, grasps his father's arm and twists it until the gun falls to the floor. The older man bends backward in startled fury and pain.] Don't you dare put your....

Robert : [laughing] : Why don't you shoot, papa? [Louder]
Why don't you shoot?

Norwood : [gasping as he struggles, fighting back] : .... Black...hands...on...you...

Robert : [hysterically, as he takes his father by the throat] :

Why don't you shoot, papa? [Norwood's hands claw the air helplessly. Robert chokes the struggling white man until his body grows limp.] Why don't you shoot? [Laughing] Why don't you shoot? Huh?

Why?" [5]

Like two interlocking realities Norwood and Robert face each other, the latter stubbornly refusing to submit to the manipulation of his life. It reminds one of Frederick Douglass who, while he was a slave, had a fight with Covey, his supervisor who wanted to force him into submission. Douglass did not kill him but told him that he could not have an upper hand. Douglass caught hold of his reality and would not let it go.

It is difficult to find a comparable example of this questioning of definition and interpretation in Dalit literature, but in a slightly subdued way, the same process could be observed in their literature too.

In the 'Poisoned Bread', a short story by Bandhumadhav, this situation is created when Yetalya a Harijan goes to the landlord Patil to beg for his share of the corn in return for the work he does on the farm. Patil treats him shabbily and even blames him for profaning religion because of which the rain-god got enraged. The grandson of Yetalya takes the interpretation of Patil head on. He asks him, "Patil, will you kindly tell me what you meant when you accused us of forgetting religion, abandoning our caste and of polluting the God? And if a religion can't tolerate one human being treating another simply as a human being, what's the use of such an inhuman religion? And if our mere touch pollutes the Gods, why were the Mahars and Mangs created at all? And who, may I know, who indeed, created them? And would you please tell me the name of the God whom the Mahars and Mangs can claim as their own?"[6] This talking back in an insolent manner by a young Mahar was too much for Patil and he was in violent anger. He defended the hierarchy supposedly created by God in which the Mahars were at the bottom. "Every one must abide by this scheme and act accordingly, put every man in his proper place as they wisely say. A chappal is never worshipped in place of God, is it?"

The young boy would not have any of that false theory. "So you think you can treat us like your footwear! But are we really like that? Aren't we also made of the same flesh and blood as the rest of you? We too are born after nine months in our mother's womb. Isn't it logical then that basically there is hardly any difference between us."[7]

The grandpa tries to pacify him so that he could get some corn at the end of it all. But the logic of the grandson gradually sinks. The hereditary land-right has trapped them and unless they get out of that trap, there will be no end to their suffering. What it means is they must stop begging. Before the grandpa dies after eating the stale crumbs he had brought from Patil's place, he tells Madhav : "never depend on the age-old-bread associated with our caste. Get as much education as you can. Take away this accursed bread from the mouths of the Mahars. This poisonous bread will finally kill the very humanness of man..."[8]

One could see this interplay of definition and interpretation in innumerable stories but there is always an element of withdrawal and acceptance in the background, although the new definition of self is more acceptable. In Babu Rao Bagul's story 'When I Concealed My Caste' one finds two levels of interpretation existing side by side. To define one's individuality, along with one's existence, involves risks. One stumbles upon social barriers which must be removed before one can have infinite possibilities of existence.

The struggle against this definition of their existence continues at various levels. William Styron wrote a novel on the Nat Turner uprising and his confessions which became a subject of a heated debate in which Black and white took different positions. It turned out to be a fight over the nature of reality, in this case questioning Styron's interpretation of Turner's *Confessions*. The Dalits are in their own way questioning the *savarna* version of human reality. In Daya Pawar's *Achut*, the protagonist was never served food along with others, as he belonged to the Dalit class and was sent on some false errand at that very moment. The attitudes of the *savarna* became apparent to him, although he had no way to counter it.

Both Richard Wright and Malcolm X, in their different ways had reached a level of consciousness which gave them hope for a better future. In fact, they had acquired a human context and they were not prepared to deny that context. Quite naturally, they faced a wall in the white man's mind when they spoke out their mind as to the career they would like to choose for themselves.

Richard Wright went to a white lady who wanted a boy (a Black boy) to do household chores for which he would get breakfast and dinner. The bread he was given for breakfast was stale and hard, and the molasses tasteless. As though this was not enough, the white lady asked him about his education and future plans.

"What grade are you in school?

"Seventh ma'am."

"Then why are you going to school? She asked in surprise.

"Well, I want to be a writer." I mumbled, unsure of myself: I had not planned to tell her that, but she had made me feel so utterly wrong and of no account that I needed to bolster myself.

"A what?" She demanded.

"A writer", I mumbled.

"For what?"

"To write stories," I mumbled defensively.

"You will never be a writer," She said.

"Who on earth put such ideas into your nigger head?"

"Nobody," I said.

"I didn't think anybody ever would," She declared indignantly.

As I walked around her house to the street, I knew that I would not go back. The woman had assaulted my ego; she had assumed that she knew my place in life, what I felt, what I ought to be, and I resented it with all my heart. Perhaps she was right; perhaps I would never be a writer, but I did not want her to say so." [9]

Similarly, when Malcolm X told his English teacher Mr. Ostrowski, that he wanted to be a lawyer, the latter was shocked. He told Malcolm, "One of life's first needs is for us to be realistic. Don't misunderstand me now. We all like you, you know that. But you have got to be realistic about being a nigger. A lawyer, that is no realistic goal for a nigger. You need to think about something you can be. You're good with your hands - making things. Everybody admires your carpentry shop work. Why don't you plan on carpentry."[10]

The whites have prescribed the limit of their experience, the limit of their ambition and the acceptance of roles that society seems to have prescribed for them. The whites cannot accept the fact that African Americans also have an inner life and can grow along different lines. Om Prakash Valmki has recorded a similar experience in his autobiography *Juthan*. The headmaster treats him as though he has no right to sit in his class. In order to make him realize that he is an Untouchable, the headmaster asks him to sweep the courtyard of the school. After two days when he sat in the class, the headmaster asks him to sweep the courtyard before coming to class. Asking questions in the class was to invite the wrath of the teacher. Once Valmiki had the courage to ask why, despite their miserable existence, no one even mentioned their name in the epics. The teacher got so enraged that he beat him with a stick, in the words of Valmiki, "wrote an epic on my back which I remembered throughout my life. All this happened after the Britishers had left the country".[11] Like Richard Wright, in Valmiki the response doesn't take a violent form. But anger and resentment against the system persist. Anger is common to all these writers. Anger to come to terms with their reality; anger to see the contradictions in the people they have to deal with; anger because they are prohibited from examining their "experience too closely by the tremendous demands and the real danger of (their) situation."[12] There are a number of challenges before African American and Dalit writers. One, carrying the burden of their unrelieved suffering; two, relating themselves to an existing or created culture; three, examining their relationship with their masters; and fourth, affirming their humanity. The burden of unrelieved suffering is the greatest challenge to them as they have to force from this burden the last drop, bitter or sweet, it can possibly yield. It is all the more important because it might deny them contact with the deeper sources of their being as also the world of emotions and feelings. It involves striking a balance between their pain and joy without compromising their unique situation. There is also the challenge of resisting the temptation of imitating white/*savarna* standards. Such writers are pulled in two different directions. On the one hand, the temptation is to make their literature an unedited transcript of reality; on the other to submit it to the structuring of it as per the demands of art. There is no doubt that the rawness of their experience and the force of their particularities give their imaginative creation distinctness of its own, but the danger is that the formal aspect may become subservient to particularities. "The concern of the artist," Baldwin wrote, "is to create out of the disorder of life that order which is art."[13]

This important issue of protest and literature, anger and art was debated among African Americans during the sixties and seventies of the last century and was debated among the Dalits in Maharashtra in the 80s and in the Hindu heartland in the 90s. In the U.S.A. both African Americans and white writers participated in the debate. It took a formal shape when it was published in the form of a book titled *Anger and Beyond* edited by Herbert Hill. The burden of their argument was that anger or protest by itself is not antithetical to art. Great literature of the world has an element of protest in it. It is what a writer makes of protest and anger. James Baldwin, in *How Long The Train's Been Gone* makes Leo, one of his characters, say "my pain is the horse that I must learn to ride."[14] This conscious desire to control it or to give it direction involves dealing with the complexity of their experience and the making of it. Ralph Ellison in his novel *Invisible Man* catches the ambiguity and irony of Black life. In it the entire social fabric in relation to the Blacks is exposed and the attitudes that the two races represent are seen in their interrelatedness. It is true that "no human personality can escape the effect of prolonged emotional rejection. The victim of this cruelty will defend himself with hatred and with dreams of vengeance and will lose perhaps for ever his normal capacity for love."[15] Rage could be taken as a necessary stage towards psychological transformation leading to full human freedom, and a more penetrating search for deeper human values. "Our humanity is our burden, our life; we need not battle for it. We need only to do what is infinitely more difficult – that is to accept it. The failure of the protest novel lies in its rejection of life, the human being, the denial of its insistence that it is his categorization alone which is real and which cannot be transcended."[16] Baldwin makes a distinction between a pamphleteer and a novelist. He considers *Uncle Tom's Cabin* a polemical piece as Uncle Tom remains a stereotype and never acquires human dimension that one finds in Jim in *The Adventures of Huckleberry Finn.* In Richard Wright's novel *Native Son,* Bigger Thomas is trapped in a world which is out to crush him. Far from being patient and forgiving, he hated "the decent and cultivated white men who from complicity or neglect shared in the responsibility of their plight."[17] It is for this reason that Irving Howe praised the "clenched militancy" of Wright's character in his essay Black Boys and Native Sons. Bigger represents the buried responses of his people as also the inner feelings of anger and hatred which no white could reach. He lives out the fantasies and prejudices of the whites and the ineffectual desire to be free of the claptrap of racial segregation that surrounds him. Deep down in him there is a desire for human love and sympathy. Despite some polemical parts, the novel exposes the insensitivity of the social structure. For Howe *Native Son* is a work of assault rather than of withdrawal. It is for this reason that the Negro violence forms an inescapable part of his existence and prevents such writers from dealing adequately with the complexity of Black existence. Howe goes a step further and says that Black writers will continue to write protest literature as long as their situation remains unchanged.[18] He praises Ralph Ellison's *Invisible Man* which is saturated with Black culture and no white man could have written such a novel. The protagonist of the novel symbolises not only Black suffering but also their desire to move beyond the constricting world in which they are placed. Howe's essay evoked sharp response from Ralph Ellison published in an essay titled the 'World and the Jug' included in his book, *Shadow and Act.*[19] Ellison's response was in two parts. The first one was a reaction to Howe's arguments given in his essay. The second part was a rejoinder after Howe had responded to Ellison's questioning of his arguments. While Ellison praised Howe's article, as it made impact upon his life and literature, he was uncomfortable with the condescending attitude of white critics towards Black literature. He also questioned the superiority of the whites to arrogate to themselves the right to interpret the variety and complexity of Black life. There is a very strong aspect of Black experience which teaches Blacks to deal with their situation and to contain pain. Besides, it is difficult to say in advance the kind of novel a Black writer should write and which aspects of his experience are to be transformed into art. Ellison was particularly critical of Howe's assertion that unrelieved suffering is the only real Black experience and that he should be taken as an abstract embodiment of living hell. Ellison felt that in his assertion Howe ignored the fact that Black life is also human life. True novels arise out of an impulse to celebrate human life and it is possible for Black writers to transcend the limits. It is in the second section of the essay that Ellison takes on the arguments of Howe point by point. Here he asserts that blackness is not an abstraction and it has its own complexity and range. Apart from that, it is rooted in historical consciousness. In *Invisible Man*, Ellison has shown the complexity of relationship between Black and white, the concealment of Black reality on the part of white and the desire and the struggle to reclaim that reality on the part of Blacks. The entire world of Black culture – its myths, its music, its folktales, its strategies – is shown in all its vibrations. Ellison asserts that there is no antagonism between protest and literature and he should be taken not only as a Black writer but also as an American writer. James Baldwin put it slightly differently when he wrote that he should be taken as a writer who happens to be Black and not merely a Black writer. Both of them wanted that they be judged not as Black writers but as writers. This is not to say that they are imitating or approximating white standards.

In an interview Ralph Ellison narrates an incident that took place at North-Western University. A young white professor asked him: "Mr. Ellison, how does it feel to be able to go to places where most Negroes can't go.' Before I could think to be polite, I answered: 'What you mean is how does it feel to go places where most white men can't go?' He was embarrassed; nevertheless, it was a teaching situation. I told him the truth. I wanted him to understand that individuality is still operative beyond the racial structuring of American society. And conversely there are many areas of Black society that are close to me while open to certain whites."[20] Ellison is rejecting the facile categorization of experience as such categorization might prevent full knowledge or better understanding of it. If one accepts the knotted and complex histories of special and interconnected experience, one will also have to accept that their experience cannot be granted a separate and special status. The uniqueness of experience can be preserved if it includes some sense of the human community and the larger whole of which it is a part. The problem is compounded at the level of structuring of that experience as it might employ devices that could be called the common properties of writers. In Richard Wright's *American Hunger* dogs are brought for experiment to a hospital and their tongues are chopped off. What the dogs are made to do cannot be separated from the entire situation. The dogs, because of their mutilated tongue, bark in a soundless wail. It is natural for one to move on to the situation of Blacks in white society. Like dogs they cannot articulate their feelings.

In *Invisible Man* the protagonist is made to work in a factory where Black employees are in a minority, although their presence cannot be called insignificant. In the process of preparing paint, ten drops of black colour are mixed in a bucket full of white paint. The Black paint seems to disappear in the white bucket but it does affect the quality of the paint. In the same novel there is a character called Rinehart who assumes protean identities or masks. He is a priest, a hustler, a political leader, a lover and a gambler. He gets his identity in relation to a specific situation he happens to be in and he acquires that identity as a result of his interaction with the larger society. What Ellison is trying to suggest is that racial situation does not dominate individual culture so absolutely as people might seem to believe. There are countless connections that override his status as African American. And at each stage of social development the complex of relationships changes, so also the points of connection. Alice Walker, Maya Angelou and Toni Morrison do not react to social and racial situation the way earlier writers did.

The anger in African American literature was fuelled by a streak of nationalism. The leadership of persons like Malcolm X, Carmichael and Eldridge Cleaver was supported by a philosophy enunciated by Frantz Fanon. The Dalit discourse that was influenced by Black discourse during the sixties and seventies did raise similar issues in India, including that of counter defence, but it was not violent enough. That is to say that they were not imitative. The philosophical basis for their struggle and literary creation was provided by Dr. Ambedkar who shunned violence. But the black discourse opened up new areas for examination and investigation. One can notice Dalit literature, particularly in Maharashtra, responding to their situation at two levels – the militant and not so militant. The two responses exist side by side, sometimes in the same writer. There is anger and there is simmering discontent with the lid on. Dalit literature in Maharashtra acquired a militant tone after the formation of the Dalit Panther Party. The founders – Dhasal and Arjun Dangle-were clear about their political and literary commitments. Dhasal made no distinction between the two. When Naipaul asked him whether he was more a poet than a politician, Dhasal categorically said: "The roles are not separate. I am against this caste system. I express it in my politics and in my poems. Poetry is a political act. Politics is part of my poetry."[21]

The language fashioned by them was shorn of old associations and given new connotations. It reflected their peculiar situation and the new way to comprehend it. It moved from the straightforward language of the earlier poems of Narayan Surve to the language that has a cutting edge. The poems of Namdeo Dhasal are like an assault. Take his poem, 'The Road to the Shrine', published in the first collection of his poems titled Golpitha:

> I was born when the sun became weak
> And slowly became extinct
> In the embrace of night.
> I was born on a footpath
> In a rug.
> And the day I was born I was an orphan.
> The one who gave me birth went to God.
> I was tired of this ghost
> Haunting me on the footpath.
> I spent most of my life
> Washing away the darkness of that sun.
> I grew like a person who has lost his fuse.
> I ate excrement and grew
> Give me five paise, give me five paise
> And take five curses in return
> I am on my way to the shrine.[22]

The tone of the poem is shrill and strident: there is an element of sadness in it. But words do not become bullets that kill, like in Le Roi Jones. Dhasal's anger takes another form in a poem entitled 'Song of the Republic and Dog'. Instead of 'tongueless dogs' we have 'leased dogs.'

> Dog, leashed dog,
> He howls and barks from time to time
> This is his constitutional right.
> He lives on stale crumbs.
> His mind is calloused with endured injustice
> If at a rebellious moment it becomes unbearable and he jerks at his leash, tries to break his chain, then he is shot.

We are becoming orphans.
Leaving our house to the winds we are returning to the burial grounds.
We dig up the bones of forty-two generations.
We sell them for four annas a kilo.
We fill the belly of the skeleton.
In the nation which spewed 'golden smoke'
The marketplace of bones is flourishing.[23]

Dhasal wanted to widen the scope of his struggle, to expand the definition of Dalits. Vijay Tendulkar refers to the inhabitants of the 'no man's land' of Dhasal's poems in his introduction to *Golpitha*. This enabled him to give expression to the "old internal cruelty of that poverty; people at the bottom, full of emotion, with no politics at that moment, just rejecting rejection."[24]

The questions are raised and converted into issues. In fact, they multiply like beggars, like slums, like people without work.

"We are turning our backs on you right now.
Right now we're becoming assassins."[25]

V.S. Naipaul compares Dhasal's career with the careers of Black Power people in the U.S.A. "...he had become someone the newspapers and magazines wrote about, and in the end he had become more famous than his cause. Yet... I felt he was the prisoner of an Indian past no one outside could truly understand. It had been harder for him to break out, to reject than it had been for Black people in the United States. And now Namdeo was again, if in a different way, a prisoner of India, with its multiplicity of movements and desperate needs; he could easily sink again. It wasn't really possible for him, as it might have been possible for a Black activist in the U.S. to withdraw to settle for ease."[26]

Because Dhasal and other Dalit writers are not able to come to terms with their past, one notices change in the level of their response. Another factor responsible for this is that most Dalit writers in Maharashtra combined Buddhism and Marxism. One reason why Dalit Panther Party split was Dhasal's commitment to Marxism. Baburao Bagul, another prominent Dalit writer, addressed himself to the issue of political role of literature in an article published in Amritadarsha. "Dalit Sahitya is not a literature of vengeance. Dalit Sahitya is not a literature which spreads hatred. Dalit Sahitya first promotes man's greatness and man's freedom and for that reason it is an historic necessity." [27] Bagul is resolving the conflict between protest and literature at the level of content itself. It is inherent in his definition of Dalit Sahitya that the celebration of man's greatness takes it beyond narrow confines of protest. Which means that protest and literature are not antithetical. In Bagul's defence of Dalit literature, literary aspect is not completely disregarded. But it must be subordinated to the larger movement in society. In fact, literature and art must bring to completion the Dalit role in social and political life. In different ways the issue has been discussed in the various issues of Amritadarsha and Arjun Dangle's collection of essays on politics and literature published in Dalit Vidroha. In fact Amritadarsha edited by Gangadhar Pantawane became a forum for Dalit literary discourse, including his book *Mulyavedh.*

In the Hindi heartland Dalit literature made its presence felt in the 70s. In its emergence Marathi Dalit literature and Ambedkar's thought played an important role. It is still in the process of establishing itself. And the issue of protest and literature is being raised now, although some of the writers are aware of its treatment in Marathi Dalit and Black literature as also comparative studies of both literatures. In spite of such studies, it was natural for Dalit writers in Hindi heartland to examine things for themselves. It is part of a process of growing up. Some of the prominent Dalit writers in Hindi are beginning to realize that oppressive situations do contain the potentials of human situation and it is the latter that ought to be celebrated.

At a seminar on 'Dalit and Black Writings: Some Recent Trends' organized by the Indian Institute of Advanced Study, Shimla in October 1997, all these issues were raised and animatedly discussed. Some eight Dalit writers, including Sharad Kumar Limbale, Dr. Dharamvir, Mohan Dass Nemishraya and Jayant Parmar participated in the seminar and presented papers. Like Namdeo Dhasal, they considered Dalit literature a political act. They asserted that Dalit writing should be seen as part of a political movement in which caste, colour and class structure are examined and a process of remaking of human situation should be set in motion. One could see the movement of their thought and struggle in a common frame of reference. This included (1) the questioning of 'symbolic violence', based on biological, hereditary or racial inequality, power and authority, whether visible or internalized; (2) the formation of a counter hegemonic discourse, leading to the perception of an alternative way of organizing human situation; (3) affirmation of a redefined identity; and (4) creation of a new aesthetics based on the hitherto neglected resources of evaluation of experience.

I would like to mention two articles – one by Dharamvir and the other by Sharad Kumar Limbale – that deal with the issue I have been discussing. Dharamvir in his article 'The Growth of Dalit thought', asks Dalit writers not to disregard formal aspect of literature. He wants Dalit writers to define Dalit Literature and literary values differently but at the same time not to neglect language and values. Dalit Sahitya should have its own art form and formal properties but it should not reject art as such. He warns Dalit writers not to fall into the trap of pamphleteers who completely disregard formal aspects in the name of Dalit reality. At the same time they must not also look up to non-Dalit writers for literary standards, as their greatness doesn't lie in measuring up to them. Dharamvir doesn't appreciate those Dalit writers who revel in their anger and ignorance. The development of art form is directly related to the depth of feelings and range of experience.[28]

Sharad Kumar Limbale in his article 'Dalit Literature and American Negro Literature' finds similarities in the emotional worlds of Dalit and Negro writers as also in their anger, revolt, hope and aspirations. Limbale sees Dalit and American Negro literature in a larger framework in which the growth of Dalit and American Negro perception of reality and their literary concerns can be studied together. The parallels he draws between the two oppressed groups are striking and should silence those critics who find no similarities between the two. Limbale quotes Yashwant Manohar, a Dalit writer who considers revolt as the most important element in literature. He then compares Yashwant's views with those of Gwendolyn Brooks, a Black American writer, who discovered seeds of creation in the centre of violent changes.[29]

According to Limbale the comparison between Dalit and Black situations is to the advantage of Dalits. The subversive nature of their literature is the outcome of the reversal of roles in which oppressors are at the receiving end. The subversion is taken not only to the level of canons of creation but also to the level of criticism. But if it is taken too far, the danger is that the elemental response to their situation might lead to the creation of a 'universe of alienation,' separating them from common sympathy and common concern.

Dalits, like Blacks, are grappling with the question of Dalit consciousness. At the seminar referred to above, most Dalit writers believed that Dalit consciousness cannot be represented by non-Dalits. Limbale was the one who did not go along with them and held that this isolationism cannot work. It is true that the intensity of their personal experience cannot be felt by non-Dalits and non-Blacks, but it can be imaginatively comprehended. There are clear two groups among Dalits: one supporting exclusivism and the other opposing it. In America this issue was raised in the sixties and has not been settled yet. A sizeable number of Dalit and Black writers hold that non-Dalits and non-Blacks can represent their consciousness provided they write in a sense of truth and beauty. In the past Black characters in mainstream American literature appeared as caricatures or as stereotypes. Similarly in India Dalit characters in non-Dalit literature were always on the periphery and never central to the theme. But some white writers exposed not only the inadequacy of white America to see the reality of Black man's life but also the humanity of Black characters. In this two prominent American writers – Mark Twain and William Faulkner – stand out. Faulkner shows in *Light in August* how a false idea planted in the minds of people – Joe Christmas was said to have Black blood in him although there was no evidence to prove it – can play havoc with the lives of Black people. The whites suffer from lack of perception and the Blacks are trapped into a situation not of their making.[30] In Mark Twain's *Huckleberry Finn* the conflict between the values of a racial society and human values is placed in the mind of the main character Huckleberry Finn. A Black character, Jim, who is the cause of growth in Huck's character, is credited with human qualities and his concern for his family puts Huck to shame.[31]

In Hindi literature Prem Chand was the first to represent Dalit consciousness much before Dalits started writing their own literature. In Prem Chand's famous story *Sadgati* the Harijan is made to work hard at the house of a Brahmin in exchange of suggesting an auspicious date for the marriage of his daughter. The Brahmin is quick to exploit the situation. He asks him to clean the barn, then after taking lunch he asks him to cut a big log into pieces with the help of a small axe and goes for an afternoon nap. The description given of the Brahmin by Prem Chand makes him vulgar and inhuman. The Harijan has not had food since morning. He cannot say no to the Brahmin. But the poor man finds the task beyond his capacity and with exhaustion and hunger drops down dead.[32] I found a comparable situation in Shanker Rao Kharat's autobiography, *Taral Antaral*. Kharat's father Anna (Ramu) gets a letter from somewhere. Since he doesn't know how to read and write, nor does any of his neighbours, he decides to go to the Brahmin teacher to know the contents of the letter. The child who accompanies him has the first experience of a Brahmin household. He unknowingly steps on to the neatly cleaned courtyard and is scolded by the wife of the teacher. Like the Brahmin in Prem Chand's story, she is quick to exploit the predicament of Ramu. Before Ramu could ask the Brahmin to read out the content of the letter, she asks him to cut the big log into small pieces for the rainy season. The Brahmin is more diplomatic and says that Ramu will never say no to such work, although he does not want to burden him with more work. Ramu says to himself that he cannot get out of the trap. So he goes to work with the axe. Ramu insists on the Brahmin to read the letter. But he finds an excuse that he will do it after taking his bath. At first Ramu is discouraged by the stack of logs of wood. The Brahmin on one excuse or another postpones reading the letter until his work is done. After the assigned work is done, he goes back to the Brahmin and requests him to read the letter for him. The Brahmin is happy at Ramu's work and then reads out the letter but not before he extracts a promise from him that next time when he comes that side he will do the work for him again. Then he tells him that his sister has passed away, and without uttering another word he throws the letter at him. On reaching home Ramu's wife reacts sharply to the exploitation of her husband by the Brahmin. She curses the teacher as she cannot tolerate such behaviour in others.[33] The only difference I found between the two situations is that Kharat's story has been narrated from a Mahar's point of view and brings out the anguish and pain that is conveyed through him. In Prem Chand's story, the inhumanity of the Brahmin is brought out admirably. After the Harijan dies, the Brahmin drags him to the river and dumps him there. I find the two situations tremendously moving. Prem Chand's portrayal of the Brahmin and the Harijan cannot be called inauthentic. Prem Chand used the log of wood as a symbol for the insensitivity of the system and the Dalit cannot make a dent in it. At best the two situations are complementary.

As Limbale also writes, in Marathi Dalit literature exclusivism that one finds in Black American and in feminists was never encouraged. In their introduction to Dalit stories, the editors Surya Kumar Ransubhey and Kamlakar Gangavane do not go along with those Dalit writers and critics who hold that Dalit literature can be written only by those who belong to the Dalit caste because they alone can convey their sensitivity, revolt, struggle and the process of change. Marxists and some liberal critics accept that Dalit consciousness cannot be the exclusive preserve of Dalits alone. But the followers of Ambedkar reject the liberal definition and hold that Dalit consciousness can be expressed only by those who have experienced the cruelty of the *chaturvarna.* Accordingly, *savarna* understanding of Dalit consciousness will either be second hand or imaginative. Besides, their tone cannot be subversive. At some point their sympathy and pity will be betrayed. If one accepts this definition of Dalit consciousness, a number of literary problems arise.

According to Ransumbhe and Gangavane, Dalit literature does not want to establish a separate tradition of short stories. In fact they see them as part of Marathi literature. They give a wider definition of Dalit consciousness and do not create categories. The criteria for representing Dalit consciousness are : emotions and feelings which are presented in all their intensity. It is immaterial who represents it.[34]

Throughout the world, literature is written on the assumption that any experience in any part of the world, once it is taken to a human level, can be understood by others. Some Dalits and Blacks deny the non-Dalits and non-Blacks the right to understand their experience because they cannot transcend their race or caste character. Edward Said takes up the question of essentialism and exclusivism and considers it in the larger context of history. "Let us begin by accepting the notion that although there is an irreducible subjective core to human experience, this experience is also historical and secular, it is accessible to analysis and interpretation and – centrally important – it is not exhausted by totalizing theories, not marked and limited by doctrinal or national lines, not confined once and all to analytic constraints. If one believes with Gramsci that an intellectual vocation is socially possible as well as desirable, then it is an inadmissible contradiction at the same time to build analyses of historical experience around exclusions, exclusions that stipulate for instance, that only women can understand feminine experience or Jews can understand Jewish suffering, only formerly colonial subjects can understand colonial experience....

"The difficulty with theories of essentialism and exclusiveness or with barriers and sides is that they give rise to polarization that absolve and forgive ignorance and demagogy more than they enable knowledge. Even the most cursory look at the recent fortunes of theories about race and the modern state, modern nationalism itself verifies this sad truth. If you know in advance that the African or Iranian or Chinese or Jewish or German experience is fundamentally integral, coherent separate and therefore comprehensible only to Africans, Chinese, Jews and Germans, you first of all posit as essential which I believe is both historically created and the result of interpretation, namely the existence of Africanness, Jewishness, or Germanness, or for that matter orientalism or occidentalism. And second, you are likely as a consequence to defend the essence or experience itself rather than promote full knowledge of it and its entanglements and dependences on other knowledge. As a result you will demote the different experience of others to a lesser status."[35]

Thus the concepts of essentialism and exclusivism ought to be examined in some depth and with circumspection. There is a whole lot of experience that lies in the intervening space between the two races or between castes. The uniqueness of experience should not be used for creating barriers but for better understanding of it. How interconnected the experiences are can be seen in what happened to Europe during the Second World War. The entire Europe went through a traumatic experience when millions of Jews were exterminated. This changed the imaginative perception of not only Jews who were the victims but also those who were not part of the Jewish race. It forced them to raise fundamental questions about human situation and human existence. In fact, the entire continent was shaken out of its complacent beliefs that human society is steadily making progress towards an ideal world and that human beings are moving towards perfection. The writers of all shades began to question the entire movement of western civilization. And some of the finest literary creations came from non-Jews. Reality became incomprehensible and unmanageable and yet the writers had an obligation to communicate this experience. There was the loss of power of the imagination to correct things and provide a moral order. In fact, the correction to this negation of existence was provided by Blacks, feminists, and I would add, Dalits.

They seemed to rehabilitate thought and a space where moral imagination could operate; and a world which was neither racist nor casteist. Dalits and African Americans have the responsibility of keeping the genuine historical memory alive and also of humanizing the oppressive system. The challenge is to go beyond these labels lest they should end up by imitating their masters. James Baldwin writes in the *Notes of a Native Son*: "The fight begins in the heart and it now had been laid to my charge to keep my heart free of hatred and despair. Distrust coupled with anger creates mental blocks, particularly in writers. I know that bitterness was folly. It was necessary to hold on to the things that matter.... The new life mattered: Blackness and Whiteness did not matter to believe that they did not acquiesce in one's destruction. Hatred which could destroy so much never failed to destroy the man who hated and this was an immutable fact."[36] But in order to affirm the things that matter, it is necessary that a meaningful dialogue is established which will not be based on concealment and subterfuge. The objective ought to be to broaden access to the critical discourse and not to take it into narrow separate grooves. It is, therefore, necessary not to repudiate the 'other' but to create, what Henry Louis Gates Jr. calls, 'critical trust' which should not only be respected but also developed. In the absence of this broadening of discourse, the sickness of mind might overpower the writer without proper intimation. As Ellison once said this is to be controlled with special care. Literature even when most pessimistic and bitter arises out of an impulse to celebrate human life.

In Marathi Dalit discourse the issues of 'anger' and 'consciousness' have been taken to a level of sophistication, but not so in Hindi Literature. In fact, in the Hindi Dalit Literature, the issues are being discussed now. A couple of years back the issue of consciousness was raised in an interview with Namwar Singh, a noted Hindi critic. According to him, much before Dalits became conscious of their predicament, Dalit consciousness was represented by Prem Chand, particularly in his short stories like Kafan, Sadgati, Price of Milk and Thakur's Well. He was unhappy at the rejection of Marxism and progressive literature by

Dalits since the concerns of such literature have been pro-Dalit.[37] This assertion of Namwar Singh was challenged by Om Prakash Valmiki, a Dalit writer in Hindi in a rejoinder to Namwar Singh's interview published in a Hindi Journal, *Hans.*[38] While Valmiki was prepared to accept allies, on his terms, of course, his skepticism prevented him from accepting the fact that there were many non-Dalit writers who had succeeded in declassing themselves. He, however, accepted the importance of Marxist literature. In fact, Marxist literature is complementary and not antagonistic to Dalit literature. In other words, their ways of resolving the contradictions in society and literature might be different but their ideals are thc same, that is the creation of a society free of exploitation and discrimination. Recently, special numbers of two journals – *Dalit Sahitya 2000* and *Kathakram 2000* – devoted to Dalit literature have come out. The contributors are both Dalits and non-Dalits although the number of the latter is not large. The two journals raise the issue of consciousness not only in relation to social and political situation but also to Dalit Literature. Some non-Dalit writers appear to be more committed than the Dalits themselves. Ramnika Gupta, for example, in her article in *Dalit Sahitya 2000* finds fault with the imaginative perception of Dalit reality in Prem Chand's *Kafan.* She finds Prem Chand emotionally and experientially ill-equipped to portray the characters of Gheesu and Madhav. In fact, she charges him with being inauthentic. She relates his inability to portray Dalit characters to his upper-caste upbringing and bias. As against this, Sharad Kumar Limbale dedicates his short stories to two great men: Dr. BabaSaheb Ambedkar who was the fountainhead of Dalit consciousness and Prem Chand who represented Dalit consciousness in his stories.[39]

In his editorial, Mudrarakshas, the editor for the special number of *Kathakram* seems to anticipate that non-Dalits would like to write on all subjects which are not even distantly related to their felt experiences. I think it is taking the issue too far. It is one thing to say that non-Dalits cannot be trusted with Dalit consciousness; it is another thing to keep them out of that exclusive club by raising unrealistic issues. No non-Dalit writer – or any writer for that matter –

can claim to have the last word on Dalit and women. This, to my mind, is creating blocks which Marathi Dalit writers don't create.

It was natural for African American and Dalit writers to move from the distinctiveness of their experience to the evaluation of experience, to its aesthetic properties. It is no longer confined to purely subjective aspects but becomes part of the social and historical processes. "It is intended to express a human dimension which the dominant version of society appears to exclude."[40] Literature is not to be studied for its own sake, for graces, for perception of beauty. Here, as in the other two issues – anger and protest and consciousness – the African Americans have taken the lead. Dalit writers in Maharashtra are grappling with the issue of an alternative aesthetics now. The question of aesthetics is directly related to cultural nationalism questioning the racist and casteist perception of reality. It is related to the question of change. The growth of Black aesthetics is linked with the new forms of writing that emerged in America during the Black Arts Movement, an extension of the Black Power Movement. This literature was based on the assumption that African American people, however dispersed in America, constituted a nation within a nation. Stokely Carmichael made it more explicit when he wrote that what they were fighting was their colonial status that was inflicted on them; and in order to free themselves of cultural domination, they must assert and preserve their cultural integrity. Thus politics and aesthetics, Black Power and Black Art went hand in hand. The New Movement became the voice of the spirit of the community. *Black Fire: An Anthology of Afro-American Writings* edited by Le Roi Jones and Larry Neal (1968) became a turning point in the history of African American Literature. It rejected the elite Western form as irrelevant to the mass of Black folks. This mood was expressed in a poem by Le Roi Jones.

We want poems that 'kills'
Assassin poems, Poems that shoot Guns.
Poems that wrestle cops into alleys
And take their weapons leaving them dead
With tongues pulled out.[41]

It is evident that literature is being written to perform a specific function in which moral, aesthetic and political cannot be separated. Even the concepts of beauty and form are being modified. The theoretical framework to Black Aesthetics was provided by Addison Gayle Jr. who edited an anthology of 33 articles written by prominent African American writers including W.E.B. DuBois, Langston Hughes and Richard Wright. He also wrote an introduction and conclusion to it. "For here we stand acknowledging those truths we would not admit at the beginning of the 20th Century: that the problem of the color line is insoluble, that the idea of an equalitarian America belongs to trash baskets of history and that the concept of an American melting pot is one to which sane men no longer adhere. In light of such realities the literature of assimilation belongs to the period of dinosaur and the mastadon."[42] It is a continuation of the concept of Black Consciousness. In fact it was part of a larger project which had deep roots in African American tradition and aimed at de-Americanizing Black Consciousness through political and artistic efforts. The new sensibility could develop after the ground had been prepared for it, which meant that the world must be free for all men. In a later book, *The Way of The New World,* Addison Gayle makes his definition of Black Aesthetic more explicit. "In more concrete terms, before beauty can be seen, felt, heard, and appreciated by a majority of the earth's people, a new world must be brought into being; the earth must be made habitable and free for all men. This is the core of the Black Aesthetic ideology and forms the major criterion for the evaluation of art. How much better has the work of art made the life of a single human being on his planet, and how functional has been the work of art in moving us toward that movement when an *ars poetica* is possible for all."[43]

The problem that had been bothering African American critics was the relationship between their culture and the mainstream culture. There were clearly two groups among African Americans: one group wanted to jettison all cultural constructs that belonged to the mainstream culture; the other group wanted to widen the scope of their aesthetics and rejected intolerance. Even among the representatives of the first, writers had started revising their views. Le Roi Jones who was the most vociferous among the Black aestheticians revised his opinion in favour of Marxism in his long essay 'Afro-American Literature and Class Struggle.' The Black situation was related to the capitalist structure and literature of 'garbage' represented by Hollywood would continue to flourish as long as the present structure continued to rule. He wrote, "the material base of racism, which allows it to exist as other than a 'bad idea', is monopoly capitalism. Its material base before the Civil War was the slave system and developing capitalism. The destruction of monopoly capitalism will allow the conditions to exist in which we begin to destroy racism and chauvinism, but no such conditions can ever exist under capitalism."[44] There were other prominent African American writers like Melvin Tolson, J. Saunders Redding, Robert Hayden, Nathan A. Scott Jr. who criticized the Black aestheticians for partisanship and philosophical incoherence. They in fact wanted Black writers to emulate the highest standards of European literature. There were others who examined the intervening ground more carefully by raising such questions as: what are the points of contact with white culture? Where does Black originality begin? Houston A. Baker and Henry Louis Gates Jr. take the discourse of Black aesthetics beyond the polemical socio-political criticism of Black aestheticians. In his book *Blues Ideology and Afro-American Literature* Baker argues that the blues comprised a mediational sight where familiar antinomies are resolved in the office of adequate cultural understanding.[45] What Baker is trying to do is to resolve the opposition between the truths of what he calls Afro-American expressive culture and its modes of representation and for this blues becomes a central metaphor. He, therefore, concentrates on the linguistic constructs of Black literature which are rooted in their culture. "The blues are 'encoded' with messages of Afro-

American Culture: the sadness, the happiness, how to survive. For those Blacks and Whites who understand the code, messages of survival – and sometimes success – are encoded covertly because it is unsafe for either Black survival or financial success for the narratives to be frank and honest."[46]

Similarly, Henry Louis Gates Jr. in *The Signifying Monkey* points out that the most distinctive feature of Afro-American Literature is its figurality. In fact, Afro-American Literature has been figurative right from the beginning. It enables Black people to survive in oppressive Western cultures. This meant that they used languagc to say one thing to mean something different. This kind of figurative use of language was part of the psyche of the Black child, to enable him to decipher complex codes. Sandra Adell questions the premise of both these Black critics and finds that the methods employed both by Baker and Gates make the very notion of such authenticity suspect. It appears that the two critics are trying to reconcile the two traditions at a sophisticated level. In other words, it is a different kind of integration in the name of broadening their access to critical discourse. Henry Gates does argue that the essentialism of Western European culture cannot be taken for granted. He finds untenable the notion that the cultures of the West are the only ones worth studying and learning.[47] But at the same time he asserts that the boundaries between Black and white cultures in America have always been fluid and porous. To pretend otherwise really perpetuates a racist fiction about American culture.[48] The greatest contribution that Black aesthetics makes is its preservation of genuine historical memory, and African Americans are not prepared to subsume it in the mainstream history which thrives on negation of history and which is the basis of their incomprehensibility. What Baker, Gates and Toni Morrison, demand is integration not on white man's terms but on their terms in which their voices get as much prominence as those of the white. In the world of literature, as Toni Morrison has shown in *Playing in the*

Dark, white imagination can't be separated from Black experience. Fisher Fishkin in her book *Was Huck Black?* has shown that the voices of white boys are quite often nourished by Black voices and they can't be separated without causing damage to the literary world. The syntax that Huck Finn, a character in *Huckleberry Finn*, uses was lifted from his Black playmates. It is evident that Black writers and critics are speaking from a position of power and authority and are asserting their contribution to white society and culture.

The effort of canonical white criticism was first to categorize African - American criticism and then try to absorb it into the main literary tradition without acknowledging the fact that their contribution enlarges the possibilities of experience and interpretation which white critics can't do. Houston A. Baker, Addison Gayle and Henry Louis Gates Jr. counter these two approaches to their literature and critical activity. Gates, for example, writes that Black literature, and its criticism "have been put to uses that were not primarily aesthetic, but they have formed part of a larger discourse on the nature of Black, and his or her role in the order of things. The integral relation between theory and a literary text, therefore, which is very often in other traditions has been a sustaining relation, in our tradition has been an extraordinarily problematical one."[49]

Thus African American critics assert that Black aesthetics must make political and artistic effort to de-Americanize Black consciousness and literature. It must try to remake the world after their goals and desire. For example, for most African American writers suffering is real and universal and the human element that is distilled out of suffering is their way of converting it into literature. Thus suffering for them is not an abstract or metaphysical reality; it is palpable and gnawing. This way of looking at suffering relates them to people similarly placed.

Here the conscious role of not only interpreting but also alleviating suffering becomes important. African American critics see literature and literary theory in a complex relation, this is because literature is not just taken as 'polite' learning or representative of grace, but as a place where contrasting constructs are contested. The critical discourse is not a parallel discourse, but a continuation of the textual discourse.

In the 80s African American critics moved from critical independence to analytic rigour. It did not mean, however, that they were reaffirming the goals of assimilation, but they were taking the discourse to a level where the existing discourse is modified. Even the concept of tragedy is redefined like Soyenka did, and for which ground was prepared by Alexander Crummell towards the end of the 19th Century. Like earlier critics of the Black Arts movement the new generation continues to write in standard English prose and to respect the exigencies of mainstream scholarship. Yet significant differences persisted in the sub-text, in the rhythm and the echoes that relate it to the oral tradition which was as rich in knowledge as the written one. Even the post structuralist African American critics refused to divorce the social from the literary text and thus refusing to submerge the vernacular in the standard tradition. The post-structuralist strategies provided Black literary critics of the 80s with a sophisticated means of dealing with the legacies of deportation and slavery.

Thus Black aesthetics incorporates three points: the painful past and its vestiges in the present; the expressive possibilities of their art, leading to a new interpretation of reality; and the point at which their experience intersects with the white world. Toni Morrison incorporates all these points in her fiction and interprets them in her critical writings.

"It should be beautiful and powerful, but it should also work. It should have something in it that enlightens; something in it that opens the door and points the way. Something in it that suggests what the conflicts are, what the problems are. But it need not solve these problems because it is not a case study, it is not a recipe. There are things that I try to incorporate into my fiction that are directly and deliberately related to what I regard as the major characteristics of Black Art, wherever it is. One of which is the ability to be both print and oral literature: to combine these two aspects so that the stories can be read in silence, of course, but one should be able to hear them as well. It should try deliberately to make you stand up and make you feel something profoundly in the same way that a Black preacher requires his congregation to speak, to join him in the sermon, to behave in a certain way, to stand up and to weep and to cry and to accede or to change and to modify to expand on the sermon that is being delivered. In the same way that a musician's music is enhanced when there is a response from the audience. Now in a book, which closes after act it is of some importance to me to try to make that connection – to try to make that happen also. And having at my disposal only the letters of the alphabet and some punctuation, I have to provide the places and spaces so that the reader can participate. Because it is the affective and participatory relationship between the artist or the speaker and the audience that is of primary importance, as it is in these art forms that I have described."[50]

Almost all elements that one should look for in fiction by an African American writer are there. The writer evokes not merely emotional response but also intellectual response, and it is done in the manner of a preacher or a musician. There is another element that Morrison finds in African American writings, that is the presence of 'ancestors' who are not parents but who are timeless people representing a certain kind of wisdom. Most writers have to come to terms with such ancestors. Baldwin was uncomfortable with this presence. In Ralph Ellison's novel *Invisible Man*, such an ancestor appears in the form of grandfather who advises *Invisible Man* how to deal with the white people. In *Song of Soloman* by Morrison, Pilate is the ancestor. The characters are judged according to their distance from the ancestor. In fact, the absence of an ancestor in their works is not only threatening but also frightening. One doesn't find such a unifying presence in the mainstream fiction where the writer exists as an individual in confrontation with society. But African American writer sees the writer as part of larger community and is both a spokesman and a witness of their collective destiny. "I am not interested", she writes in the same essay, "in indulging myself in some private, closed exercise of my imagination that fulfils the obligation of my personal dreams – which is to say yes, the work must be political. It must have that as its thrust. That is a pejorative term in critical circles now: if a work of art has any political influence in it, somehow it is tainted. My feeling is just the opposite: if it has none, it is tainted."[51]

The Black aesthetics is part of a larger movement in which the social and political structures are also reorganized. Until that happens the alternative aesthetics will not achieve its purpose. It will be bogged down in the same dichotomies with which it began in the early 20th Century. Sandra Adell raises the seminal question in the conclusion of her book. Have the African American writers succeeded in "loosening the double bind that threatens to impede that progress or have we, in our concern elaborating a more coherent theory of Black writing, only succeeded in providing a basis for more theoretical incoherency?"[52] The two issues that of questioning the hegemony of the Euro-centric discourse and the fusing of the two traditions could not be easily resolved because they are part and yet apart from the Euro-centric discourse. It is for this reason that "Black literature and Black criticism returns again and again to the problem of double consciousness and attendant problem, identity, in all its aspects. The preoccupation with identity, this desire for the reconciliation of the two 'warring ideals' signified by the hyphenated name, by the African American, by the Negro-African(e), is what marks much of the literature of the African diaspora as thoroughly modern."[53]

In India Dalit writers, particularly in Maharashtra are now dealing with the issue of Dalit aesthetics. Sharad Kumar Limbale has brought out *The Aesthetics of Dalit*

Literature in which, along with theoretical issues, the criteria for evaluating Dalit literature are also discussed. It seeks to include the upward movement of Dalit Literature, its character and objective, its philosophical and ideological basis in the context of Ambedkar and Marx, different approaches to it, both Dalit and non-Dalit and Dalit aesthetics which forms the last chapter of the book. The important aspect of this book is its attempt to broaden the Dalit discourse by comparing it with African American Aesthetics (Limbale prefers to call it Negro Aesthetics).[54]

Some of the issues included in Limbale's book could be found scattered in Marathi Dalit Literature but here they have been put together. Thus the book builds up on the ground that had already been prepared by prominent Dalit writers during and after the Dalit Panther Movement suggesting theoretical issues, their suffering and strategies for giving dimension to their experience and criteria for evaluation. The ground for Dalit Aesthetics was provided by two contending ideologies one represented by the followers of Ambedkar and the other by the followers of Marx. The Ambedkar-Buddhist thought was a potent force even during the black Panther movement. Since Ambedkar was critical of the communists, the movement split into two. On one hand there were leaders like Raja Dhale and Vijai Sonwane whose guiding force was Ambedkar supported by Buddhism; on the other there were writers like Namdeo Dhasal, Baburao Bagul, Daya Pawar, Arjun Dangle and Narayan Survey whose guiding force was Marxism. The Dalit discourse suffered to that extent as the two groups failed to discover a common ground, although there were points of similarity between the two. For example, both were progressive; both kept man at the centre of their struggle; and both worked against exploitation/discrimination based on class/caste formation; and both worked for change leading to a human order. An important book that contributed to the discourse was the *Aesthetics of Non-Brahmin Literature* by Sharad Patil which came out in 1988.[55] He was the first to point out similarities between the New Buddhist and Marxist Aesthetics. The book is in Marathi and has not been translated so far either into Hindi or English. Patil's book establishes two significant points:

1. Dalit discourse cannot be considered independent of politico-ideological dimensions;
2. Dalit writers must develop their own aesthetics in the absence of which they will continue to depend on Non-Dalit aesthetics.

According to Patil India's socio-cultural agonies are in essence caste and class agonies. The holistic vision of India's tragic history and its literary and aesthetic reflection must be grounded upon a Marxian-Phule-Ambedkarite viewpoint. Only this view point can show them the way to liberating the suppressed and the oppressed millions in the country. And this could bring together all the revolutionary and progressive literatures on a cultural programme.

Limbale extends this discourse further. He deals with the question of Dalit Aesthetics at three levels: (1) At the level of non-Dalit Aesthetics and its inability to see the revolutionary character of Dalit literature as also its inability to modify or expand the accepted criteria for evaluating literature; (2) at the level of forming a Dalit Aesthetics which will reflect not only social conditions but also the possibility of change; (3) at the level of reception of their literature and how it affects both Dalit and non-Dalit readers, although it has not been sufficiently developed. In order to establish a point Limbale goes to the extent of saying that non-Dalit aesthetics deals exclusively with pleasure and by implication has nothing to do with real life situation. To dub all non-Dalit aesthetics as reactionary, abstract and spiritualist is to beat a dead horse. It has already been given up and part of it is based on elements that initiate a process of change. Besides, artistic pleasure grows out of a combination of human relations, world view and human values. The sense of liberation that one experiences grows out of this combination. Yaswant Manohar, whom Limbale quotes, at one place writes that great human values and artistic values will combine in Dalit literature of the future.[56] At places it appears that Dalit aestheticians are moving towards a kind of reconciliation between the Dalit and non-Dalit aesthetics. In his book, Limbale lists four criteria for evaluating Dalit Literature. These are:

1. A writer's experience must be authentic;
2. His experience must be generalized;
3. His experience must transcend the situation in which the writer is placed;
4. His experience must appeal to people in all ages.[57]

I don't think most non-Dalit aestheticians would disagree with these criteria. In fact, these criteria could be applied to literature written by non-Dalits. In what way will Dalit critics judge eternal values that are enshrined in canonical literature? Like Sharad Patil, Limbale pleads for an aesthetics that combines both Ambedkarite and Marxist approaches. For that reason he doesn't subscribe to the view that Dalit consciousness and class consciousness belong to two separate categories. The Dalit aesthetics has yet to move into areas that explore the expressive power of language, like Baker and Gates Jr. do, and the framework within which it is to be placed. Some critics have examined the use of Buddhist terminology by Dalit writers committed to Ambedkarite and Buddhist thought, but by itself it doesn't explain the subversive aspect of their use.

In Hindi Dalit Literature the issues are still being formulated. In an article, 'Some Theoretical Aspects of Dalit Sahitya', Dr. Harish Chandra Srivastava discusses the broad framework of Dalit Aesthetics which is oppositional in nature. For this reason academic criteria cannot be applied to this literature.[58]

References

1. Lucian Goldmann, "Dogmatism in Literature" in The Dialectics of Liberation, ed. David Cooper, Penguin Books, 1969, p.128.
2. Carolyn F. Gerald, "The Black Writer and His Role" in African American literary Criticism 1773-2000 ed. Hazel Arnett Ervin, Twayne Publishers 1999 p.113.

3. Le Roi Jones, Home: Social Essays, William Morrow & Co. 1966, p. 639.
4. Toward Black Literature, Massachusetts Review, 1966, p. 639.
5. Langston Hughes, "Mulatto", in Three Negro Plays, Penguin Books 1969, pp. 38, 46, 48.
6. Bandumadhav, "The Poisoned Bread" in Homeless in My Land, ed. Arjun Dangle, Disha Books, 1992, p. 2.
7. *Ibid.*, p. 3.
8. *Ibid.*, p. 7.
9. Richard Wright, Black Boy, Harper & Row, New York 1945, pp. 162-163.
10. The Autobiography of Malcolm X, Penguin Books 1976, p. 118.
11. Om Prakash Valmiki, Juthan, Radha Krishna Prakashan, Delhi, 1997.
12. James Baldwin, Notes of Native Son, Dial Press, 1964, p. 5.
13. *Ibid.*
14. James Baldwin, Tell Me How Long The Train's Been Gone, Dell, New York, 1973, p. 76.
15. Robert Bone, The Negro Novel in America, Yale University Press, New Haven, 1965, p. 229.
16. Notes of a Native Son, p. 17.
17. Irving Howe, "Black Boys and Native Sons" in A World More Attractive, Horizon Press, New York.
18. *Ibid.*, p. 102.
19. R. Ellison, Shadow and Act, New York, Random House, 1964, p. 54.
20. John Hersey, 20th Century Views on Ralph Ellison, Prentice Hall, New Jersey, 1975, pp. 11-12.
21. V.S. Naipaul, India : A Million Mutinies Now, Minerva, 1990, p. 116.
22. Quoted by V.S. Naipaul, India : A Million Mutinies Now, pp. 96-97.
23. Mulk Raj Anand and Eleanor Zelliot (ed) An Anthology of Dalit Literature, Gyan Publishing House, New Delhi, 1992, pp. 68-71.
24. India: A Million Mutinies Now, p. 119.
25. An Anthology of Dalit Literature, p. 51.
26. A Million Mutinies Now, p. 116.
27. Dalit Literature: Man's Great Freedom, Amritadarsha, VI:I, 1973, pp. 56-57.
28. Dharamvir, The Growth of Dalit Literature, paper presented at the IIAS, Shimla, Oct. 1997.

29. Limbale, Dalit and American Negro Literature, paper presented at the IIAS, Shimla, Oct. 1997.
30. William Faulkner, Light in August, Penguin Modern Classics, 1973.
31. Mark Twain, The Adventures of Huckleberry Finn, Penguin, 1954.
32. Prem Chand, "Sadgati" in Katha Prasun, Panchsheel Prakashan, Jaipur, 2000.
33. Shanker Rao Kharat, Taral Antaral, National Publishing House, New Delhi, 1987, pp. 3-8.
34. Suryanarayan Ranshubhe and Kamlakar Gangavane, (eds) Dalit Stories, Panchsheel Prakashan, Jaipur, 1981 Introduction, p. 18.
35. Edward Said, Culture and Imperialism. Alfred A. Knoff, 1993, pp. 31-32.
36. James Baldwin, Notes of a Native Son, p. 13.
37. Naya Path (Hindi) June 1998.
38. Hans (Hindi) June 1998.
39. Dalit Sahitya 2000 edited Jai Prakash Kardam, Delhi
40. Sharad Kumar Limbale, Devta Admi, Pratibha Prakashan, New Delhi, 1994, p. 5.
41. Quoted by Vincent B. Leitch, American Literary Criticism from the 30s to the 80s, Columbia University Press, 1988, p. 339.
42. Addison Gayle Jr., The Black Aesthetic, Double Day, New York, 1971, p. 418.
43. Addison Gayle Jr., The Way of the New World : The Black Novel in America, New York, Double Day, 1976, p. 379.
44. Black American Literature Forum, ed. Joe Weixlmann, 14 : 1 (1980), p. 10.
45. Houston A. Baker, Blues, Ideology and Afro-American Literature, Chicago, 1984, p. 6.
46. Reginald Martin, The New Black Aesthetic Critics and Their Exclusion in American Mainstream Criticism in College English, Vol. 50, No.4, April 88, p. 378.
47. Larry W. Ward, Interview with Henry Louis Gates Jr., New Literary History, Vol. 22, Autumn, 1991, p. 932.
48. *Ibid.*, p. 933.
49. H. Gates Jr. "Authority (White) Power and The Black Critic" in the Future of Literary Theory ed. Ralph Cohen, New York, 1989, p. 331.
50. Toni Morrison, "Rootedness" in African American Literary Criticism, 1773-2000, Twayne Publishers, New York, 1999, p. 200.
51. *Ibid.*, p. 202.

52. Sandra Adell, Double Consciousness and Double Bind, University of Illinois Press, 1994, p. 140.
53. *Ibid*, p. 139.
54. S.K. Limbale, The Aesthetics of Dalit Literature (translated into Hindi by Ramnika Gupta), Vani Prakashan, Delhi, 2000.
55. Sharad Patil, The Aesthetics of Non-Brahmin Literature, 1988, Sugava Publishers, Pune (translated for me by Dr. Sharad Rajimwale).
56. Limbale, p. 74.
57. *Ibid.*, p. 117.
58. Kathakram, Dalit Special Number, Nov. 2000, ed. Mudra Rakshas, Lucknow, pp. 88-89.

4
The World Within and Without the Veil

The Negro writer who seeks to function within his race as a powerful agent has a serious responsibility in order to do justice to his subject matter in order to depict Negro life in all its manifold and interrelated relationships, a deep, informed and complex consciousness is necessary, a consciousness which draws for its strength upon the fluid love of a great people and moulds this love with the concepts that move and direct the forces of history today.... by his ability to fuse and articulate the experience of man because his writing possesses the potential cunning to steal into the utmost recesses of the human heart.

R. Wright quoted in
The Crisis of Negro Intellectual,
Harold Cruse, William Morrow &
Co. New York, 1964

Real freedom will only have arrived when critics from ethnic minorities feel able to attack their own culture as well as celebrate them, with all the privileges currently monopolized by those, who often have little enough to lose from doing so.

Terry Eagleton
Theory in the Space between
Culture and Capitalism
T.L.S. July 15, 1994

In Dusk of Dawn, DuBois tries to capture the mechanism of racism through an elaborate imagery. "It is difficult to let others see the full psychological meaning of caste segregation. It is as though one looking out from a dark cave in a side of an impending mountain, sees the world passing and speaks to it; speaks courteously and persuasively, showing them how these entombed souls are hindered in their natural movement, expression and development, and how their loosening from prison would be a matter not simply of courtesy, sympathy and help to them, but aid to all the world. One talks on evenly and logically in this way, but notices that the passing throng does not even turn its head, or if it does, glances curiously and walks on. It gradually penetrates the minds of the prisoners that the people passing do not hear, but some thick sheet of invisible but horribly tangible plate glass is between them and the world. They get excited; they talk louder; they gesticulate. Some of the passing world stop in curiosity; these gesticulations seem so pointless; they laugh and pass on. They still either do not hear at all, or hear but dimly and even what they hear, they do not understand. Then the people within may become hysterical. They may scream and hurl themselves against the barriers, hardly realizing in their bewilderment that they are screaming in a vacuum unheard and that their antics may actually seem funny to those outside looking in. they may even, here and there, break through in blood and disfigurement, and find themselves faced by a horrified, implacable and quite overwhelming mob of people frightened for their own very existence."[1]

The passage beautifully brings out the intense and ineffectual desire of the segregated people to communicate with the outside world and, at the same time, their inability to do so because of the insensitivity of those who have created an invisible wall between them and the world. Their early literary creation – in fact it was a cry of their soul – was to draw the attention of the world to their predicament and how they felt about it. It was in the nature of supplication – white/*savarna* men listen. But the urge to communicate and to make sense of the world could not be contained. And some of them at least break through the invisible wall to force them to see their reality but find that the outside mob looks on with fear. It is obvious that the diabolical contrivance in the form of race and caste segregation caused psychological imprisonment. The masters through carefully designed means had destroyed their self-determination and along with it their creative power. It is a miracle how they fought to save the human grain. It took them quite some time to come out of that cloistered place and to breathe in free air and see the world through their own eyes.

Since the reality of the segregated people was not part of the imaginative world of the masters, it was never reflected in their literature. The universality in their literature was separated from the large part of the experience of the segregated people and was projected as given. But when the latter established contact with the particularities of their existence, they discovered that they had a force of their own. Besides, the universality that grew out of them exposed the contradiction of which particularities were made. That is why the newness of their experience and the freshness of their approach to it shock the 'cultivated minds' fed on the stale diet. "Their literature thus becomes the organized search for the truth of the oppressed."[2]

It is for this reason that freedom is a powerful concept for them – freedom from physical and psychological bondage as also freedom to choose a kind of world that they would like to live in. In America this quest for freedom began with slave narratives which became a powerful form of self expression for them. These were the first stirrings of their soul and have undergone innumerable mutations in other forms. Freedom is still an important component of their imaginative perception of reality.

In Dalit Literature, ever since Chokhamela raised his voice against social inequality, freedom has been the central motif, although it was sought to be resolved in religious equality. It became a central concern, in its secular form, in the 20th Century. The quest for freedom, like in America, was pitted against the formidable and intricate mechanism of caste hierarchy. Yashwant Manohar's powerful poem 'I'm Ready for Revolt' brings out the irresistible desire for freedom.

> I am burning with a feeling of revolt and I call out to you.
> I will write the poem of revolt on your sword
> Today I have become a storm – come with me!
> I reach out to you – give me your hand!
> I have become the sun, my friend – sing with me!
> I have become the fire, today I am afire with fire –
> Give voice to the volcano within you!
> I'm out of my senses, out of control
> Make me a limitless sky with words
> I will hurl myself into the battle
> If I should win, shout out my victory!
> If I should break, bury me deep!
> If I come to your door confused, try to understand me!
> If I return bloodied, hold me to your breast!
> If I die out there, take my body in your arms!
> Some one make me believe I am and will be yours!
> Shed a few tears and remember me forever![3]

There is a ceaseless yearning for freedom and the fear that it might not be achieved during his lifetime. One notices the same anguish in Ambedkar when he responded to Gandhiji's claim that Dalits were as much part of the country's heritage as anybody else. He said: "Gandhiji, I have no homeland." The gravity of this statement could not have been lost on Gandhiji.

Arjun Dangle's poem 'Revolution' similarly, is an indictment of the ambivalent and duplicitous enterprise to restore human dignity to Dalits. The Untouchables had some semblance of peace when they followed the caste code.

> "When clay pots hung from our necks, brooms tied to our rumps."

The elite were not disturbed as long as they fought

with animals –for their share of the dead cattle.
"They used to love us then."

In the changed context, the animals, crows, jackals, dogs, vultures, kites – are no longer their enemies. The irony is that the elite shout 'victory to Revolution' but those who actually work for it are burned.[4]

The simmering discontent begins to surface in their literature. Along with it there are rumblings that they are not willing to accept the situation for long. One can see this restiveness in a poem by Langston Hughes.

We run
We run
We can not stand these shadows
Give us the sun.
We were not made
For shade
For heavy shade
And narrow space of stifling air
That those white things have made.[5]

One can find the same pattern of discontent and restiveness in Dalit literature. Take the poem, 'The City' by Daya Pawar. In this he tries to visualise a 20th Century city from the perspective of the future.

The city lies buried and in excavation some interesting
things are brought to light.
One day some one dug up a twentieth-century city.
It's lying there now like a wade of paper
Crumpled by a gigantic fist
In it are traces of the machine age
Wheels, pieces of metal
Smokestacks like old cigarette butts.
If it weren't for these
The place would be another Mohanjodaro.
Pick a spot, any spot, and dig a foot down
You'll find stones, rocks, images covered with ochre,
Some with elephant trunks sticking out of their faces,
Some with tails hanging from their behinds.
Good! The museums will be filled this year.

Why don't we stuff these holy puppets for future generations?
Here is an interesting inscription:
'This water tap is open to all castes and religions.'
What could it have meant?
That this society was divided?
That some were high while others were low?
Well, all right, then this city deserved burying -
Why did they call it the machine age?
Seems like the stone age in the twentieth-century."[6]

The struggle to separate their reality from the controlled reality in which they were made to live can be seen in both these poems. Whereas Langston Hughes wants to get out of the narrow space of stifling air, Daya Pawar wants to bury the society based on hierarchy. While questioning the contradictions in their situation, they also question the over-determined use of 'word' which contains those contradictions because of the association they carry. "Not long ago" Sartre wrote in Introduction to *The Wretched of the Earth*", the earth was numbered two thousand million inhabitants: five hundred million men, and one thousand five hundred million natives. The former had the Word; the other had the use of it. Between the two there were hired kinglets, overlord and a bourgeoisie, sham from beginning to end, which served as go-between."[7]

The simple connection between the Word and its use was disturbed and the Word was mediated by theories, mythologies and ideologies. But there comes a moment in the life of the natives, Dalits and African Americans, when they question not only the use of the Word but also the Word itself, which means its composition. It carries an entire ideology that conceals their real existence. The process of retrieving the Word involves the questioning of the entire experience and the legitimacy provided to it. This is the process of reconstruction of the Word and its use. [8]

Once they lift the veil behind which they were condemned to live, they find that the entire world is there for them to acquire. In *American Hunger*, Richard Wright conveys this through an image of devocalized dogs who were the object of experiments for the benefit of the white patients. "Each Saturday morning I assisted a young Jewish doctor in slitting the vocal chords of a fresh batch of dogs from the city pound. The object was to devocalize the dogs so that their howls would not disturb the patients in the other parts of the hospital. I held each dog as the doctor injected nembutal into its veins to make it unconscious; then I held the dog's jaws open as the doctor inserted the scalpel and severed the vocal chords. Later when the dogs came to, they would lift their heads to the ceiling and gape in a soundless wail. The sight became lodged in my imagination as a symbol of silent suffering."[9]

Wright calls the four Negroes who were huddled together in the underworld corridors of the hospital as close kins of the animals. They were "separated by a vast psychological distance from the significant processes of the rest of the hospital – just as America had kept us locked in the dark underworld of American life for three hundred years – and we had made our own code of ethics, values, loyalty."[10]

The process creating psychological distance has to be reversed and the programming of their mind must be stopped. This is exposed in a poem titled Speech by Arun Kamle.

Bone-chewing granpus
at burning ghat
permanent resident
of my heart
with weight of tradition
behind his back
Yells, 'Sadding bastard, I
tell you',
stutter 'with our tongue!'
Picking through the *Vedas*
buttering his queue
Brahmin teacher at school
Bellows, 'speak my pure tongue,

whoreson!'
Now you tell me which speech
am I to tongue?[11]

Clearly there are two choices put before him: either he suppresses his voice or he accepts the sanctioned voice which is full of contradictions and ambivalence. Apparently, his voice cannot be suppressed for long for it is part of his quest for a deeper buried self.

The same process can be observed in African American literature. "Inside Black folks' soul there is this tension, because the voices from the larger society are still heard. And voices are there from behind the veil."[12] Can the voices from the larger society be completely eliminated? Yet they cannot be a substitute for their voice. Take the following poem, 'Theme For English B', by Langston Hughes:

The instructor said,
Go home and write
a page tonight
And let that page come out of you-
Then it will be true.
I wonder if it is that simple?
I am twenty two, colored, born in Wingsten Salem,
I went to school there, then Durham then here
to this college on the hill among Harlem.
I'm the only Colored student in my class.
The steps from the hill lead down into Harlem,
Through a park, then I cross St. Nicolas
Eighth Avenue, Seventh, and I come to Y
The Harlem branch Y, where I take the elevator
Upto my room, sit down and write this page.
It is not easy to know what is true for you or me.
At twenty two, my age. But guess I'm what
I feel and see and hear, Harlem, I hear you:
hear you, hear me – we too – you, me, talk on this page
(I hear New York, too) Me – who?
Well, I like to eat, sleep, drink and be in love
I like to work, read, learn and understand life
I like a pipe for a Christmas present,

Or records – Bessie, Bop or Back.
I guess being colored doesn't make me not like
the same things other folks like who are other races.
So will my page be colored that I write?
Being me, it will not be white
But it will be a part of you, instructor
You are white –
You are a part of us, as I am a part of you.
That's American.
Sometimes, perhaps you don't want to be a part of us.
Nor do I often want to be a part of you
But we are that is true!
As I learn from you,
I guess, you learn from me –
although you're older and white –
and somewhat more free.
This is my page for English B.[13]

Langston Hughes' page is his page, although part of the page is used by the white. The voice of the poem is the voice of those who feel, see and hear Harlem. But this voice moves from his reality to the reality of being American.

African American literature has been fed by oral poetry that the slaves composed while working on the plantation. In its format it was the expression of their pain and anguish leading to some kind of resolution. The blues thus became a form of affirmation in the midst of darkness and thunder. There were two aspects to such compositions. In one they wrestled with themselves; in the other they wrestled with the outside world. Besides, they reflected the rhythm of their lives while preserving their creative urge. They also drew upon the untapped emotional resources in a language that was not always imitative. The white masters were taken in by the duplicity of meaning in such songs. Cannan, for example, in their blues conveyed Biblical meaning to the white but to their people it was a symbol of free states in America. "Thus the blues revealed the tension in which they stood to the white world and the relationship in which they stood to each other. This was the double-edgedness that was an integral part of their existence".[14]

Dalit literature did not have a tradition like that of the blues in African American literature, although some researches on the folk songs and the variation of the epic theme have been made. Zelliott quotes an article by Egnor in which 'crying songs' of the untouchable castes have been described.[15] But there is no significant form that points to 'cultural segregation.' Even the 'crying songs' and their version of the epic do not substantially separate them from the mainstream literature. Ambedkar and others tried to rehabilitate themselves in a tradition by claiming that the writers of epics were in fact untouchables. It is for this reason that rejection of the idea of pollution – from Chokhamela to the present day – has been a dominant theme in their tradition.

The effort to acquire a different voice is the beginning of other problems for Dalit/African American writers. Since they are estranged from the dominant culture and live a garbled form of that culture within them, they have to fight the battle within themselves. And the world within has been fractured beyond limit and the effort to put it together forces them to separate the real from the conditioned part of the self. Here they have to devise ways that are morally, intellectually and aesthetically satisfying. The same fracturing is to be corrected in the outside world. Time and again they are made to realize that the profession of the ideals of equality and fraternity are hollow, in fact they do not exist for them. Richard Wright had a taste of it when he went to attend a meeting of the Communist Party in which the future of the John Reed Club was to be discussed. He hoped that in the Communist Party he would not have to face colour prejudice. But he was proved wrong by the person at the reception who expressed his inability to give him accommodation in the hostel where other members were housed. It was an unusual demand from a Black comrade. He should have behaved. Finally, with the help of a Chicago Club member he could find accommodation for the night at a white member's place. This provoked Wright into saying to himself: "Could a Negro ever live half way like a human being in this goddamn country."[16]

Along with this, they face the problem of finding literary equivalents for this experience. Surprisingly and understandably there are no models for giving shape to this experience available. James Baldwin calls himself a bastard of the West. When he followed the line of his past, he found himself not in Europe but in Africa. For this reason, he could not relate himself to the great models of literature and other forms of art in the manner the Europeans could. His problem was how to create a space for his special attitude in the scheme of things. "The difficulty for me of being a Negro writer was the fact that I was in effect prohibited from examining my own experience too closely by the tremendous demands and the very real danger of my situation."[17] The unreconciled contradictory feelings in him did not let him maintain the distance that is necessary to the creation of literature.

Arjun Dangle's story 'Promotion' exemplifies how the world within doesn't yield to imaginative creation so easily. It is the story of Baghmare who gets promotion under the reserved category. He becomes an A.P. O. in the Railways superseding a large number of non-reservationists. His problems begin from this point: problems in relation to himself and problems in relation to the outside world. His subordinates, who belong to the *savarna* class and are senior in service, do not cooperate with him on technical grounds. Baghmare hesitates to take action against them for fear that his action might not be supported by his seniors and also that he might become unpopular. He is so tangled up that he grants leave, reluctantly though, to an employee to visit the shrine of Shirdi Sai Baba and what is more gives her money for offering on his behalf. He tries to maintain the necessary distance from his subordinates including his caste fellows by travelling first. At home his changed status in society creates other problems. On reaching home he finds an ill-clad woman, with her shabbily dressed children, sitting in the drawing room watching the television. He chides his wife for her 'human action' and asks her to do things befitting the status of a 'Babu', even when his wife tells him that the lady was her aunt who lived in a nearby slum. His artificially created status gets a shock when he learns from his son, who came home with an injured knee, that he was pushed by a potter's wife for daring to drink water from her pot. At the end of the story Baghmare stands divested of his assumed self.[18]

Lorraine Hansberry in her play, 'A Raisin in the Sun', warns the young African American against the pitfalls of the rising mercantile class among the people of their race. Hair straightener and skin lightner have pushed the African American towards the values of the white middle class. Those who move up the social ladder abdicate their responsibility towards their own people. In the play Mama Younger does not let America define her. But her son has been completely taken over by the lure for money.

Mama	How come you talk so much about money?
Walter	Because it's life, Mama.
Mama	Oh! So now it is life. Money is life. Once upon a time freedom used to be life – now it is money. I guess the world really do change.
Walter	No – it was always money, Mama. We just didn't know about it.
Mama	No...something has changed. You something new, boy. In my time we was worried about not being lynched and getting to the North if we could and how to stay alive and still have a pinch of dignity too....... Now here come you and Beneatha – talking about things we ain't never even thought about hardly, me and your daddy. You ain't satisfied or proud of nothing we done. I mean that you had a home; that we kept you out of trouble till you was grown; that you don't have to ride to work

> on the back of nobody's streetcar – you my children – but how different we done become."[19]

Hansberry takes the conflict to a level where the differences in values become explicit. It is not only about material needs and aspirations but about the basic issues that concern all Black families in the ghetto of America. Are African Americans going to be transformed by their acquisitiveness into mindless consumerism like the whites or should they be concerned about human dignity? It doesn't mean, however, that they should not have a "more comfortable material base for their lives; they desperately need an hourly sacrifice for clean homes, decent food, personal and group dignity and the abolition of terroristic violence as their children's heritage."[20]

Hansberry doesn't subscribe to the myth that Blacks have wanted nothing more than to be a poor copy of the white. In fact she is providing a critique of the entire American enterprise in which people remain satisfied only with tinsel. She wants her people to define themselves differently and in the process modify the ideals that the American Society has placed before them. In her plays Hansberry exemplifies the conflict in dramatic terms what Frantz Fanon calls Black Skin and White Masks. Walter towards the end of the play 'A Raisin in the Sun' decides to move in the house in the white neighbourhood. Some critics have seen it as a confirmation of the American Dream through integration. But they miss the simple fact that Walter is asserting his right as a human being. He doesn't "acquiesce to restrictions placed upon him by others, particularly if those restrictions are based solely on race or religion."[21]

Their literature becomes more complex when they deal with the social environment of ideas and customs that has defined their place in the world. It is more complex because they share that environment with the dominant group. The literature of Dalits and African Americans provides a critique of the socio-political system, the complexities of inter-personal relations and the suggestion of a more humane order. The consciousness of their situation carries the consciousness of the larger group. The full range of their experience is expressed in autobiographies as they provide a large canvas for analysing different levels of their adjustment with the larger group. The range of their experience widens when they realise that they have as much stake in the system as those who claim to monopolise it. The question they pose to themselves quite often is: could they lead a full existence in a racialised/casteist society? The basic theme of such autobiographies was freedom, that is how the idea of freedom germinated in them, what devices they invented to move towards freedom, the concept of freedom itself, the limited sense in which freedom was experienced and the ideal of freedom. F. Douglass who quite early in life started questioning the entire social machinery that had kept him a slave, made speeches on political and social system which are historical documents and show that a Black man can analyse the system as analytically as any white man can, or even better. In one of his speeches he talks of the economic basis of slavery in which he is a property just as a horse is a property. The fruits of his labour are collected by his master.

"He is industrious that another may live in idleness; he eats bolted meal that another may eat the bread of fine flour; he labors in chains at home, under a burning sun and biting lash that another may rise in ease and splendor abroad; he lives in ignorance that another may be educated."[22] Slavery/discrimination would persist as long as it remained a permanent and hereditary condition of a class of human beings in the U.S.A. With slight variation it could apply to the Dalits in India. One can hear the echo of this denunciation in Ambedkar's speeches. Even after they became free, the principles of natural justice and political freedom did not apply in their case. These anomalies were effectively and forcefully brought out by Douglass in a lecture he gave in Rochester, New York entitled, 'What to the Slave is the Fourth of July!' The U.S.A. continued to deny equal manhood to another race. "To drag a man in tatters into the grand illuminated temple of liberty, and call upon him to join you in joyous anthems were inhuman mockery and sacrilegious irony.... To him your celebration is a sham; your boasted liberty, an unholy license; your national greatness, swelling vanity; your sounds of rejoicing are empty and heartless; your denunciations of tyrants, brass-fronted impudence; your shouts of liberty and equality hollow mockery; your prayers and hymns, your sermons and thanksgiving with all your religious parade and solemnity are to him mere bombasts, fraud, deception, impiety and hypocrisy, a thin veil to cover up crime which would disgrace a nation of savages."[23]

Almost all important African American writers and thinkers wrote autobiographies, and although the basic theme remains the same, the variations are provided by the context of historical situation.

Forcing the white to see their reality is one aspect of dealing with their situation. The other aspect deals with their real self within a larger framework of the national self. In Richard Wright the assertion of his self began when he was in school. At the valedictory function he refused to read out the speech written by the Principal. He told him: "I know that I am not educated, Professor. But the people are coming to hear the students and I won't make a speech that you have written."[24] At times he debated within himself whether he should resort to violence against the white and even against his own people. He had developed a hunger for life, for books which kept him alive in a vital way. Through his reading he had come to realize that words could be used to challenge the authority of the white provided one had the courage to use them that way.

Richard Wright also examined the larger issues that concerned the American civilization. He wrote in *American Hunger*: "Culturally the Negro represents a paradox. Though he is an organic part of the nation, he is excluded by the entire type and direction of American culture. Frankly, it is felt to be right to exclude him, and it is felt to be wrong to admit him freely. Therefore, if, within the confines of its present culture, the nation ever seeks to purge itself of its color hate, it will find itself at war with itself, convulsed by a spasm of emotional and moral confusion. If the nation ever finds itself examining its real relation to the Negro, it will find itself doing infinitely more than that; for the anti-Negro attitude of whites represents but a tiny part – though a symbolically significant one – of the moral attitude of the nation. Our too young and too-new America, lusty because it is lonely, aggressive because it is afraid, insists upon seeing the world in terms of good and bad, the holy and the evil, the high and the low, the white and the Black; our America is frightened of fact, of history, of process, of necessity. It hugs the easy way of damning those it cannot understand, of excluding those who look different and it salves its conscience with a self-draped cloak of righteousness... and I really do not really think that America, adolescent and cocksure, a stranger to suffering and travail, an enemy of passion and sacrifice is ready to probe into its most fundamental beliefs."[25]

In Malcolm X this probing into their fundamental beliefs has been clinical, almost brutal. In fact, he gave it a political edge. He was categorical in his denunciation of the murky beliefs of the white race. For this reason he was against the limited integration between the liberal whites and chosen Blacks. He demanded "human rights! Respect as human beings' that was what America's Black masses want. That's the real problem. The Black masses want not be walled up in slums, in the ghettoes, like animals. They want to live in an open, free society where they can walk with their heads up like men and women."[26]

James Baldwin examines the beliefs in human terms. His greatness lies in his ability to express the situation of being a Negro, of being white and of being human. In his autobiographical essays collected in *The Price of the Ticket*, he examines the entire range of their experience, including the concept of American Dream and segregation. First of all he questions the right of the white Americans to arrogate to themselves the position of superiority. Then he questions their right to choose the ideals for their society. The ideals would be chosen by whites, Blacks and other ethnic groups who were unwilling immigrants to America. From here he moves on to the vital question of the very creation of America which, for quite some time, was supposed to be an extension of Europe. "The price the white American paid for his ticket was to become white-: and, in the main, nothing more than that, or, as he was to insist, nothing less. This incredibly limited, not to say dim-witted ambition, has choked many a human being to death here: and this, I contend, is because the white American has never accepted the real reasons for his journey. I know very well that my ancestors had no desire to come to this place: but neither did the ancestors of the people who became white and who require of my captivity a song. They require of me a song less to celebrate my captivity than to justify their own."[27]

He also questions the conscious negation of history which is at the core of the entire American enterprise. This negation of history finds expression in the way the relationship between the individual and society is defined. The Americans believe that it is possible to consider the person apart from all the forces which have produced him, leading to alienation of the entire people from their forbears. In a very strange manner the individual past has been separated from the common past. They believe that an individual can create his own destiny which has thrust upon them such a troubling role. "The truth about that past is not that it is too brief, or too superficial, but only that we, having turned our faces so resolutely away from it, have never demanded from it what it has to give."[28]

Baldwin believes that if there was any purpose to their adventure in America it must be related to the common past which both the Blacks and whites have created. Surprisingly, Baldwin discovered this when he decided to live in Paris where he was considered an

American and not a Negro. There he could move about without crutches, without invisible walls and without fear of being different from other Americans. "Any honest examination of the national life proves how far we are from the standard of human freedom with which we began. The recovery of this standard demands of everyone who loves this country a hard look at himself for the greatest achievements must begin somewhere and they always begin with a person. If we are not capable of this examination we may yet become one of the most distinguished and monumental failures in the history of nations."[29]

Thus the battle against "hidden laws and unspoken and profound assumptions" to achieve standards of human freedom must be fought in the minds of individuals both Black and white. When the Black man breaks the sociological and sentimental image of him, the whites are panic stricken because they are not prepared to come out of the accepted categories of thought and customs. When Bigger Thomas, a character in *Native Son*, questions those categories, he in fact is questioning the relationship in which he stands to all other Americans. In addition, he points to the reality which is indivisible from white reality as also its dehumanization, which is in direct proportion to the dehumanization of Blacks in America. Not only this – the Blacks will also have to accept the fact that their relationship to Africa is sentimental and they will have to adopt the vesture of their adopted land.

Baldwin is categorical in his assertion that "Negroes are Americans and their destiny is the country's destiny. They have no other experience besides their experience on this continent and it is an experience which cannot be rejected, which yet remains to be embraced. If, as I believe, no American Negro exists who doesn't have his private Bigger Thomas living in the skull, then what most significantly fails to be illuminated here is the paradoxical adjustment which is perpetually made, the Negro being compelled to accept the fact that this dark and dangerous and unloved stranger is part of himself for ever."[30]

Denying this complex nature of their experience will push them towards provincialism. A retreat into the African past as has been advocated by Marcus Garvey and others is impossible as that would mean denying 400 years of their experience in America. Baldwin put it very graphically in an interview with Michael Clark recalling his school days. One day when he returned home, his mother asked him whether his teacher was colored or white. Baldwin replied that she was a little bit colored and a little bit white. "That is part of the dilemma of being a Negro; that one is a little bit coloured and a little bit white and not only in physical terms but in the head and the heart."[31]

The same concept has been artistically conceived in his novel, *Tell Me How Long The Train's Been Gone*. In a conversation between the brothers, after they were ill-treated by the cops, one of them, Caleb, said that he had never come across a good white man. Leo, the other brother said their mother was almost white. "Almost don't get it," Caleb said. "Our Mama is almost white but that don't make her white. You got to be all white to be white."[32]

The nagging question of Black identity cannot be discussed without reference to white society. They seem to occupy a no man's land and this situation would continue until the terms of reference of their identity were spelt out. The terms of reference become clearer when Alex Haley goes back to Juffure and is confronted with the natives, the descendents of his forebear. Although he was a symbol of the 25 million Black people whom the people of Juffure had never seen, he could not identify himself with them because of the barriers of language and culture. "I remember thinking, down on my knees, after I have found out where I came from, I can't understand a word they are saying."[33] The distance of four centuries has not only made his blood impure but has also rooted him in a different cultural and social soil. It was, therefore, impossible to go back to Africa except for emotional satisfaction.

Baldwin believes that America would have to be rediscovered, freed from the myths which have nothing to do with laws they live by; otherwise they would continue to live in a fantasy world. "There were always contradictions but we assumed that they would be taken care of; and since never before have we been in quite so important a position in the world, the contradictions have never been quite so glaring before. Something has gone wrong, no one quite knows where; no one knows where we are going; we seem to be headed in several directions at once – the strain is made a good deal more unbearable by the fact that, Americans passionately believe in their avowed ideals, amorphous as they are, and are terrified of waking from a radiant dream."[34]

Thus the past is examined in terms of what it yields to the making of life in the present. Along with it other areas of human experience, which were earlier pushed into the background, are being brought into focus. Some recent African writers have shown that past should be treated in such a manner that it doesn't become oppressive. They also take into account the fact that forms of evil exist independent of the uneasy relationship between the two races. They reject the simple categorization of experience and create a space which is not constricting and in which common humanity could be rehabilitated. In *A Raisin in The Sun*, a Black character, Walter plans to start business with two Black partners and gives sixty five hundred dollars as his share to one of the partners. Willy who was supposed to get the license made for the liquor shop, disappears with the money, and the entire family is crestfallen. Beneatha, his sister discusses this with her friend Asagai. She questions Asagai's idealism and dreams about Africa and independence. "Independence and then what? What about all the crooks and petty thieves and just plain idiots who will come into power to steal and plunder the same as before – only now they will be Black and do it in the name of the new Independence."[35]

It is the same evil that DuBois did not take into account while prescribing an idealistic role for the

Talented Tenth. Accepting this aspect of their experience will mean creating a larger truth in which not only their bruised spirits will be healed but there will also be a sober acceptance of the basic human inadequacy. Maya Aangelou in a conversation with Cornel West quotes Terence, a one-time slave during the Roman empire. He said : "I am a human being. Nothing human can be alien to me."[36] This kind of assertion can come with a sense of security which leads to the affirmation of humanity, or evil, in others. At that point there cannot be categories of being human. If one confines oneself to a selective sense of human, one will remain warped and will narrow oneself down in some tunnel without any light from the other end. Unlike James Baldwin, who felt uncomfortable with great writers of the West, Maya Angelou feels comfortable in the company of Shakespeare who provides succour to one who is disgraced.

> When in disgrace with fortunes in men's eyes,
> I all alone bemoan my outcast fate
> And trouble a deaf heaven with my bootless cries.
> And look upon myself and curse my fate,
> Wishing me like the one rich in hope.
> Featured like him, like him with friends possessed,
> I'm desiring that man's heart and that man's scope.
> And with what I most enjoy, contented least."

Angelou comments on this. "So here is a white man who wrote that in England and I, a Black girl on the dirt roads of Arkansas, used it for hope.[37]

Toni Morrison emphasizes other aspects of their experience. She says that the past should be accepted not only with its pain and suffering but also with qualities of endurance, resilience and acceptance which the people developed during the period of slavery. The whole problem of dealing with the past, according to Toni Morrison, has to do with two things: "To live for something bigger than yourself, to nurture something and also to sabotage yourself."[38] One way to survive the ravages of the past is to think about one another, to share their comfort and joy a small remnant of which can sometimes be seen in Black churches where people participate in the chorus.

Such a participation provides a sense of community and togetherness and also generates a sense of value which one finds missing in the outside world. This makes their life individual as well as representative.

The experience is not only corroborated but also confirmed through participation. This is the kind of relationship in which a Black writer stands to his people. He is thus both a participator and a witness in the sense in which white writers are not. At the same time he needs the support of his people so that the energy emanating from his art can suffuse all of them and change things. When this support is missing, the process of change is halted and the artist no longer remains their spokesman.

The participatory role of the artist is evident in Dalit Literature as well although the analogy cannot be completely established. Limbale considers his self-told story representative of his people, just as DuBois considers his autobiography as part of collective experience; in fact he goes to the extent of saying that he derives his strength from the commonality of experience. The Dalit writers, thus, examine the world within and the world without in a common framework of a casteless social order. One could add a classless social order with the difference that in Dalit literature the world within occupies most of the space, though the sources of its conflict emanate from the world outside. The pressure of the complexity of caste machination is such that the larger ordering of the world outside is somewhat tampered.

The African Americans had a reference point in Africa, a baseline by which they compared their situation in America. This reference point enabled them to question the goals of American society. For Dalits such a baseline was provided by Ambedkar in the form of Buddhist thought. Later Ambedkar himself became a reference point. (See *Akkarmashi* pp 145-149, Taral – Antaral, pp 254-255, 274, 277, 286-287, and *Our Life* by Baby Kamle, pp 117-118, *Paraya* by Laxman Mane, pp 92-94) In Shanker Rao Kharat's autobiography which he would have preferred to call the story of the Untouchables, one comes across the two forms of struggle. The intricate working of caste is revealed through points of contact with other people. The maid servant who comes to work at their place belongs to another caste and is discouraged by her brother from working at a Mahar house. Similarly, the girl from the neighbourhood who would willingly accept tea at their house, suddenly changes her attitude and refuses to take tea. The people at her place had made her conscious of caste reality. Kharat also shows the tenacity to move up the social ladder, despite all odds. The speech that he made when he took over as Vice-Chancellor is significant as it shows the contact between the two worlds. "The reason why I accepted the Vice-Chancellorship lay in my experience at school. When in primary class, I was made to sit outside the classroom and later even when I moved to Class III and was made to sit inside the class room, it was close to the door so that I did not touch other students and teachers. It is a matter of honour and privilege for me, and for the entire Dalit community that an untouchable has become a Vice-Chancellor. This fact is an important event in the life of the nation. Hopefully, this flow of change will not be confined to me but will be a reality for the larger community, particularly the depressed and the oppressed classes."[39]

The same pattern is repeated in Laxman Mane's *Paraya* (The Outsider). The separation of Laxman Mane and his caste becomes apparent at each stage of their movement. The homeless Banjaras carry the entire home with them, and with this rootlessness and homelessness. The struggle to gain education and to acquire an identity becomes more acute. The extension of experience in his case comes when he becomes part of the Dalit movement started by Ambedkar. He begins to take part in social and political stirrings – the agitation against Shankaracharya of Jagannathpuri is an example – and gets some idea of the working of the social system and what it has done to them. He seems to be moving in some direction but the goal is not very clear to him. His life is an example of growth and regression. The questions of poverty and exploitation are added to the question of caste. There are moments when he gets disgusted with the treatment he receives in the outside world and thinks of going back to his village. He has yet to learn to cope with the complex world of the city where the two realities are always in conflict.

There are two more aspects to his situation that reveal its complexity. On the one hand there were people like Dabhole, Patangaonkar, Bapusaheb Deshpande who went all out to support him in his bold step of intercaste marriage to a Maratha girl, on the other there were those, including his friends, who wanted him to operate within the existing system. For the first time, in the company of Bapusaheb, Dabhole, Narayan and others, he realized that he was not just a caste symbol but a human being like others. What is more, his aspirations also matter. And surprisingly, it was not condescension on the part of some *savarnas*, but a sense of duty. Shashi whom Mane marries belongs to a well-to-do family. It was her commitment to a relationship that forces her to reject a secure environment with an assured future. In fact, it was a revolutionary act, with all the risks involved. Mane's crusade against narrow caste distinctions is halted by his own people. His parents and other members of the family persuade him to come back to the caste fold so that his sisters could be married off without any hassles. His resolve is weakened and much against his will, he goes back to the village where the Panchayat admits him into the caste once again with elaborate rituals. His wife is adopted by Mane's uncles so that she is acceptable to the caste people. Even the problem of the coming child is solved by arranging a fake marriage and the Panchayat seems satisfied. "I wanted to remove the stain of caste," Mane writes, "but it became darker. I felt sad. For Shashi everything was new. It was like getting up from an oppressive sorrow."[40]

In Sharan Kumar Limbale's *Akkarmashi* this intricate relationship is enlarged to include the problem of identity. Limbale is a bastard. His father doesn't own him and consequently he has no claim on him. The problem of identity raises the issues of history, tradition, culture, religion and all those practices that contribute to the wholeness of life. He keeps shuttling between acceptance and defiance. Small incidents in his life make him realise how difficult it is for him, and others like him, to get a human existence. The policeman to whom Limbale and his friend complain about discrimination at the restaurant is cautious while dealing with them. When they threaten to write to the Prime Minister,[41] he relents. Limbale realises that it is not an individual problem but of the entire community. But this awareness of injustice does not take him to open rebellion. His experience in college intensifies his awareness. It acquires a new dimension which finally takes the form of a movement. But his struggle against the system doesn't move in a single direction.

It is surprising how the caste problem becomes more menacing once he gets some foothold in life. He becomes a telephone operator and with it begins the process of concealment of his caste and the acceptance of the mask of a Dalit brahmin. The force of Ambedkar ideology which filled him with anger and revolt is now weakened and he begins to devise ways of dealing with the system. Earlier Limbale greeted his Dalit friends with 'Jai Bhim' but now he greets them with 'namaskar'. He requests his friends not to mention 'Jai Bhim' or 'Baba Saheb' in their letters to him lest people should know his caste. He hides Ambedkar literature and his photograph in his suitcase. He feels gratified when people mistake him for a Lingayat. Among the Mahars he feels impure. Ambedkar, though a Mahar, belonged to the Sombanshi caste. Limbale being an Akkarmashi adds to his problems. Not knowing that he was an Akkarmashi, some Dalits approach him for support for their candidate on the occasion of Ambedkar Jayanti. Limbale could not tell them that he was not Baramashi. His artificially created world would be punctured and he would feel terribly lonely if he told them the truth of his being an Akkarmashi.

When his grandmother comes to his hostel to inform him of his sister's marriage, he keeps her at a distance as she is not decently clad and he doesn't want his hostel mates to know the relationship between them. "I was Akkarmashi but living like a Lingayat. I was ashamed of the poverty of Santamai and Dada."[42]

To wear the mask of a superior caste appeared to be an easy way out of that situation. This is how Limbale rationalises it.

"The benefits given to Dalits by the system; the consciousness of their identity and self-respect as a consequence of education; the rebellious youth shaped by the Dalit movement; the sense of security because of an assured job; rejection of the age-old duties assigned to them in the name of religion: all these had annoyed the *savarnas*. They could not digest the fact that Dalits could stand up to them, who until recently lived like animals. Naturally they resented this change and the acquisition of a new identity by them. My natural response was to conceal my caste."[43]

An important aspect in which the book stands out is the bracketing of the three oppressed groups – Dalit, Women and Muslims. Limbale discusses common elements in their process of liberation, but women and Muslims have not been subjected to deeper analysis. His mother's situation fills him with indignation. She is a plaything for Patel who would visit her during the night but would not even recognise her during the day. As a result Limbale had no claim on him. He always wondered if he would be accepted in his father's house if he went there. What rankled in him was that he was deprived of the affection of his father. The exploitation did not end with his mother. His sister is lured into a similar relationship by Patel's son, Chander, who eventually marries her.

The treatment of Muslim as a member of a Dalit family in a caste-ridden society adds another dimension to the autobiography. For all practical purposes, Dada is his grandfather although the relationship has not been sanctified. But he gives Limbale all the affection and care he needed when he was growing up. Limbale admits the relationship even at the cost of earning the displeasure of his caste fellows.

The question of caste remains unanswered to the end of the book. His friend, Chandya has completely accepted the role of a Dalit brahmin. When he visits the town, he does not want to stay with his sisters who live in the slums but stays in a lodge instead. Limbale does not suggest any way to deal with this immoral act. The predicament of his mother, grandmother and Dada are brought together in the last paragraph of the book.

"Who will take Dada's coffin to the graveyard? Will the Muslims do his last rites? Where will his bones be interred? Where was his graveyard? Who will join in the last rites of Santama and Masama! Why has this web of caste system been created this way? If my birth itself was declared immoral, what rules should I follow?"[44]

Daya Pawar's book, *Achoot*, deals with a more complex social world in which inter-caste, even inter-religion relationships are as prominently analysed as the relationship within one's caste. Thus it steers clear of the pitfall of caste obsession. It also suggests, in not too explicit a manner, that personal and social/political realities cannot be easily separated. The intricate relationship of people within the caste with their sorrows, grief, anguish, struggle and acceptance of life is broadened to include the *savarnas* with whom the protagonist interacts. The result is that caste analysis is not so one sided as one finds in other books. The consciousness of his situation came to him quite early when he was in school. It was a practice there that on the last day of S.S.C. class the school administration was run by students and the roles were reversed. For a change, students became teachers. In his lecture on history, Pawar spoke on the caste system, criticised *Manusmriti* which was naturally not liked by his Brahmin teachers who were sitting in the class. Later he explained that he got his ideas from Ambedkar's book on Shudras. This understanding gives him some kind of self-respect and in this education played an important role.[45] The interlocking realities represented by the appellations 'Harijan' and 'Mahar' are brought into sharper focus.[46] There is also assertion of identity when the Mahars insist on sharing the same well with the other castes.[47]

The Ambedkar ideology is always in the background when he deals with caste and class realities which are not antagonistic categories but are presented in overlapping interrelatedness. For example, Pawar doesn't reveal his relationship with his mother when she is employed as cook at the hostel he was staying in. In fact, she becomes an object of double exploitation. When Dada Saheb became minister he wrote to him. "So far all those ministers who represented Dalits were corrupt and infamous. You will have to create a leader who will work for the betterment of Dalits."[48]

The district in which Pawar lived was the centre of communist movement. But the communists were obsessed with the issue of class and did not realize that the Dalits had their own problems which ought to be tackled along with class issue. Besides, they never questioned the cultural values that sustained the oppressive social system. Pawar was never able to choose between the rightists and the leftists, for neither were committed to the common man although they professed to represent him. They themselves had not given up social practices that were the offshoots of the rituals performed by the brahmins. The rich men in the village, whether socialists or communists, had a condescending attitude towards the lower classes. When after conversion to Buddhism, the Dalits refused to perform the traditional work assigned to them, they were ostracized. There was ambivalence on the part of the communists while dealing with the caste reality. The Dalits were caught in a strange situation and for the communists it was not part of their political agenda. "On the one hand Mahars were giving up their old ways and were rejecting the deadening brahmin religion, on the other they had no place in the production system."[49] Even the movement for land distribution started by Dada Saheb Gaekwar and supported by Baba Saheb Ambedkar did not make much headway. The movement received a set back after the death of Ambedkar. The compromise between the Republican Party and the Congress sealed its fate.

Pawar gives his individual suffering a wider meaning by relating it to the suffering of people similarly placed. Instead of suffering, he uses the world deprivation. And the deprived people, whatever might be the source of their deprivation, are always scared of the system and those who control it. He felt scared during the Emergency but could muster up courage to turn down an invitation to participate in a National Writers' Conference in Delhi. The restoration of democracy; which he calls "second independence", did not bring material change in his situation. His faith in the system could not be restored and be continued to feel scared. And the uncertainty about his future added to his uneasiness. What worried him more was the future of his children. He ends his novel with his own poem which conveys his deep sorrow and restiveness.

"This tree I saw mangled with sorrow had roots as deep down as the Bodhi Tree's. But the Bodhi tree flowered and, this tree through all seasons is barren."[50]

The suffering of the deprived people and their inconsequential struggle to get some economic security is the subject of two books, *Uthaigeer* by Laxman Gaekwad and *We Also Exist* by Anil Avchat. The deprived people are exploited on both counts: on the count of poverty and on the count of their caste situation. Even when they get some stability in life, their caste situation continues to dog them. In *Uthaigeer* the moneyed and the powerful succeed in curbing Laxman's spirit but not completely destroying it. He tries to organize people of freed tribes – no longer branded in independent India – but at each step his efforts are thwarted by the corrupt and biased social and administrative system. He creates group consciousness among factory workers and initially succeeds in wresting some gains for his people but in the end the factory owners prove smarter and succeed in isolating him from his coworkers. He is suspended and is beaten up by hired goondas of the management with the result that he leaves the job. But his spirit is not crushed and he again organizes the branded or those who are subjected to police brutality. Five orphans of the slain 'pardhis' who belonged to a branded caste, were beaten up by the Police Inspector because they had the caste label. In other cases some people were tortured to own the crime which they had never committed. The surprising thing was that even after the real culprit was arrested, the police officer never felt sorry about it; and never returned the money he had taken from them. He was frank enough to admit that he collected the money in order to entertain his superior and he couldn't do that within his income. No action was taken against such officers. The boys who were struggling to get decent existence in society, were pushed back into the world of crime.

The most shocking experience that he had was when he agreed to contest the Assembly election on the Bahujan Samaj Party ticket. The Party promised to provide funds for election work but the money never came and Laxman found himself in a difficult situation. He had hired loud speakers and rickshaw-wallas but he couldn't pay them as the promised financial support never came. When the workers and those who worked for electioneering demanded money, he had no option but to withdraw his candidature from the fray in favour of the Congress Party candidate. He took seven thousand rupees from them to pay for loud speakers and vehicles and also an assurance that they would protect the interests of his people. But instead of understanding his predicament, his own people turned against him and accused him of betraying them by selling himself and making money in the bargain. The people of such tribes remained where they were earlier. "I was thinking that it was not enough to be a good and honest candidate; it is also necessary to be a member of a good family with financial support. Besides, one should indulge in other activities, taking the support of goondas making false promises and resort to violence. One can't contest elections without such support."[51]

He is forced to compromise with the system but keeps the spark of struggle alive. In order to survive as a contractor he pays 'percentage' in the divisional office for getting his bill passed. The man who once raised voice against injustice is now part of the system.

Laxman's brother and father kept struggling to break the mould within which they were imprisoned. But despite his political consciousness of the falsity of it all and the need to organize his people, he doesn't succeed much. But through his efforts he has shown that there are some basic differences between his approach to the problems of his people and of those who have assumed the leadership of such classes. He is cleverly used by them and is never allowed to take over the leadership. His awareness is sharpened by the communist leader Bhagwanrao Deshpande and the literature that he reads. Even after set backs he doesn't give up the fight. The novel ends with a resolve and determination that he will continue to work for change in the condition of the oppressed and suppressed people by enlarging the scope of their struggle and bringing all oppressed groups together despite caste categories.[52]

In Avchat's reportage 'We Also Exist' it is difficult to put a dividing line between caste and economic issues. Yet the oppressed never form themselves into an organized class group. They simply exist like animals around them and don't live, except for some who live comfortably. The acceptance of their fate and the pressure of earning the minimum wages that help them survive have been so oppressive that they don't even think of changing it. Any effort to organize them doesn't succeed partly because of the organized way in which the oppressors shield themselves and partly because of lack of support from the outside world. One displaced person who has come to the city for some work has this to say: "We know you are working for our good and we do support you but we cannot go along with you to the end of this struggle. When we see our children at home crying for food, we can't think of anything else. In that situation we are willing to do anything, agree to work on subsistence wages so that we are able to feed our children." On this Avchat comments, "I accept everything they say. It means that they can have political consciousness only after their basic needs are satisfied."[53] It is hypocritical to praise the great and liberal culture when people do not have resources to feed their family for a day. Slogans of 'total revolution' only help conceal the hypocrisy and greed of the moneyed class. Avchat emphasizes the need to combine the two issues that in fact are one.

One of the unfortunate parts of Dalit movement in the country has been that it has projected Ambedkar as anti-Marx. It is true that he did not approve of the ways of Bombay Marxists who discriminated between workers on caste lines; it is also true that he shared some common points with Marx which were never highlighted by his followers. Even Ambedkar projected Marxism as an alternative to Buddhism should Buddhism fail to bring about a casteless and classless society. Marxists, until recently, never analysed the Dalit situation including the caste issue. They went to the extent of opposing Ambedkar. May be a new Ambedkar will emerge some day and will not only organize and educate his people but also prepare them for a long fight against the two monsters.

Dalit literature has now reached a stage where it is prepared to deal with experiences that are part of the general human condition. It is a sign of maturity that Dalit writers are now prepared to take the risk of running the full gamut of their humanity. They are not averse to presenting those aspects of their people that reveal their evil propensities. In Daya Pawar's story 'Vultures', the old lady who lives all by herself in a village is the object of the predatory designs of both the Patel of the village and her own nephew. The Patel offers her ten thousand rupees for the patch of land. At the same time her nephew appears on the scene and lures her into transferring the land in his name. She knows that she is being tricked into it but doesn't know how to counter it. She has the fear that she may not get the same respect from her nephew as she is getting now once the land is transferred in his name.[54] In another story by Sharan Kumar Limbale titled 'Rape-Within and Without' evil propensities in a Dalit Brahmin are exposed. A young lady was raped by a corporator who had put her on job and the people were agitated. Since they failed to get any support from the police and administration they came to the Dalit Brahmin who is a journalist and who lives in comfort in a decent house. The conflict is presented at two levels : one between his situation and of those who have not risen in social ladder; and the other is between his own act of raping his maid servant and that of supporting a woman who has been raped by the corporator. His wife doesn't even have an inkling of what is going on within him. She is concerned only about how her colleague praises the sweets she has made at home and her colleague exclaims 'how horrible' when he hears the story of rape.[55]

Refereces

1 W.E.B. DuBois, Dusk of Dawn: An Autobiography of a Race concept, Schoken Books New York, 1968, pp. 131-132.

2 Richard Wright, American Hunger, Harper & Row, 1977, p. 62.

3 Anand and Zelliot, An Anthology of Dalit Literature, pp. 43-44.

4 Yashwant Manohar, 'I'm Ready for Revolution' in An Anthology of Dalit Literature, p. 113.

5 Arjun Dangle, 'Revolution' in An Anthology of Dalit Literature, pp. 43-44.

6 An Anthology of Dalit Literature, pp. 129-130.

7 Jean Paul Sartre, Preface to The Wretched of the Earth, Penguin, 1963, p. 7.

8 Sartre p. 8

9 R. Wright, American Hunger, p. 48.

10 *Ibid.*, p. 59.

11 Dalit Anthology, p. 85.

12 Restoring Hope, p. 92.

13 The Poetry of the Negro ed. Larry Neal, 1746-1970, p. 204.

14 The Price of the Ticket, p. 57.

15 Eleanor Zelliot, from Untouchables to Dalit, p. 318.

16 R. Wright, American Hunger, p. 97.
17 James Baldwin, Notes of a Native Son, p. 5.
18 Arjun Dangle, 'Promotion' in Dalit Stories edited by Surya Narayan Ransubhe and Kamlakar Gangavane, Panchsheel Prakashan, Jaipur, 1981, pp. 149-156.
19 Lorraine Hansberry, A Raisin in the Sun, A Signet Book, 1960, New American Library, p. 61.
20 Julius Lester, Introduction to Les Blancs, The Collected Last Plays of Lorraine Hansberry, Random House, New York, 1972, p. 11.
21 *Ibid.*, p. 13.
22 Fredrick Douglass, My Bondage My Freedom, Arno Press, New York, 1968, p. 430.
23 *Ibid.*, pp. 441, 445.
24 Richard Wright, Black Boy, Harper & Row, New York, 1945, p. 193.
25 Richard Wright, American Hunger, pp. 13-14.
26 The Autobiography of Malcolm X, p. 378.
27 The Price of the Ticket, p. XX.
28 *Ibid.*, p. 99.
29 *Ibid.*, p. 193.
30 James Baldwin - Notes of a Native Son, p. 33.
31 Three Interviews, edited Kenneth B. Clark, Middletown, Wesley University Press, 1985, p. 54.
32 James Baldwin, Tell Me How Long The Train's Been Gone, Dell Books 1973, p. 47.
33 Alex Haley, Roots, p. 680.
34 The Price of the Ticket, p. 16.
35 A Raisin in the Sun, pp. 114-115.
36 Restoring Hope, Cornel West, Conversations on The Future of Black American, Beacon Press, Boston, 1997, p. 190.
37 *Ibid.*, p. 207.
38 Toni Morrison, Conversations, p. 254.
39 S.R. Kharat, Taral Antaral, National Publishing House, New Delhi, 1987, p. 284.
40 Laxman Mane, Paraya, Sahitya Akademy, New Delhi, 1997, p. 93.
41 Sharan Kumar Limbale, Akkarmashi, p. 110.
42 *Ibid.*, p. 146.
43 *Ibid.*, p. 145-146.
44 *Ibid.*, p. 159.
45 Daya Pawar, Achoot, p. 177.
46 *Ibid.*, p. 136-137.
47 *Ibid.*, p. 110.
48 *Ibid.*, p. 135.

49 *Ibid.*, p. 204.
50 *Ibid.*, p. 241.
51 Laxman Gaekwar, Uthaigeer, Sahitya Akademi, New Delhi, 1992, p. 169.
52 *Ibid.*, p. 171.
53 Anil Avchat, We Aslo Exist, Radhakrishan Prakashan, New Delhi, 1991, p. 37.
54 Daya Pawar, 'Vultures', in Dalit Charchit Kahaniya, ed. Kusum Viyogi, Lalit Prakashan, Delhi, 1997, pp. 44-49.
55 S.K. Limbale, Rape Within and Without in Devta Aadmi, Pratibha Pratishthan, New Delhi, 1994, pp. 135-141.

5
Conclusion

..... We have got the courage to be on the one hand, and we have the courage to tell the truth about America in relation not just to white supremacy but to other forms of evil.

Maya Angelou
in
Restoring Hope

The history of the oppressed throughout the world – Dalits and African Americans in particular – has not been identical. Yet the broad framework of their struggle for liberation has been, more or less, the same. The differences are caused by the conditions of their existence, ideological formation of the dominant group and the strategies devised by them to keep the oppressed in their place. The oppressed, despite hostile conditions, devised their own strategies, in most cases unknown to the oppressor, to survive in a human way. There were differences in the manner their lives were manipulated – theories of race and caste were invented for the purpose – and the limits of their ambitions fixed; similarly, there were differences in the manner resistance, whether violent or feeble, was provided to such manipulation. The process of liberation depended upon the manner the oppressed acquired awareness of their predicament in a racialised or casteist society.

Their struggle to acquire a human status has run through three stages: one, the consciousness that they were victims of a calculated inhuman design; two, the questioning of the right of the oppressors to have complete control over their lives; and three, the rejection of the definition given of their existence and an effort to redefine it. These stages are also reflected in their literature.

Thus their history has been a struggle to reclaim the human space which the dominant group systematically denied them for centuries. The struggle has been painful and agonising. The cry of a Douglas or a Limbale reverberates through the corridors of history. An important stage in their struggle comes when they discover that it was no longer an individual problem but a group problem because they had suffered the same affliction and shared the same aspirations. It is at this crucial stage of their struggle that they throw up a leader – DuBois in America and Dr. Ambedkar in India – who becomes the spokesman of their collective voice. He not only analyses their situation, devises strategies for their liberation but also gives direction to achieve self – conscious manhood.

The resistance to their situation is directly related to the level of conditioning. In the case of Dalits, the process of reaching the level of awareness was protracted because of deeper conditioning, what Daya Pawar calls, 'psychological imprisonment'. In the case of African Americans it was not so protracted because they never accepted their situation of slavery. Even when the Dalits reached the level of awareness, their resistance never took a violent form. In the entire history of Dalits in India there are no extant records of insurrection or violent revolts against their situation, barring some tribals. The African Americans revolted against their forceful enslavement even while on ships and later on landing in America. By the end of the 18th Century more than fifty actual or anticipated insurrections had been recorded.

In India resistance took the form of petitions and protests. The direct action for getting water from tank or for entry in temples was never violent enough. Even the burning of *Manusmriti* was not accompanied by violence. It was in the nature of passive resistance and peaceful defiance. Even the Dalit Panther movement – a poor copy of the Black Panthers in the U.S.A. – did not have enough fangs and soon petered out. One reason why Ambedkar refused to align himself with the communists was the latter's indulgence in wholesale violence to achieve their ends. Although Ambedkar demanded human rights for his people like Malcolm X did, his demand, unlike Malcolm X's, was never backed by violence. The struggle of both these groups has been to expose the lies on which the entire citadel of racism and casteism was raised and to reject the devices which gave validity to the lies so that the consequences of such lies could be contained, if not completely eliminated. In Lorraine Hansberry's play 'Les Blancs', Charlie, a white character accuses a black character, Tshembe of being obsessed with race. Tshembe explains how the lie of race has played havoc with their lives. It is a device, or a means, an invention that of itself explains nothing but has been used to justify the rule of someone over others. Thus the device is not so innocuous. Tshembe explains it further: "I am simply saying that a device is a device, but it also has consequences. Once invented it takes on a life of its own. So in one century, men invoke the device of religion to cloak their conquests. In another, race. Now, in both cases you and I may recognize the fraudulence of the device, but the fact remains that a man who has a sword run through him because he refuses to become a Moslem or a Christian – or who is shot in Zatembe or Mississippi because he is black is suffering the utter reality of the device. And it is pointless to pretend that it doesn't exist – merely because it is a lie."[1]

Since the victims even now suffer the bitter reality in everyday life, the argument that racism or casteism was invented to deal with a particular situation and that it was necessary at that particular point of time and that in the changed political climate it is no longer necessary, does not hold. A device thus invented does not suddenly disappear with the change in historical situation. The resultant attitudes persist as the device acquires associations and a mythical and even rational justification. And its consequences have further consequences. This is what Pierre Bordean meant when he called these consequences "internalized oppressive beliefs". The U.S.A. took four centuries to realize that a human being is a human being despite his racial stock. In India we took millenniums to realize this simple fact or have we?

Ambedkar was aware of the consequences of the lies of caste created in the past but he doesn't present them in dramatic terms. He wanted to knock out the support that provided sanction to those lies. "The power of the privileged classes rests upon lies which are sedulously propagated among the masses. No resistance to power is possible while the sanctioning lies are accepted as valid. While the lie, which is the first and the chief line of defence remains unbroken there can be no revolt. Before any injustice, any abuse or oppression can be resisted, the lie upon which it is founded must be unmasked, must be clearly recognized for what it is."[2]

The cultural consequences of the manipulation of lies of their existence have been immense. The worst of it was that their creative power was destroyed and along with it the springs of human life. In literature, as in life, they began with a zero image of themselves which meant the repression of their self-hood. Since they could not represent themselves, they were represented by others but only marginally. Such representation was not ideologically neutral; in fact, it only reaffirmed the attitude of the mainstream culture towards them, although not without general human concern. But this concern was devoid of specificity of their existence. Their specificity seemed of no consequences. When the oppressed found their voice and began to make sense of the chaos of their life, the first thing they did was to rehabilitate their specificity in their imaginative creation. This process also gave them an insight into the pretence, the ambivalence and the duplicity of the dominant culture. Thus their literature acquired a different tone, subverted the accepted attitudes and invaded the imagination of their readers in the manner mainstream literature never did.

Literature for them becomes an act of analysing and remaking of their lives. It is no longer a mysterious phenomenon unrelated to the problems of their existence. It is taken as a historical category and as a part of a larger discourse in which knowledge and power cannot be separated. For this reason it is a rationally precise and imaginatively coherent expression of problems that confront them in their daily lives. It plays a definite role of consciousness raising and initiating a process of change. In this sense it is a continuation of their struggle in real life. In fact, it is now part of a larger social and political churning taking place throughout the world in which issues based on social hierarchy, race, caste and gender are challenged in the framework of social justice and social well being. There is interrelatedness of literature and social and political processes which can no longer be put in separate categories unrelated to each other.

The first expression of the victims when they acquire their voice is to make themselves visible (*Invisible Man* and *Akkarmashi*) so that the whites and the *savarnas* know that they have been blind to this aspect of reality. Then their voice takes the form of anger and protest so that the masters know how they feel about their existence and how unsatisfied they are with it. The masters on their part are at first amused but when the consequences of their attitudes supported by the lie are thrown back into their face, they are frightened. The voices of African Americans and Dalits become strident and recalcitrant when they try to establish a connection between their existence and the unjust social and political order. A new process of establishing connection between words and meaning begins. The word of the master is shown to be what it is, divested of its meaning and connotation; it is then redefined and relocated so as to give it new meaning and new connotations that have relevance to their existence. An entire world is being dismantled and restructured, deconstructed and reconstructed.

The purists among the elite group dismiss African Americans and Dalit literature as of no consequence but even they do not fail to recognize the intensity of their feelings and the freshness of their content and method. What is more, African Americans and Dalits do not want to measure up to the standards set by the purists and are setting their own standards. They are out to create their own aesthetics, which will draw on their history, range of experience and its interrelatedness and evaluation in the context of change.

The acquisition of a different voice gives them a peep into the complexity of their existence. They realize that the world within has been fractured to such an extent that they find it difficult to separate the real from the conditioned part of their being. The shuttling between the real and the conditioned has been the source of most of their writings. There is also the problem of relating it to the larger experience of which their experience is a part. In Bagul's story, 'When I concealed my Caste', two options are clearly given but it is not easy to move from one to the other. The options are the concealment of one's caste and the assertion of it daring others to treat them differently. In Laxman Mane's 'The Outsider', the problem of caste has been presented in all its oppressiveness. Throughout his life Laxman keeps fighting the ugly reality of caste oppression but towards the end he is sucked into it. His sister cannot be married off unless he and his wife are accepted once again into the caste fold. Another option is to become part of the middle class respectability and looking down upon even close relations. The hierarchy within caste, the caste factor and the economic aspect have been presented in Dangle's powerful story, 'Promotion'.

The African Americans deal with the internalized oppressive beliefs in terms of the distorted vision of themselves given by the white and not in terms of hierarchy within their race. It enables them to concretize their attitudes *vis-à-vis* whites easily. Thus duplicity and violence, covert and overt, play important role in their attitude towards the other race. Frederick.

Douglass, when he was a slave, took on his supervisor, Covey, and overpowered him physically as though to prove that the colour itself did not give him the right to power. Even when free, he did not submit himself to the mould created for his lectures by the Garrisonians. Richard Wright in 'Black Boy' refuses to fit into the "nigger being-a-good-natured-boy-in-the-presence of a-white-man-pattern."[3] Unable to communicate with the white on equal terms, he decided to grow internally and lived a parallel existence unknown to the whites. The important thing was to save himself. In this the books helped him, although they created a distance between him and the world. Despite the oppressive environment, he was able to kill the imposed self within him and replace it by a self that gave him a human status. He knew that words alone could not bring about a revolution, but he trusted the efficacy of the words. He hurled them in the void, waiting for an echo.

Ralph Ellison converts this internalized self into a metaphor of invisibility. White people working with Blacks consider them as part of the landscape and take no notice of their real existence. The effort to acquire visibility or a human status reveals the distortion in the eyes of the whites. *Invisible Man* took time to see through this colour game. He runs through the entire spectrum of American life but finds that he doesn't have what the whites take for granted. Even the communists do not help him get that status. At the end of the novel, he withdraws himself into the cellar waiting for favourable environment. The destruction of the imposed self and the creation of another self can be seen in Toni Morrison's novels. This process is seen in the presence of an ancestor who is not only representative in nature but also is the repository of some kind of wisdom. This presence can be seen in Ralph Ellison or Toni Cade Bambara or Henry Dumas. In some way or the other the characters have to come to terms with that presence.

The struggle to come to terms with one's self is as difficult as to come to terms with the larger world. Most African American writers are not satisfied with surface adjustments but long for changing the world of ideas and customs to make it more humane. In the U.S.A. writers from Douglass through DuBois, Richard Wright, James Baldwin, Ralph Ellison, Maya Angelou, Alice Walker to Toni Morrison provide a critique of the ideals of the American society. They also suggest an alternative ideal not only for their people but for the entire country. In a piece Richard Wright wrote for delivery to a French audience, he presented a modified ideal for the people: "I am an American but I dream of being able to live in a world where race, dollars and status are not the final definition of human life."[4] According to Baldwin, America is the strongest nation in the Western world because it has the capacity to move beyond the Old World concepts of race, class and caste and to create a nation of the ideal that the people had when they thought of the New World. "But the price of this is a long look backward whence we came and an unflinching assessment of the record."[5]

While the Dalit writers are dissatisfied with the social and political structure in the country, they do not deal with the larger world as forcefully as the African Americans do. Apart from the dismantling of the inhuman caste system, no distinct alternative vision emerges from the Dalit writings. They deal with ideals in so far as they impinge upon their inner caste world. Daya Pawar and Om Prakash Valmiki and Sharad Kumar Limbale expose the impediments in human relations but treat the larger world, including political issues only marginally. In this Pawar's *Achut* is different from the others.

In African American history there are two different strains: one leaning on nationalism leading to separatism and the other towards assimilationism. Sometimes one is in ascendancy, sometimes the other. The stream of nationalism was represented by DuBois, Marcus Garvey, Elija Mohammed, Malcolm X and in more recent times, by Louis Farrakhan. African American slaves, however managed to forge an alternative world view capable of supporting either a spiritual or 'national' liberation movement. The process began with the collection of accurate information about their group history and culture.[6] Some of them went to the extent of saying that they were a separate nation within a nation. Dalit struggle has no such pronounced streak of nationalism or separatism. One reason could be that they did not belong to a separate racial stock. Dr. Ambedkar refuted Jyotiba Phule's thesis that the Dalits were the natives and the Aryans came from outside and subjugated them. Besides, they have found solace in the cultural strength of Hindu religion minus caste. Some efforts have, however, been made as is revealed in the book, *History of Hindu Imperialism* by Swami Dharma Theertha but this never developed into a movement. The literature written by Kabir, Chokhamela, Nandnar, Ravi Das and others is claimed equally by Dalits and non-Dalits. Their goal was never separatism but integration on more human terms. A spurt of it can be seen in Dr. Ambedkar's demand for a separate electorate and he succeeded in getting it from the Britishers. But Gandhi opposed it on the ground that Dalits were an integral part of Hindu religion and thus there was no need for a separate electorate for them. Dr. Ambedkar relented when Gandhiji went on a fast unto death. But Ambedkar was convinced that "only when the Hindu society becomes a casteless society that it can hope to have the strength enough to defend itself. Without such internal strength swaraj for Hindus may turn out to be only a step towards slavery."[7]

The mood of African American has swung towards reconciliation. Even Louis Farrakhan realized the inability of African Americans to effect the establishment of a separate nation – state. He formed an organization, Nation of Islam's People Organized and Working for Economic Rebirth (P.O.W.E.R.). The blending of race specific theology and economic power is significant. Toni Morrison, Cornel West, Henry Louis Gates Jr. and others work for a society in which they will be both African and American. They want to clear the pallid stream of American life, its lust for wealth, its market morality, and humanize America so that they have their place in America like any other ethnic group.

The reconciliation in Dalit writers is not overt as it did not grow out of the streak of nationalism or separatism. It is implicit in their literature. Even when they are critical of the *varna* / caste system, they want a better deal within the larger system. Even Ambedkar's conversion to Buddhism is not seen as an act of separatism. Buddhism is now accepted as an extension of Hinduism and Buddha is considered as one of the *avatars*. The best one can say is that reconciliation is inherent in their literature. Like the Blacks they do not have to work for it, if only the caste system was demolished.

It is apparent that the Dalits in India and African Americans in the U.S.A. are no longer at the receiving end. They have spelt out the terms on which they would like to be integrated into the larger system. They carry a great responsibility on their shoulders, that of redefining not only their people but also those who have defined their lives for centuries. They will in this way create conditions in which a new social and political order can grow. Their creative act involves the analysing the meaning of their existence *vis-à-vis* the other as also the making of it. Dalit literature and African literature are no longer seen as literature of vengeance. According to Baburao Bagul "dalit sahitya is not a literature which spreads hatred. Dalit sahitya first promotes man's freedom and for that reason it is an historic necessity."[8]

Alice Walker was once asked what she thought was the major difference between the literature written by black and by white Americans. She said that "for the most part, white American writers tended to end their books and their characters' lives as if there was no better existence for which to struggle. The gloom of defeat is thick. By, comparison, black writers seem always involved in a moral and/or psychological struggle, the result of which is expected to be some kind of larger freedom. Perhaps this is because our literary tradition is based on the slave narrative when escape for the body and freedom for the soul went together or perhaps this is because black people have never felt themselves guilty of global, cosmic sins."[9]

References

1. Lorraine Hansberry, Les Blancs in The Collected Last Play of Lorraine Hansberry, Random House, New York, 1972, p. 122.
2. Ambedkar, Writing & Speeches. Vol. I, p. 399.
3. Richard Wright, Black Boy, p. 256.
4. Quoted by Michel Fabre, "Wright in Exile' in Richard Wright : Impressions and Perspectives, p.138.
5. James Baldwin, The Price of the ticket, p. 320.
6. William L. Van and De Burg Eds. Modern Black Nationalism, New York University Press, 1997, p. 5.
7. Ambedkar, Writings & Speeches, Vol. I, p. 80.
8. Asmitadarsh, VI-I, 1973, pp. 56-57.
9. Alice Walker, Saving the Life that is Your Own : The Importance of Models in the Artist's Life in African American Literary Criticism, 1773 to 2000, ed. Hazel Arnett Ervin, p. 156.

Appendix - I

B. R. Ambedkar, W.E.B. DuBois And the Process of Liberation

In one of the essays, 'The American Experience of Dr. Ambedkar', included in her book, *From Untouchable to Dalit,* Eleanor Zelliot writes: "A direct comparison between the Negroes of America and Untouchable of India does not appear in Ambedkar's writings." She may be right, in a way, but Ambedkar does make comparison between 'Slaves and Untouchables', cites parallel cases and also shows how Hindus lack social and public conscience as against the white Americans.[1] The reason why Zelliot finds no direct comparison between the two oppressed groups is that Ambedkar found no racial basis for untouchability. From this she deduces that Dr. Ambedkar was not influenced by the struggle of Negroes (they prefer to call themselves African Americans or Blacks) in America but used his "knowledge of American culture to analyse his own country's social situation". Thus, according to her, the American experience of Dr. Ambedkar "seems to be chiefly in developing his commitment to a pragmatic, flexible democratic system". Zelliot seems to limit Dr. Ambedkar's interest in

---

* Initially presented at a Seminar on The Literature of The Oppressed organized by the Department of English, Lachoo Memorial College and Roopayan Sansthan, Jodhpur in January 2001. The revised and enlarged version, which is included in Appendix-I, has been published in Economic and Political Weekly, December 27-January 2, 2004.

America to the effort made by white Americans to create an egalitarian democracy.[2] For her Ambedkar's experience of Black Americans counts for nothing.

Apart from the trappings of American democracy to which Dr. Ambedkar was exposed, there was another reality, the Black American reality, that was struggling to assert itself. I believe that the Black American component of his American experience has been glossed over or has not been sufficiently researched. Since Black struggle is integral to American experience, it is difficult to keep this part out of Ambedkar's experience of America.

The period of Ambedkar's stay at Columbia University (1913-16) coincided with the most crucial period in Black American history. It was the period of Harlem Renaissance when Black American writers and thinkers were trying to separate those aspects of their existence that made them different from the whites. In fact, they were struggling to free themselves from the white imagination which had defined their existence for them. Their struggle did not end with the Civil War and the Fourteenth Amendment of the Constitution of the U.S.A. It continued long after the period of Reconstruction both in the South and the North. Malcolm X, in the first chapter of his autobiography titled 'Nightmare', mentions the warnings and threats given by the Ku klux Klan raiders to his family that they better leave the town. Malcolm's father was a dedicated organizer for Marcus Aurelius Garvey's Universal Negro Improvement Association. Malcolm X was still in his mother's womb when the incident took place.[3] The struggle intensified in the 50s and the 60s moving from Civil Rights (non-violent struggle of Martin Luther King Jr.) to Human Rights (violent struggle represented by Malcolm X). Black Power Movement bordering on separatism and Black Muslim Movement were the other manifestations of that struggle. As late as 1992 Arthur Schlesinger Jr. wrote that "racism has been a great national tragedy".[4] It is not surprising, therefore, that in India a large number of Dalit writers, particularly in Maharashtra, compared their struggle with that of Blacks in America. The Dalit Panther Movement was modelled on Black Panther Movement. V. S. Naipaul writes in *India: A Million Mutinies Now* that Namdeo Dhasal's career was like the career of a number of Black Power people in the U.S.A.[5] Sharad Kumar Limbale, one of the prominent Dalit writers, has written his Ph.D. dissertation on Negroes and Dalits.

Even if it is conceded that the Untouchables in India were of the same racial stock as the caste Hindus, although it has not been conclusively established as yet, it does not follow that the comparison between the two cannot be made. James Baldwin, while emphasizing the uniqueness of Black experience in America, finds similarities between the Blacks and the oppressed groups in other countries. In a piece on James Baldwin Stephen Spender writes: "If the Negro problem is resolvable, the only useful way of discussing it is to consider American Negroes in a situation comparable to that of workers and Negroes elsewhere [like Dalits in India]. To write as though Negroes do not exist anywhere except in America is to induce despair, to suggest than in America, white and black, cannot become integrated to the (rather limited) extent to which they have been, for example, in Brazil. It is in fact playing in the hands of Black Muslims whose position is that America – world even – has to choose between having but black or nothing but white people by which it is meant that it would be undemocratic to have nothing but the black majority."[6] The comparison between the oppressed groups is natural despite different historical situations because the process of liberation is almost similar. Although the direct comparison between the Blacks and Untouchables is rather limited in Ambedkar's writings, the influence of America, including Black America, goes deeper than direct comparisons can snow. I find marked similarities between W.E.B. DuBois and B. R. Ambedkar in the process of liberation of their people. It is here that the comparison is valid and ought to be considered.

In an essay, Slaves and Untouchables, Ambedkar compares the two inhuman systems pointing out the level of segregation and the degree of psychological damage caused by them. "Slavery was never obligatory. But untouchability is obligatory. The law of slavery permitted emancipation. Once a slave always a slave was not the fate of the slave. In untouchability there is no escape. Once an Untouchable always an Untouchable. The other difference is that untouchability is an indirect form of slavery. A deprivation of a man's freedom by an open and direct way is a preferable form of enslavement. It makes the slave conscious of his enslavement and to become conscious of slavery is the first and most important step in the battle for freedom. But if a man is deprived of his liberty indirectly he has no consciousness of his enslavement. Untouchability is an indirect form of slavery".[7]

Columbia University, where Ambedkar was working for his degree, was close to Harlem, and it seems unlikely that he had no knowledge of the stirrings going on there. Besides, there were two prominent Black leaders whose approaches to Black problems were diametrically opposed. They were Booker T. Washington and W.E.B. DuBois who disagreed not only over the nature of education Blacks should receive but also the direction their struggle should take. Washington wanted his people not to aspire to be like white but be satisfied with things they could do. In other words, he was for the status quo. It was reflected in his famous slogan 'cast your bucket where you are.' (Up From Slavery) Dhananjay Keer in his biography, *Dr. Ambedkar: Life and Mission* and W. N. Kuber in *B. R. Ambedkar* mention Booker T. Washington and the good work he had done at Tuskegee Institute.[9] A.N. Rajsekhariah in his book, *B.R. Ambedkar: The politics of Emancipation*, mentions, not only Booker T. Washington but also W.E.B. DuBois. Rajsekhariah writes about Washington: "One of the most remarkable men America has produced, a man born in slavery but lifted by his own vision and perseverance to a position of leadership and power. The son of a slave woman, Booker T. Washington struggled to acquire an education for himself, then dedicated his life to educating others. His is the story of almost unbelievable devotion and selflessness, an inspiration to people all over the world as long as men recognize the value of courage and human dignity". Rajsekhariah adds: "How could Ambedkar escape the influence of such a silent revolution that was brought about by Booker T. Washington, about whom he had learnt so much while in America."[10] Rajsekhariah does not mention DuBois in such glowing terms although he was doing much more revolutionary work than Washington. DuBois wanted his people to educate themselves in the best manner possible – not just for mechanical work which was the object of Tuskegee institute – and work for change so that they could not only compete with the white on equal footing but also help raise their unfortunate brethren. Towards the end of his book Rajsekhariah mentions DuBois to whom Ambedkar had sent a letter exploring the possibility of taking the question of the Untouchables to the newly born United Nations Organization. The letter was sent to the University of Atlanta, Georgia, U.S.A. where DuBois was working as a professor. The letter was despatched on July 2, 1946.[11] Ambedkar probably had no time to pursue the matter as soon after the British Government announced that it would hand over power to Indian leaders by June 1948. I do not think it was a sudden revelation to Ambedkar that DuBois was a prominent Black leader and could help him in his crusade against Untouchability. It appeals to reason that he must have known DuBois or read his books during his stay in the U.S.A. DuBois published his important book, *The Souls of Black Folk*, in 1903 and it became an instant success. Its readers were impressed by the fresh approach to the Black problem. Saunders Redding wrote that the book "may be seen as fixing that moment in history when the American Negro began to reject the idea of the world's belonging to white people only, and to think of himself as a potential force in the organization or society".[12] Ambedkar was a bibliophile and, according to Dhananjaya Keer, he bought about 2,000 old books in New York itself. It is unlikely that Ambedkar wouldn't have seen the book or even bought it. It is said that the steamer in which Ambedkar had sent his pile of books was destroyed by a submarine. Some of the precious books were lost this way. He had also sent some books with his friends returning from America but not all books finally reached him. I am sure some future scholar who will have access to the pile of papers still lying unpublished, will come across the name of DuBois and other Black American writers.

In polite conversation quite often we advance the argument that since law has taken care of casteism and racism, it is pointless to talk about it. But a single incident in Los Angeles or in a remote village in Rajasthan or Bihar exposes the falsity of this argument. Similarly, it is facile to argue that racism and casteism were invented to deal with a particular historical situation and it was necessary at that particular point of time. Ambedkar argues that a division of labour eventually became a division of labourers and became the basis of graded inequality. A system thus invented does not suddenly disappear with a change in historical situation. It acquires association and mythical, even rational, justification. The power of the privileged whether in India or the U.S.A. rests upon lies which are propagated in such a manner that they get internalized. Even after the lie, on which the entire structure of racism and casteism is based is exposed, it continues to exist in the minds of people.

Dalit in India took a long time, as compared to Blacks in America, in reaching the level of awareness of their predicament. And even when they did reach that level, their awareness was still enmeshed in the complex hierarchy of caste within their own group. In Laxman Mane's *Outsider* the protagonist fights against the stranglehold of caste throughout his life but ends up by accepting the same debasing and limiting system against which he had earlier revolted. It is another thing that he did this to please his father. One is tempted to ask whether it is the expression of related intolerance or a kind of assimilation into the larger world of caste. A character in Lorraine Hansberry's play Les Blancs has this to say about racism, and it could be applied to casteism as well. "Race-racism is a device. No more, No less. It explains nothing .... I am simply saying that a device is a device but it also has consequences; once invented it takes on a life, a reality of its own. So in one century, men invoke the device of religion to cloak their conquests. In another race [or caste]. Now in both cases you and I may recognize the fraudulence of the device, but the fact remains that a man who has a sword run through him because he refuses to become a Muslim or Christian – or who is shot in Zatembe or Mississippi [or refuses to follow the caste code in a remote village in India] because he is Black [or Dalit] is suffering the bitter reality of the device. And it is pointless to say that it doesn't exist."[13]

The process of liberation of Dalits and Black Americans from invisibility to visibility, from a non-human to a human existence, has not been simple and linear. It is characterized by growth and difficulty. In fact it has been painful and prolonged. It has been painful because at each stage of their struggle they are reminded of their lurid past; it has been prolonged because they have to fight against an invisible wall of segregation, supported by racially or religiously sanctioned entrenched attitudes. The attitudes that racism and casteism have put in them cannot be jettisoned out of the system at will. Besides, the ruling ideology in its innumerable manifestations does not concede the human space to them. The history of Black Americans since 1866 when slavery was legally abolished and of Dalits since 1948, when through an Act of Parliament untouchability was abolished, shows how difficult the path for equality has been. The psychological distance in both cases is not allowed to be bridged and ever new ways are devised to maintain the status quo. The fight is now against an unknown terror as against a known terror.

It takes a long time before the oppressed group throws up a thinker who gives direction to their struggle. In America such a thinker emerged in the person of W.E.B. DuBois; in India, in the person of B.R. Ambedkar.

The task of such a thinker is momentous since he derives his strength from his people. He has to analyse the entire gamut of their experience, the forces that were responsible for their predicament, the strategies to deal with those forces and then to project an ideal order in which the one-time victims can realize their full potential as human beings.

The first task of a thinker is to give his people 'group consciousness' that is to tell them that it is not an individual problem but a group problem. Since they have had a common history, have shared a common memory and have suffered a common disaster, they must fight it collectively. The battle for liberation begins when group consciousness gets crystallized. DuBois wrote in his autobiography, Dusk of *Dawn*, that his life derives its significance from the community and not otherwise. Ambedkar wrote letters for Mook Nayak in which he emphasized the need for unity among all the innumerable untouchable castes. He once said that he would survive as long as it was necessary for the welfare of the Depressed Classes. "If I fail to do away with the thralldom and inhuman injustice under which the class, into which I was born, has been groaning, I will put an end to my life with a bullet."[14] He was impatient to get his people dignity and human status. He kept on goading his people to come out of the ghetto of their existence and unitedly fight against the monster of caste discrimination and those who denied them a decent existence. In order that they did not relapse into the same pattern of passive acceptance of their existence, he organized satyagraha, first against the denial of access to Chawadar Tank, then against entry to the Kalaram temple and finally the burning of *Manusmriti* which was for him a symbol of inequality.

A precondition for forging group consciousness was to systematically examine the past. Both DuBois and Ambedkar were intellectually equipped to do so. DuBois had done his research on The Suppression of The European Slave Trade; Ambedkar began his intellectual journey by writing a paper on 'Castes in India: Their

Mechanism and Development' for the Anthropological Seminar at the Columbia University. DuBois took this inquiry further in *The Souls of Black Folk*; Ambedkar examined the concept of caste in his well-researched paper, Annihilation of Caste, which he wrote as a Presidential address for the Jat Pat Todak Mandal, Lahore.

In Dusk of Dawn: An Essay Toward an Autobiography of a Race Concept DuBois tries to capture the mechanism of Racism through an elaborate imagery. "It is difficult to let others see the full psychological meaning of caste segregation. It is as though one, looking out from a dark cave in a side of an impending mountain, sees the world passing and speaks to it courteously and persuasively, showing them how these entombed souls are hindered in their natural movement, expression and development; and how their loosening from prison would be a matter not simply of courtesy, sympathy and help to them, but aid to all the world. One talks on evenly and logically in this way, but notices that the passing throng does not even turn its head, or if it does, glances curiously and walks on. It gradually penetrates the minds of the prisoners that the people passing do not hear, that some thick sheet invisible but horribly tangible plate glass is between them and the world. They get excited; they talk louder; they gesticulate. Some of the passing worlds stop in curiosity; these gesticulations seem so pointless; they laugh and pass on. They still either do not hear at all, or hear but dimly and even what they hear, they do not understand. Then the people within may become hysterical. They may scream and hurl themselves against the barriers, hardly realizing on their bewilderment that they are screaming in a vacuum unheard and that their antics may actually seem funny to those outside looking in. They may even, here and there, break through in blood and disfigurement, and find themselves faced by a horrified, implacable and quite overwhelming mob of people frightened for their own very existence."[15]

Similarly, in the second issue of his paper Mook Nayak, Ambedkar conveys this reality of segregation through the imagery of a tower. "Hindu society was just like a tower which had several storeys without a ladder or an entrance. One was to die in the storey in which one was born."[16]

DuBois moves on to show the intellectual and psychological interaction with the situation of the Blacks who had their lives shaped and manipulated by the way the white world treated them. And the interpretation of their situation kept changing: it was social, biological or cultural. DuBois proved through his character and achievements that such an interpretation was a contrivance. He could beat them in every department of life in which he participated. Similarly, Ambedkar questioned and rejected the religious interpretation of the Depressed Classes based on the theory of birth and *karma.* He called such an interpretation a ruse to keep his people in thraldom. In fact, he went to the extent of saying that "if Hindu religion is to be their religion, it must become a religion of social equality."[17] Not many *savarnas* could match his scholarship. He could stand up to any *savarna* leader and interacted with them on the level of equality. Until Gandhi met Ambedkar he thought that he was a *savarna* fighting for the cause of the Depressed Classes. The speech he made at the Round Table Conference for self-governance and communal award was praised by all, including the Britishers.

Having exposed the falsity of interpretation, DuBois moves on to deal with the real problem which began with Reconstruction: how to deal with the damaged psyche, the 'double consciousness, the twoness of their existence. There were "two un-reconciled strivings, two warring ideals in one dark body whose dogged strength alone keeps it from being torn asunder. The history of the American Negro is the history of this strife, this longing to attain self-conscious manhood, to merge his double self into a better and truer self. In this merging he wishes neither of the older selves to be lost. He would not Africanize America, for America has too much to teach the world and Africa. He would not bleach his Negro soul in a flood of white Americanism, for he knows that Negro world has a message to the world. He simply wishes to make it possible for a man to be both a Negro and an American without being cursed and spit upon by his fellows, without having the doors of opportunity closed roughly in his face."[18]

The problem of reconciling the two selves could not be solved so easily. A large majority of Blacks wallowed in misery and ignorance and time and again, despite the fact that they were now free, relapsed into the old pattern of submissiveness of the 'Yes Sir, Massa' variety. DuBois knew that the only way they could understand their situation and the possibilities of existence was through education. And the kind of education he had in mind was different from the kind of education Booker T. Washington was propagating, that is technical skill. DuBois was very clear in his mind that technical skills produced only artisans and not men. "Men we shall have if we make manhood the object of the work of the schools – intelligence, broad sympathy, knowledge of the world that was and is, and of the relation of men to it – this is the curriculum of that Higher Education that must underlie true life."[19] He did not leave education entirely to school; he wanted family and social group to contribute to their growth. For this he had a specific plan in mind which he outlined in his famous essay, The Talented Tenth. The plan was that 10 per cent of bright young Black would be trained in the best manner possible so that they in their turn bring the others up and provide leadership. "Men of America," DuBois said, "the problem is plain before you. Here is a race transplanted through the criminal foolishness of your fathers. Whether you like it or not, the millions are here, and here they will remain. It is if you do not lift them up, they will pull you down. Education and work are the levers to lift a people. Work will not do it unless inspired by the right ideals and guided by intelligence. Education must not simply teach work; it must teach life. The Talented Tenth of the Negro race must be made leaders of thought and missionaries of culture among other people. No other can do this work and the Negro colleges must train men in it. The Negro race, like all other races, is going to be saved by its exceptional men."[20]

The assumption was that the elite of their race would be alive to their social and ethical obligations and would provide an overall leadership, directing their thought and movements. DuBois had obviously placed responsibilities in them which they were not equipped to bear. The danger in such a plan was that they might end up by imitating the standards of the other race placing their interest above the interest of their community. DuBois was later charged with encouraging elitism and was forced to examine his thesis, which he did in a memorial lecture at the Grand Bouls Conclave in 1948. Among other things he said: "I assumed that with knowledge sacrifice would automatically follow. In my youth and idealism, I did not realize that selfishness is even more natural than sacrifice. I made this assumption of its wide availability because of the spirit of sacrifice learned in my mission school training."[21]

In his modified lecture he moved from individuals motivated by personal freedom to group leadership. Such a leadership, he believed, would take care of economic and cultural aspects of their race. Lest people misunderstand him, he made it explicit that he was not advocating pride in biological race but pride in a culture group, integrated and expanded by developed ideals. In such a leadership, it would not remain a simple thing of colour but would include a deeper and broader matter of social conditions, including economic conditions. "Here comes a new idea for a talented tenth: the concept of a group leadership, not simply educated and self-sacrificing, but with clear vision of present world conditions and dangers, and conducting American Negros to alliance with culture groups in Europe, America, Asia and Africa, and looking towards a new world culture."[22]

Like DuBois, Ambedkar identified the problem of his people in his longish essay, Annihilation of Caste, which was initially written as a presidential address but later published by Ambedkar on his own. The booklet was sold out immediately and, what was more, was translated into a number of Indian languages. According to him "caste is a notion, it is a state of the mind. The destruction of caste does not therefore mean the destruction of a physical barrier. It means a notional change. Caste may be bad, caste may lead to conduct so gross as to be called man's inhumanity to man. All the same, it must be recognized that the Hindus observe caste because they are deeply religious." Thus he attacked the religious basis of caste. Fighting against it involved fighting against the authority of the *Shastras*. This religious sanction was responsible for creating not only separate enclosures in society but also separate enclosures in the mind. Despite the fact that the Jat Pat Todak Mandal was working against the annihilation of caste, it did not go along with Ambedkar in denouncing religion, at least the parts that sanction untouchability. Pushed to the wall, they gave excuses and finally cancelled the meeting.

Gandhiji agreed with Ambedkar that caste was evil and must go but he made a subtle distinction between caste and *varna* and said that the latter was the basis of Hindu society and had nothing to do with caste. Even Sant Ramji of Jat Pat Todak Mandal questioned this distinction. In a letter to Gandhi he wrote: I wish to bring to your notice that your philosophical difference between caste and *varna* is too subtle to be grasped by people in general, because for all practical purposes in the Hindu society caste and *varna* are one and the same thing, for the function of both of them is one and the same i.e. to restrict inter-caste marriages and interdining."[24] Ambedkar was more forthright. He accused Gandhi of 'terminological inexactitude'. He countered this distinction at a more rational level. Questioning Gandhi's emphasis of following ancestral calling, he wrote: "When can a calling be deemed to have become an ancestral calling so as to make it binding on a man. Must one follow his ancestral calling even when it does not suit his capacities, even when it has ceased to be profitable? Must one live by his ancestral calling even if he finds it to be immoral? To me the ideal of following one's ancestral calling is not only an impossible and impractical ideal but it is also morally an indefensible one."[25] Nor can the distinction between *varna* and caste on the basis of worth and birth be defended. Besides, who is going to decide and in what manner the existence of worth in a person. Thus, for all practical purposes, worth is associated with birth and that is what has happened all along.

That is why he did not go along with Gandhiji, despite the latter's messianic zeal, in the abolition of untouchability. The basis of caste is a lie and must be exposed for what it is. It is to be fought not only in the minds of the people but also in the realm of the abstract which is so dear to Hindus. Like Jyotiba Phule, he saw the danger of following the line of converting a social problem into a moral problem. It is a social problem supported by religion and must be accepted without prevarication. "The power of the privileged class," he wrote in the same essay, "rests upon lies, which are sedulously propagated among the masses. No resistance to power is possible while the sanctioning lies, which justify the power, are accepted as valid. While the lie which is the chief line of defense remains unbroken there can be no revolt. Before any injustice, any abuse of oppression can be resisted, the lie upon which it is founded must be unmasked, must be clearly recognized for what it is. This can happen with education."[26]

Ambedkar, like DuBois, believed that part of their problems emanated from ignorance. They must be brought to a level where they become critically aware of their environment. The consciousness-raising strategy could be effectively achieved through education. As early as 1924 he helped establish Bahishkrit Hitkari Sabha which, among other things, aimed at promoting education among the Depressed classes. Apart from starting Industrial and Agricultural schools, it also opened libraries, social centers and study circles and through them promoted the spread of culture. He firmly believed in a kind of education that helps people to blow up the caste system. "Giving education to those who want to blow up the caste system will improve the prospect of Democracy in India and put Democracy in safer hands."[27]

Later Ambedkar helped establish the People's Education Society and schools and colleges under its aegis. Once people began to see things for themselves, formed ideas of their own, they would willingly cooperate in creating a common front, which would lead to agitation. In the field of education Ambedkar was following the broad direction that DuBois had given in his famous essay on The Talented Tenth. His hope that the educated men of his community would take up the leadership of the people was belied. Most of them forgot all about their obligation and moved to become 'Dalit Brahmins.' They lacked commitment and fell into the trap of middle class respectability. Like DuBois, who edited *The Crisis*, Ambedkar also brought out a fortnightly paper called *Mook Nayak*, although he was not its official editor. It underwent a number of mutations: it became *Bahishkrit Bharat, Samta, Janata* and finally *Prabuddha Bharat*. He also prepared a blueprint for the formation of a political party, The Republican Party of India, which was formed after his death in 1956.

Ambedkar was convinced that without social emancipation of the Depressed classes, political emancipation had no meaning. He went to the extent of saying that no economic or political reform would be successful unless the monster of caste was destroyed. For this it was imperative that the Depressed classes were treated not as a religious minority but as a political minority. Here the approaches of DuBois and Ambedkar towards the .liberation of their people diverge. Whereas DuBois emphasized cultural and racial aspects, not completely ignoring the political aspect, Ambedkar believed that liberation could be achieved through political means. His demand for a separate electorate for his people which was conceded by the British and his disagreement with Gandhi over it shows the direction in which he wanted his struggle to move. One doesn't know what direction Dalit politics would have taken if the communal award had been implemented, but the course of Dalit situation would have certainly been different. Under moral pressure from the people throughout the country following Gandhi's fast unto death, he was forced to sign the Poona Pact instead of the Communal Award announced by the British Government. Ambedkar had already earned the displeasure of the people and the charge was that he was working against the interests of the country. Even when he sought support of the British for getting political power for his people, he knew that they were helping him out of political compulsions. I believe Ambedkar was more sinned against than sinning. It is true that the cause of his people was uppermost in his mind but time and again he had given evidence of his loyalty to the country. The letter that Ambedkar wrote to Alexander, a member of the Cabinet Commission and somewhat sympathetic to the cause Ambedkar represented, after the British had decided not to give representation to the Depressed classes in the Interim Government, shows Ambedkar's bitterness and the wily character of the British. He wrote: "The despotism of the Hindu continued as ever before. Far from being curbed by the British High Command, it was pampered. From a social point of view, the British accepted the arrangements as they found them and preserved them faithfully in the manner of the tailor who, when given an old coat as pattern, produced with pride an exact replica, rents and patches and all. The result is that though 200 years have elapsed since the establishment of the British rule the Indian wrongs remained unaddressed and their progress hampered at every stage."[28]

Like DuBois, Ambedkar was impatient to get his people not only Civil Rights but also Human Rights. Despite the fact that Nehru made efforts to secularize Indian politics, Ambedkar was skeptical of the role of caste Hindus. He saw some hope to translate his ideals into practice when he was called upon to be the Chairman of the Constitution Drafting Committee. He firmly believed that through the statutes and law the status of his people as equal citizens would be upheld which would pave the way for their final assimilation into the Hindu society. Then the slogans of equality, liberty and fraternity would become facts of life. His speech at the Constituent Assembly spelt that out. "These principles of liberty, equality and fraternity are not to be treated as separate items in a trinity. They form a union of trinity in the sense that to divorce one from the other is to defeat the very purpose of democracy.... We must begin by acknowledging the fact that there is a complete absence of two things in Indian society. One of them is equality. On the social plane, we have in India a society based on the principle of graded inequality which means elevation for some and degradation for others. On the economic plane, we have a society in which there are some who have immense wealth as against many who live in abject poverty. On the 26th January 1950, we are going to enter into a life of contradictions. In politics we will have equality and in social and economic life we will have inequality. In politics we will be recognizing the principle of one man one vote and one vote one value. In our social and economic life, we shall, by reason of our social and economic structure, continue to deny the principle of one man one value. How long shall we continue to live this life of contradictions?. How long shall we continue to deny equality in our social and economic life? If we continue to deny it for long, we will do so only by putting our political democracy at peril. We must remove this contradiction at the earliest possible moment or else those who suffer from inequality will blow up the structure of political democracy which this Assembly so laboriously built up."[29]

It is apparent that Ambedkar was redefining the concepts in the light of his reading in Buddhist philosophy and his experience as a leader of the Depressed Classes. He not only pointed out the contradictions in social and political life but also identified the two enemies that had come in the way of their liberation. The two enemies were: Brahminism and Capitalism. By Brahminism he meant not Brahmins as a community but all those who negated the spirit of trinity. And such people could be found in all sections of society including the communists who were at times guided by the spirit of Brahminism.

Ambedkar knew that economic deprivation was as real as social degradation. And he made a beginning in this regard when he collaborated with the communist in the strike against the Industrial Disputes Act. But such collaboration was short lived.

True, he realized the limitations of the liberal democracy but kept on working within its framework for whatever benefits he could get for his people. Besides, those who were at the helm of affairs in the ruling party were not radical enough to bring about revolutionary change in their situation. He became painfully aware of this when he piloted the Hindu Code Bill through which he wanted to correct some of the ills of Hindu society. Initially he had the support of Nehru but when the Parliamentary Party opposed it, he was forced to modify it and finally withdraw it at the behest of Nehru himself. The orthodox elements were too powerful for him to resist. On this issue he resigned from the Cabinet,

Both DuBois and Ambedkar were working within the Enlightenment worldview - Ambedkar modifying it a bit but still reposing faith in liberal democracy – which defined man and society in human terms. Both worked indefatigably for change in the social, political and economic conditions of their people without spelling out institutional change. DuBois unwittingly became part of the elitist culture which aimed at correcting things through excellence for which criteria came from the others. Cornel West in his reevaluation of DuBois points out two defects in his endeavours. "First he believed that the highbrow culture was inherently humanizing and that exposure to and immersion in great works produce good people. The other was that the educated elite he had put his faith in could transcend their individual and class interests and move easily on behalf of the common good than the educated classes."[30]

Ambedkar is being subjected to a similar reevaluation. Anand Teltumbde is one such critic. But he is guarded in his reevaluation although he denounces those who have used different icons of Ambedkar to further their own ends. According to Teltumbde "although there cannot be any doubt that he stood against capitalism, he could not articulate a sound theoretical basis for doing so." At another place he writes: "Babasaheb Ambedkar, in his own way, has been in search of a suitable ideological carrier for the Dalit movement."[31] The consequence has been that in the post - Ambedkar Dalit movement the revolutionary character of Ambedkar has been overshadowed by "prejudiced social identities in worn-out casteist phraseology."[32]

But Ambedkar could not be charged with elitism as he always kept contact with his people who came to him in large numbers for advice and guidance. According to Keer "he was the voice of their woes, their view and their vows."[33] Ambedkar's tragedy was that he trusted for a while the existing political system to go along with his line of thought. Despite the fact that he never gave up his fight against economic exploitation, he could not free himself from the stranglehold that Hindu social system had created for his class. He looked for and found some solace in religion. At best he shuttled between religious and economic reorganization of society which could not be combined as one finds in his comparison between Buddha and Karl Marx. In one of his speeches in 1953 Ambedkar said that the present generation and the future generation would have to chose between the gospel of Buddha and the gospel of Marx. But if one chose the former, which some of them did, one could not change the material conditions of people except through moral force.

The strategies adopted by both DuBois and Ambedkar did not emanate from an ideological framework that encompassed all aspects of human activity. That was one reason why they were disillusioned towards the end of their life. At the ripe age of 91 DuBois left America for Africa. He wrote in a letter: "I cannot take any more of the country's treatment. We leave for Ghana October 5th and I set no date for return. ... Chin up and fight on but realize that American Negroes can't win."[34] He died soon after.

Ambedkar was similarly disillusioned with the system after he was made to withdraw the Hindu Code Bill. After resigning as Minister of Law he wanted to make a statement but he was not allowed to do so by the Deputy Speaker on the ground that he had not submitted a copy of his statement earlier. When Mr. Kunzru and Mr. Kamath, two members of the House, pointed out that it amounted to pre-censorship, the Deputy Speaker said since he was the custodian of the rights and privileges of Parliament, it was necessary for him to see that the statement contained nothing irrelevant and libelous. On this Ambedkar left the House and immediately afterwords gave his statement to the newspapers. His faith in Parliamentary Democracy was shaken. His end came soon after.

References

1. See Volume 5 of Ambedkar Writing and Speeches compiled by Vasant Moon, Education Department, Government of Maharashtra, 1989.
2. Initially written in 1977, revised in 1979 and later included in her book From Untouchable to Dalit, Manohar 1988, pp. 79-85.
3. The Autobiography of Malcolm X, Penguin 1976, pp. 79-102.
4. Arthur Schlesinger Jr., The Disuniting of America, Norton Edition, USA, 1992, p.19.
5. V.S. Naipaul: India: A Million Mutinies Now. Minerva, India, 1990, p. 115.
6. Fred L. Standly & Nancy V. Burt (ed) Critical Essay on James Baldwin, C.K. Hall & Co. Boston, 1988, p. 256.
7. Ambedkar Speeches and Writings, Vol. 5, p. 15.
8. Dhananjaya Keer, Dr. Ambedkar: Life and Mission, Popular Prakashan, Bombay, 1994, p. 31.
9. W.N. Kuber, B.R. Ambedkar : Builders of Modern India Series, Publications Division, Ministry of Information and Broadcasting, Government of India, December 1990, p. 22.
10. A.K. Rajsekhariah, B.R. Ambedkar: The Politics of Emancipation, Sindhu Publication Pvt. Ltd., Bombay, 1971, p. 11.
11. Ibid., p. 216 Rajshekhariah found this letter in the files containing his correspondence with the Cabinet Mission

and with other leaders at Siddharth College Library, Bombay.

12. W.E.B. DuBois, The Souls of Black Folk, A.C. McClurg & Co. Chicago, 1931, P. 1X.
13. Lorraine Hansberry, The Last Collected Plays of Lorraine Hansberry, Random House, New York, 1972, p. 122.
14 Keer, p. 525.
15. W.E.B. DuBois, Dusk of Dawn: An Essay Toward an Autobiography of a Race Concept, Shocken Books, New York, 1968, pp. 131-132, by Keer, p. 41.
16. Quoted by Keer, p. 41.
17. Quoted by Keer, p. 229.
18. The Souls of Black Folk, pp. 3-4.
19. Henry Gates Jr. & Cornel West (ed), The Future of the Race, Alfred A. Knopf N.Y., 1996, p. 132.
20. Ibid., pp. 156-157.
21. Ibid., p. 161.
22. Ibid., p. 168.
23. Ambedkar Writings and Speeches, Vol. 1, p. 68.
24. Ibid., p. 84.
25. Ibid., p. 90.
26. Ambedkar Writings and Speeches, Vol. 5, p. 399.
27. Quoted by Keer, p. 491.
28. Ambedkar Writings and Speeches, Vol. 10, pp. 497-498.
29. Quoted by V.R. Krishna Aiyer, Ambedkar and the Dalit Future, B.R. Publishing Corporation, New Delhi, 1990, pp. 32-33.
30. The Future of the Race, p. 68.
31. Anand Teltumbde, Ambedkar in and for the Post Ambedkar Dalit Movement, Sugawa Prakashan, Pune, 1997, pp. 55.
32. *Ibid.*, p. 23.
33. Keer, pp. 302-303.
34. The Future of the Race, p. 118.

Appendix - II

Internalized Oppressive Beliefs and The Creation of a Just Social Order*

My claim to be participating in this seminar is that I am presently working on a U.G.C project on Dalit and African American. Since the subject of the seminar leaves enough scope to talk about the dispossessed and the deprived and their predicament, I think I fit in here. The subject suggests some thing negative, that is that the existing social order is not just and that we do not discharge our responsibility in bringing about a just social order. There are visible and invisible impediments. Law can provide a basis for direction, for change for a better social order, but it cannot knock out beliefs, myths, attitudes which govern human relationships. It requires sustained social and political effort to create new beliefs, and myths and resultant changed attitude. "It is true that every type of association – social, political or economic – has some philosophy behind it. And when these associations change, the philosophical foundation must also change in order to give it rootedness and utilize them to the best advantage. Usually the philosophy

* This paper was presented at a U.G.C. Seminar on Law and a just Social Order organized by the Law Faculty, JNV University, Jodhpur in 2000. A Hindi version of the paper was published in Pratishruti, Bhartiya Vidya Bhavan, Jodhpur Kendra April - June 2001.

lags behind the course of events and this lag creates all the trouble." (Nehru, *Autobiography,* p. 528)

Philosophy deals with the entire framework that governs human relationships. Even when political and social situations change or indicate change, the vestiges of earlier philosophy remain and do not disappear at one stroke. In England the challenge to the absolute authority of the State and Church began with Magna Carta (13th century) and attained fruition in Enlightenment when the bases of human relationships were redefined and reestablished. A new class – the middle class – replaced the earlier class of feudal lords and kings and new associations developed. The entire complex of relationships changed. Words acquired new connotations. Raymond Williams defined certain key words – art, culture, democracy, industry and personality – which indicated not only change in content but also the direction of change. (*Culture and Society*).

Responsibility towards a just social order must be understood in the context of this change and the vestiges of the earlier order. Whether one likes it or not responsibility cannot be completely codified. Individuals are guided by their worldview and perception about human society and human relationships. Even silence and indifference can be part of one's attitude, and the individual may be right in his perception. Sometimes there is a conflict between two contradictory perceptions placed in the same person. The conflict may be painful as well as revealing. When it takes concrete shape – when human rights are violated – it comes in conflict with law. One may treat a person belonging to another class with bitter contempt without uttering a single word. It is not only a conflict between two social formations but also of two frameworks, religious as well as rational. It has been made more complicated by our insistence that religious duty is as much a part of our attitude to life as rational. One can move easily from one to the other. As William James once said that in vital matters the mind does not take us very far. "If your heart does not want to your head will assuredly never make you believe. The emotions govern the general outlook and control the mind." (Quoted by Nehru in his *Autobiography* p. 516).

In order to see the working of this process of change, one will have to examine the attitudes that play a crucial role in this transition. And attitudes cannot be easily separated from the philosophical basis that supported them. There is always residual attitude which has got to be taken into account before it submits itself to the new attitude that will eventually be formed. There are people who carry the mindset of the earlier social formation; there are people who face a conflict between the entrenched attitude and the changed attitude; and then there are people who have been completely changed by the new ideological framework. Thus there is a grey area between the enactment of law and the creation of a just social order. In America after the Civil War when the Blacks became legally free, they did not know, at least for the time being, what to do with their freedom, and some of them went back to their masters. Those who accepted the changed relationship between the Blacks and the whites treated them well. But there were masters who took advantage of this confusion. What I am suggesting is that the rejection of the old basis of discrimination, the stratification of castes with labels attached to them is a prolonged process. Whenever a situation arises, the attitudes formed over centuries come into operation, despite the fact that some of them are actuated by human values as can be seen in Mark Twain's *The Adventures of Huckleberry Finn.* There is a very powerful short story by Prem Chand. It is titled the 'Price of Milk'. It deals with the categories of caste, the Zamindar and the Harijan, with their areas of operation clearly defined. Any effort to transgress it is sure to invoke the wrath of the caste people. A peculiar situation arises when the Zamindar's wife gives birth to a son but is unable to feed him. At the same time a Harijan lady also gives birth to a son. Since there was no way to save the life of the Zamindar's son without mother's milk – at that time tinned milk was not available – the Zamindar asked the Harijan lady to feed his child. She obediently did that even at the cost of not feeding her own child. Soon after the Harijan lady died leaving her child to the mercy of the landlord who condescendingly looked after him. The two boys were of the same age and played together like normal children. In the game they played the Harijan boy always became the horse and the Zamindar's son, the rider. One day the Harijan boy said that for once he should be the rider, a very natural demand. As was expected, the Zamindar's son objected to it and reported the matter to the father. The entrenched attitudes came into operation and centuries of conditioning came in the way of normal human relationship. The Zamindar decided that his son would no longer play with the Harijan boy. In demanding a different role, he had transgressed the limits. The Harijan lady was obliged to help the landlord but he had no obligation towards her son. The price of milk was rejection and discrimination and not gratitude.

The philosophy behind caste discrimination cannot be wished away for it was rooted in a religious framework. It requires a sustained political and social programme to contest it as it has become part of our psyche. Gandhiji who fought unceasingly for the uplift of the Harijans would not agree to reconsider the role of *varna* in supporting the caste system. According to him the *varna* system was an integral part of Hinduism and had nothing to do with caste. This was contested by Dr. Ambedkar. (See Dr. Ambedkar's longish essay, 'Annihilation of Caste', which was written as a Presidential address for the Jatpat Todak Society but was published later and the correspondence between Gandhiji and Dr. Ambedkar on this issue. (Dr. Baba Sahib Ambedkar – Writings and Speeches Vol. I). Gandhiji believed that a change of heart in the other castes would solve the problems of the untouchables in the country. In fact, he would ask the rich to serve the masses not so much to raise them materially as to go down to their level and mix with them on equal terms. The rich should live no better than the depressed classes and make a conscious effort to approach that level to the best of their ability. According-ing to Nehru, Gandhiji carried the outlook of a medieval saint. " In the old world it was difficult to think of raising the general material level of the masses. The poor were with us. The handful of rich men were then an essential part of the social fabric, they were necessary to the production system. And so the moralist and the reformer and the sensitive men accepted them, but at the same time tried to impress them with their obligations to their needy brethren. They were trustees of the poor." (Nehru, *Autobiography* p.518). The rich felt virtuous; they built temples and dharamshalas to show that they were charitable. This religious attitude went with the world of the medieval period when poor people pinned their hope in the life to come. In the modern age conditions are such that even common man can reach the level of prosperity. The earlier world-view sounds anachronistic. The rich people "are no longer a necessary or desirable part of the productive system or of society as a whole." (Ibid. p. 520) Nehru went to the extent of saying that to apply ancient methods and formulae to the complex problems of the modern world leads to confusion. The right to ownership and private property has undergone a sea change. The rise of the Dalit movement and feminist movement are the direct outcome of that shift in thought. The modern society has means to eliminate poverty and discrimination, if political system is organized to that end. It is no longer an ethical or moral problem but a social and economic problem.

As I said earlier, I would like to talk of the intervening ground between conception and its realization – law and a just social order, a ground which deals with grey areas, with attitudes, with contradictions and with internalized oppressive beliefs. At the level of conscious thought we accept the new rational basis of human relationship, but relapse into the old categories of thought at the slightest provocation. It is at this level that the effort is to be directed. I would like to quote here a French thinker Pierre Bordeau who has done significant work in this field. "There are many things people accept without knowing. I will give you an example from our society. When you ask a sample of students what are the main factors of achievement at school, the further you go down the social scale, the more they believe that those who are successful are naturally endowed with intellectual capacities. And the more they accept their exclusion the more they say 'yes', I was no good at English.... Now, it is a fact, and in my view an appalling fact, one that individuals do not like to accept. It does not mean that the dominated individuals tolerate everything; but they assent to much more than they know. It is a formidable mechanism, like the imperial system, a wonderful instrument of ideology, much bigger and more powerful than television or propaganda. This is internalization of oppressive beliefs." (*New Left Review No,* 191). The creation of a just social order must be understood in this background of internalized oppressive beliefs.

The creation of a just social order is related to the formation of consciousness, that is awareness of their predicament and what the system has done to them. W.E.B. DuBois coined a picturesque phrase – double consciousness – for this phase of African American struggle for liberation. It meant that they lived a double existence; one was after the image of the white that is what the white expected of them, and the other was what they thought of themselves. The struggle between the two continues until they reach a stage where they reject the false image foisted on them and then move towards a human image. This process leads them to the assertion of their manhood. As is evident, it is a long and protracted process as the entrenched forces make efforts through carefully designed means to obstruct or deflect this process. Apart from the role of the dominant group, the Dalits themselves create categories and sometimes move in different directions. Once they reach the point of awareness there are two choices available to them. I shall explain this with the help of a story by Baburao Bagul, 'When I Concealed My Caste'. The first choice is the assertion of one's identity even at the cost of risking one's life, without any sense of inferiority; the other is the suppressed desire to become part of the middle class respectability by concealing one's caste. The first choice is born out of anger and resentment against the system and a strong desire to change it. Since ideological goals are lost right of in this assertion, it develops its own logic and mechanism. It happened in the U.S.A. during the Black Power movement when this assertion of their identity took them to the extreme of rejecting every thing that belonged to the white race or that could be claimed by both races. Separating themselves from the larger culture, they took pride in whatever belonged to them, their music, their folk culture, their history, their literature. They even decided to have a separate university with their own curricula, keeping out the culture and history of the dominant race. But in a decade they had to retrace their steps and decided to open up to other experiences and other ideas. But the pressure they exerted on the dominant culture could not be disregarded. Now Black literature - Black studies - is part of the academic programme of Yale and Harvard universities, two prominent institutions of the U.S.A. This opening up of the premier universities to Black studies might lead to a kind of change in the basis of society so that the history of racial segregation becomes a thing of the past and both Black and white and other racial stock look at the same reality from different angle. The second choice is difficult to resist as it offers a dream of comfortable, secure existence once one moves up the social ladder. There has been a very significant section in India - as in America - that has striven to become part of the middle class respectability. Once they are there, they do not bother about their unfortunate brethren, who have not had the opportunity they had. In fact, they soon acquire the attitudes of the new class. They begin to maintain distance from their close relatives. This movement satisfies a psychological need, and they feel happy that they are part of the dominant class. Both these choices are available in Bagul's story. There are two Dalit characters in the story, surrounded by upper class people, Kshatriyas and the Brahmins. One Dalit, Kashinath, displays the caste label and dares the caste people to treat him differently. He becomes a terror to them. He is so aggressive that the upper-caste people are scared of him. The other character, who is also a Dalit carefully conceals his caste, poses to be a Brahmin in speech and dress, although all along he feels uncomfortable with this mask. His behaviour convinces the two upper caste characters that he is a Brahmin and he is treated like one. He is given a room in a Kshatriya household and is treated with respect given to a Brahmin by his landlord. Another character who is taken in by his projection of a different self is a Brahmin who adores him and wants to understand poetry and learn other graces from him. He feels uncomfortable with this mask and wishes he could act and behave like Kashinath, but he secretly admires Kashinath's courage. He knows he cannot conceal it for long, as he has to produce his certificate. He thinks of resigning and going back to Bombay but the fear of poverty prevents him from resigning. Ramcharan the Brahmin invites him to his place for food. At his house, his wife touches his feet. Ramcharan gives him a bath and both feed him with respect. He is given a bed and sleeps comfortably. But people get wind that he is a Dalit and not what he has been taken to be. They barge into Ramcharan's house and beat him up mercilessly, his wife meekly complaining that it was not his fault. At that very moment, out of nowhere Kashinath, his caste fellow, appears on the scene and rescues him from the caste fanatics. The story ends there but it raises deeper psychological contradictions which are to be resolved since they have been internalized. Those who are committed to creating an egalitarian and casteless society ought to devise ways of dealing with these cicatrices in the consciousness of the Dalits. The fight against this internalized oppressive beliefs has to be waged at two levels. (1) At the level of ideology which will slowly create a climate for consciousness that emanates from human relationships. The ideology is not for reference or occasional reiteration, like most political leaders do, but has to be worked for so that the forces that are required to bridge the gap and to create a human environment get the right support. The entrenched ideology is so powerful that it has succeeded in diverting the forces of the third front in the form of Janta Dal that emerged in the Indian polity in the eighties. It has now fragmented into innumerable groups. But these set backs are part of the ongoing struggle. (2) The other level is that of human relationship. There are people in upper castes who have succeeded in declassing themselves and treat the Dalits on the level of equality. What Dr. Ambedkar once said holds true even today. The caste problem will continue to plague our society until there are free inter-dining and inter-marriages, where the distinction is not even noticed. Caste discrimination will not disappear only by giving awards to those who take this bold step. It is necessary that the source of stigma must go. The politicians in our country, instead of removing this discrimination, have created more fissures. The caste people, I believe, are as much victim of the system as the Dalits, only the level is different. They are not whole. I sometimes feel ashamed that my ancestors heaped so much misery on them. It is not that the basic issues are not being addressed by intellectuals, but their reach is limited to a small coterie. Vikram Seth in his massive novel, *A Suitable Boy*, which is a fictionalized narrative of post independence history raises, along with the problem of the peasants and the minorities, the issue of the Dalits. In particular he raises the issue of *Varna* system. It is examined from the point of view of a cobbler who questions the desirability of a person following the profession of his parents and caste. He also questions the right of the upper caste – the Kshatriyas have been condescendingly included in it by the Brahmins – to take part in the Ramlila enactment. The invisible line between the upper and the lower castes still exists, despite laws to the contrary. It is this invisible line between them that annoys and irritates the Dalits and it is this that has to be consciously removed by the upper castes.

In Arundhati Roy's novel, *The God of Small Things* the relationship between the lower and the upper castes has been taken to a deeper level. Velutha is a Dalit and Ammu, an upper caste Christian divorcee. Even Christianity has not succeeded in removing the label fixed on Velutha, a Paravan. The two enter into a relationship which is not sanctioned by the custodians of society's morality. When it is known to Ammu's family, they are livid and all social forces controlled by the upper castes join hands in keeping Velutha in his place. Even the police, called the henchmen of history, and the communist leader collaborate with them. In a frame up, he is charged with kidnapping the children and beaten up mercilessly until he becomes unconscious. His crime was that he demanded the human right to love and be loved. Ammu who loves him raises her voice against this inhuman treatment but before she could assert herself, the children were made to say that they were kidnapped, apparently to save the mother from going to jail.

Arundhati through these two characters shows how internalized oppressive beliefs operate in human relationship, and they cannot be easily eliminated given the attitude of people. The children think differently and raise some hope.

It is evident that the Dalits cannot fight the battle all by themselves. They need allies who are willing to support them at crucial moment. Pillai, a comrade in Roy's novel doesn't lend support, although Velutha was a card-holding member of the Communist Party. The issue was animatedly, discussed at a seminar on Dalit and Black Writings : Some recent trends held some two years back at the Indian Institute of Advanced Studies, Shimla. It was felt that exclusivism will not take us very far. But are the upper caste people ready to overcome their prejudice and see the human face beyond the claptrap of caste. But the burden of creating human situation is on the upper caste people and not on the Dalits, for this will mean asking the victim to set things right. A just social order can be created only when the two individuals are free to enter into human relationship without fear of persecution.

References

1. The Autobiography of J.L. Nehru.
2. New Left Review - 191.
3. Dalit Short Stories ed. Surya Narayan Ranshubhe & Kamlakar - Gangavane.
4. Vikram Seth: A Suitable Boy.
5. Arundhati Roy: The God of Small Things.
6. Annihilation of caste: Dr. Baba Sahib Ambedkar's Writing & Speeches Vol. I.

Bibliography

1. A.M. Rajasekhariah: *B.R. Ambedkar, The Politics of Emancipation*, Sindhu Publication, Bombay, 1971.
2. Addison Gayle jr., *The Black Aesthetics*, Double Day, New York, 1971.
3. Addison Gayle jr., *The way of the New World: The Black Novel in America*, New York, Double Day, 1976.
4. Albert Galloway Keler, *Colonization*, Boston, 1907.
5. Alex Haley, *Roots, Picador*, 1997.
6. Alexis de Tocqueville, *Democracy in America, Double Day Anchor*, New York, 1969, Original 1838, Vol. 2.
7. *Ambedkar at Ramlila Ground*, Agra March 18, 1956.
8. 'Ambedkarism' : *The Theory of Dalit Liberation in Gail Omvedt: Dalit & and the Democractic Revolution*, Sage Publication, New Delhi: 1994.
9. *American Literary Criticism from the 30s to the 80s*, Columbia University Press, 1988.
10. *An Anthology of Dalit Literature*, Gyan Publishing House, New Delhi, 1992.
11. Anil Avchat, *We Also Exist*, Radhakrishan Prakashan, New Delhi, 1991.
12. Arjun Dangle, *"Promotion" in Dalit Stories* edited by Surya Narayan Ransubhe and Kamlakar Gangavane, Panchsheel Prakashan, Jaipur, 19981.
13. Arjun Dangle, *"Revolution" in An Anthology of Dalit Literature.*
14. Bandhumadhav, *"The Poisoned Bread" in Homeless in My Land*, ed. Arjun Dangle, Disha Books, 1992.
15. Baren Ray, *Gandhi's Campaign Against Untouchability, 1933-34, Gandhi Peace Foundation*, New Delhi, 1996.

16. *Black American Literature Forum*, ed. Joe Weiximann, 14:1 (1980).
17. Carolyn F. Gerald, *"the Black Writer and His role" in African American Literary Criticism*, 1773 – 2000 Ed. Hazel Arnett Ervin, Twayne Publishers 1999.
18. Chokhamela, in *An Anthology of Dalit Literature* ed. Mulk Raj Anand and Eleanor Zelliot, Gyan Publishing House, New Delhi, 1992.
19. *Collected works of Mahatma Jotirao Phule, vol. II*, Education Department, Govt. of Maharashtra, Bombay, 1991.
20. *Commentary* Feb. 1967.
21. Cornel West and Henry Louis Gates Jr. Eds. *The Future of the Race*, Alfred A Knoff, N.Y., 1996.
22. Czeslaw Milosz, *The Southern Review*, 1985.
23. D.D. Kosambi, *An Introduction to the Study of Indian History*, Bombay, 1956.
24. *Dalit Literature: Man's Great Freedom, Asmitadarsh, VI:I*, 1973.
25. *Dalit Sahitya 2000* edited Jai Prakash Kardam, New Delhi.
26. *Danielle Taylor Gutherie (ed) Conversations with Toni Morrison*, University of Massachusetts Press, 1994.
27. Daya Pawar, *"Vultures", in Dalit Charchit Kahiniya*, ed. Kusum Viyogi, Lalit Prakashan, Delhi, 1997.
28. Daya Pawar, *Achoot*, Radhakrishna Paperbacks, New Delhi, 1998.
29. Dharamvir, *The Growth of Dalit Literature*, paper presented at the IIAS, Shimla, Oct. 1997.
30. Dr. Babasaheb Ambedkar, *Writings and Speeches*, Education Department, Government of Maharashtra, 1989, vols. 1,2,3,5,7,10,13.
31. Edward Said, *Culture and Imperialism*. Alfred A. Knoff, 1993.
32. Frantz Fanon, *The Wretched of the Earth*, Penguin 1973
33. Fred L. Standley and Nancy V. Burt, (ed.) *Critical Essays on James Baldwin*, C.K. Hall & Co., Boston, 1988.
34. Frederick Douglass: *Life and Times of Frederick Douglass : The complete Autobiography*, Rept., 1962, Collier Books.
35. Frederick Douglass: *My Bondage and My Freedom*, Arno Press, New York, 1968.

36. Frederick Douglass, *quoted in The Future of the Race* by Henry Louis Gates Jr. and Cornel West, Alfred Knoff, New York, 1996.
37. *From Untouchable to Dalit*, Manohar Publishers, New Delhi, 1998 (Rep).
38. G. Aloysius, *Nationalism Without a Nation in India*, O.U.P., 1994.
39. Gail Omvedt, *Dalits and the Democratic Revolution*, Sage Publications, New Delhi, 1994.
40. Gore Vidal, *At Home: New York*, Random House, 1988.
41. H. Gates Jr. *"Authority (White) Power and The Black Critic" in the Future of Literary Theory* ed. Ralph Cohen, New York, 1989.
42. *Hans (Hindi)*, June, 1998.
43. Harold Cruse, *The Crisis of the Negro Intellectual: From its Origin to the present*, William Morrow & Co., 1967.
44. Houston A. Baker, *Blues, Ideology and Afro-American Literature*, Chicago, 1984.
45. *India : Another Millennium*, ed. Romila Thapar, Viking 2000.
46. V.S. Naipaul, *India: A Million Mutinies Now*, Menerva, 1990.
47. Irfan Habib, *Essays in Indian History*, Tulika, 1979.
48. Irving Howe, *"Black Boys and Native Sons" in a World More Attractive*, Horizon Press, New York, 1975.
49. J.Hector St. John Crevecoeur, *Letters from an American Farmer, Gloucester, Mass*, Peter Smith, 1968.
50. James Baldwin: *The Price of the ticket*, St. Matin marek, 1985.
51. James Baldwin, *Notes of a Native Son*, Dial Press, 1964.
52. James Baldwin, *Tell Me How Long the Train's Been Gone*, Dell publishing, New York, 1973.
53. James Baldwin, *The Fire Next Time*, New York, Dell Publishing Co., 1964.
54. James M. Clarke: *Lineaments of Wrath: Race, Violent Crime in American Culture*, Transaction Publishers, New Jersey, 1998.
55. Jean Paul Sartre, *Preface to The Wretched Earth*, Penguin, 1963.
56. Jennifer L. Hochschild: *Class and the Soul of the Nation: Facing upto the American Dream*, Princeton University

Press, N. Jersey, 1995.

57. John Hersey, *20th Century Views on Ralph Ellison,* Prentice Hall, New Jersey, 1975.
58. John Hope Franklin, *"A Brief History of the Negro in the United States"* in The American Negro Reference Book, ed. John P. Davis, Prentice Hall, New Jersey, 1967.
59. Juan Comas, *Racial Myths,* Ionesco, Paris, 1953.
60. Julius Lester, *Introduction to Les Blancs, The Collected Last Plays of Lorraine Hansberry,* Random House, New York, 1972.
61. Justice V.R. Krishna Iyer : *Dr. Ambedkar and The Dalit Future B.R. Publishing Corporation,* Delhi, 1990.
62. Kancha Illaiaih, *Why I am Not a Hindu,* Somya, 1996, Preface.
63. Kathakram, *Dalit Special Number,* Nov. 2000, ed. Mudra Rakshas, Lucknow
64. Langston Hughes, *"Mulatto".* In Three Negro Plays, Penguin Books, 1969.
65. Langston Hughes, *quoted in The Black American,* Ed. Fishel and Quarles jr.
66. Larry Neal & Le Roi Jones, *Black Fire : An Anthology of African American Writing,* William Morrow & Co., 1968.
67. Larry W. Ward, *Interview with Henry Louis Gates Jr., New Literary History, Vol.22,* Autumn, 1991.
68. Lata Murugukar, *Dalit Panther Movement in Maharashtra,* Popular Prakashan, Bombay, 1991.
69. Laxman Gaekwar, *Uthaigeer,* Sahitya Akademi, New Delhi, 1992.
70. Laxman Mane, *Paraya,* Sahitya Akademy, New Delhi, 1997.
71. Le Roi Jones, *Home: Social Essays,* New York, William Morrow and co., 1960.
72. Leslie Fishel Jr. and Benjamin Quarles, *The Black American : A documentary History,* Glen View, Illinois, Scott Foresman, 1970.
73. Limbale, *Dalit and American Negro Literature,* paper presented at the IIAS, Shimla, Oct. 1997.
74. Lorraine Hansberry, *A Raisin in the Sun,* A Signet Book, 1960, New American Library.
75. Lucian Goldmann, *"Dogmatism in Literature" in The Dialectics of Liberation,* ed. David Cooper Penguin Books,

1969.

76. M. Andrew Scott, Henry George, *Henry Adams and The Dominant American Ideology*, SAC – 76, 1977.
77. M.A. Gopalkrishnanad, *Periyar: The Father of the Tamil Race, Emerald Publishers*, Madras, 1996.
78. M.S. Gore, *The Social Context of an Ideology*, Sage Publication, 1993.
79. Malcolm X, *The Man & His Times*, P. XXIII in Introduction to the Autobiography of Malcolm X.
80. *Manusmriti*, Introduction by R.N. Sharma, Chaukhamba Sanskrit Sansthan, Delhi, 1998.
81. *Mark Twain: The Autobiography* ed. Charles Neider, A Perennial Classic, 1959.
82. Mark Twain, *The Adventures of Huckleberry Finn*, Penguin, 1954.
83. Mulk Raj Anand and Eleanor Zelliot (ed.) *An Anthology of Dalit Literature*, Gyan Publishing House, New Delhi, 1992.
84. *Naya Path (Hindi)*, June 1998.
85. *New Left Review*, No. 191.
86. *Octavio Paz*, Partisan Review (1), 1986.
87. Om Prakash Valmiki, *Juthan*, Radhakrishna Publication, 1997.
88. Pavan K. Varma: *The Great Indian Middle Class*, Penguin, 1988.
89. Prem Chand, *"Sadgati" in Katha Prasun*, Panchsheel Prakashan, Jaipur, 2000.
90. R. Ellison, *Shadow and Act*, New York, Random House, 1964.
91. Randall Kenan, *Walking on Water: Black American Lives at the Turn of the 21st Century*, Alfred Knoff, New York, 1999.
92. Reginald, *Mainstream Criticism in College English, Vol. 50*, No.4, April 1988.
93. *Restoring Hope: Cornel West in Conversation on the Future of Black America.* ed. Kelvin Shawn Sealey, Beacon Press, Boston, 1997.
94. Richard Wright, *Black Boy, Harper & Row*, New York, 1945.
95. Richard Wright, *American Hunger, Harper and Row*, 1977.

96. Robert Bone, *the Negro Novel in America*, Yale University Press, New Haven 1965.
97. S.D. Kapoor, *"Aspects of Violence"*, in Jodhpur Studies in English Vols. III & IV, 1990.
98. S.D. Kapoor: *"American Dream and Black Experience"* in The Utopian Imagination eds. Jasbir Jain and Santosh Gupta, Printwell Jaipur, 1991.
99. Sharad Patil, T*he Aesthetics of Non-Brahmin Literature*, 1988, Sugava Publishers, Pune (translated for me by Dr. Sharad Rajimwale).
100. Sharan Kumar Limbale, *Akkarmashi*, Granth Akademy, New Delhi, 1991.
101. S.K. Limbale, *Rape Within and Without in Devta Aadmi*, Pratibha Pratishthan, New Delhi, 1994.
102. S.K. Limbale, *The Aesthetics of Dalit Literature (translated into Hindi by Ramnika Gupta)*, Vani Prakashan, Delhi, 2000.
103. Sandra Adell, *Double Consciousness and Double Bind*, University of Illinois Press, 1994.
104. *Saunders Redding in Introduction to the Study of The Souls of Black Folk* by W.E.B. Du Bois, Chicago, 1931.
105. Shanker Rao Kharat, *Taral Antaral*, National Publishing House, New Delhi, 1987.
106. Sharan Kumar Limbale, *Devta Admi*, Pratibha Prakashan, new Delhi,1994.
107. Suryanarayan Ranshubhe and Kamlakar Gangavane, (eds.) *Dalit Stories*, Panchsheel Prakashan, Jaipur, 1981 Introduction.
108. Tark Tirth Lakshman Shastri, *Jyotiba Phule*, national Book Trust India, 1996.
109. *The Autobiography of Malcolm X (with the assistance of Alex Haley)*, Rept. Penguin Books 1976.
110. *The Poetry of the Negro* ed. Larry Neal, 1946-1970.
111. *The Times of India*, July 18, 1993.
112. *Three Interviews*, edited Kenneth B. Clark, Middletown, Wesley University Press, 1985.
113. Toni Morrison, *"Rootedness" in African American Literary Criticism*, 1773-2000, Twayne Publishers, New York, 1999.
114. Thomas Jefferson, *Notes on the State of Virginia, Boston*, 1801.

115. Todd Gitlin: *The Twilight of American Dream,* Metropolitan books, 1995.
116. Toni Morrison, *Playing in the Dark, Whiteness and Literary Imagination: William Morrow,* New York, 1992.
117. *Toward Black literature, Massachusetts Review,* 1966.
118. U.G.Weatherby, *"The West Indies as a Sociological Laboratory"* in American Journal of Sociology XXIX, 1923-24.
119. W.E.B. Du Bois: *The Souls of Black Folk,* G.McClug, 1931.
120. W.E.B.Du Bois: *The Talented Tenth,* published in The Future of the Race.
121. W.E.B.Du Bois: *Dusk of Dawn: An Essay Toward an Autobiography of a Race Concept,* Shocken books, New York, 1968.
122. William Faulkner, *Light in August,* Penguin Modern Classes, 1973.
123. William L. Van De Burg, (ed.) *Modern Black Nationalism,* New York University Press, 1997.
124. Yashwant Manohar, *"I'm Ready for Revolution" in An Anthology of Dalit Literature.*

Index

N

O

P

W

Z